8700 East Via De Ventura I Suite 300 I Scottsdale, AZ 85258
toll free: 888.422.7714 I testeachers.com

MW00608052

Dear Insurance Licensing Candidate,

**Welcome to the insurance profession!!**

Your state Department of Insurance is empowered by law to qualify individuals who wish to become insurance agents. To become licensed, you must pass an examination that covers the Life and Health (Disability) insurance products you will be selling as well as the laws and regulations that apply in insurance sales. The scope of coverage and passing scores for each license qualification examination are set at levels designed to ensure that passing applicants possess **at least the minimum** degree of knowledge necessary **to protect the insurance-buying public**.

The study material presented in this book (Book 1) of this two book set is specific to the product portion of your state Life and Health (Disability) Agent's or Producer's examination. Please note that the insurance laws and regulations specific to your state are discussed in Book 2.

Most states present these exams on computer, and upon completion, you will be given your results immediately. An overall score of 70% is required to pass in most states. However, passing your exam does not constitute licensing. You must still apply for licensing with your state insurance department.

All questions and requests for information about required pre-license training, examination content outlines, examination scheduling and locations or obtaining your license should be directed to either your sales manager or the organization that administers the state exam in your state.

For states using **Prometric**, please visit their website at www.prometric.com to find out how to schedule your exam. For states using **Pearson VUE**, visit their website at www.pearsonvue.com to find out how to schedule your exam. For states using **PSI**, visit their website at www.psiexams.com.

While we believe these study materials are excellent, the **ultimate responsibility for understanding them is yours**. The various topics discussed in this text have been the subject of previous state examination questions. However, since the examinations are conceptual, you should realize that much of the material contained herein will not appear on your actual examination exactly as written.

Therefore, it is imperative that your goal should be to completely understand the materials, rather than just know the answer to the specific practice examination questions. You should know the right answer, why it is correct, and what is wrong with the other answers!

Good Luck!

8700 East Via De Ventura I Suite 300 I Scottsdale, AZ 85258
toll free: 888.422.7714 I testeachers.com

# PRE-STUDY PROCEDURES FOR LIFE AND HEALTH

FIRST, review the Licensing Information BULLETIN or HANDBOOK as it relates to your examination. This bulletin or Handbook is available on-line from the company that administers the exam in your state (www.prometric.com, www.pearsonvue.com or www.psiexams.com), and it outlines the various areas on which you will be tested.

NEXT, read Section 2 relating to the study of GENERAL insurance contained in Book 1 of this 2 book set, paying particular attention to the areas underlined. After reviewing the Key Facts located at the end of the Section, take the Section exam on an OPEN-BOOK basis, writing your answers on a separate piece of paper. Note that Section 2 relates to both Life and Health insurance.

DON'T GUESS! If you are not sure of the answer, learn it by reading the rationales immediately following each exam. Then take the exam again, CLOSED-BOOK, until you can score at least 90%. You should know the correct answers and why, and what is wrong with the incorrect answers!

NEXT, proceed with Sections 3 through 8 on the same basis. Once you are able to score 90% or better on all of the LIFE Section exams, proceed to LIFE Insurance Final Exams A and B and study them in the same manner. Your goal is to understand the concepts, not to memorize the questions.

THEN, proceed to HEALTH insurance Sections 3 through 10 in Book 1 and study them exactly the same way. When you are done with your review of HEALTH insurance, take HEALTH Insurance Final Exams A and B until you can score at least 90%.

NEXT, proceed to Book 2 of this 2 book set and study the INSURANCE LAWS & REGULATIONS specific to your state's LIFE & HEALTH insurance exam in the same manner as indicated above.

FINALLY, be sure to review all the various KEY FACTS in both Books 1 & 2 again just prior to taking your state exam. Knowing these KEY FACTS can be the difference between passing and failing your exam!

WHILE it is imperative that you review all of the text material in both Books 1 & 2, especially the underlined areas, key facts and glossary, the real key to passing is understanding and practicing the Section and Final exams until you know and understand the concepts.

GOOD LUCK!

P. S. To further enhance your studies, try our TESTUTOR DVD program, TESTAKER EXAM SIMULATION computer disc and/or our TESTELLER audio CD

# LIFE AND HEALTH (DISABILITY) INSURANCE

# TABLE OF CONTENTS

**LIFE INSURANCE**

*Section 2 – General Insurance Concepts relates to both Life and Health Insurance

# HEALTH INSURANCE

*Section 2 – General Insurance Concepts relates to both Life and Health Insurance

# SECTION 2

# General Insurance Concepts

**Note to Students**: This section of the course relates to both Life and Health insurance.

## CONCEPTS

Insurance is a social device for spreading the chance of financial loss among a large number of people. By purchasing insurance, a person shares risk with a group of others, reducing the individual potential for disastrous consequences.

The insurance company, or <u>insurer</u>, receives relatively small amounts of money, referred to as <u>premium</u>, from each of the large number of people buying insurance. <u>A large, uncertain loss is traded in this way for a small, certain loss, the premium.</u>

The <u>agreement between the insurer and the insured</u>, the person who is covered by the insurance, is established in a legal document referred to as a contract of insurance, or a <u>policy</u>. The insurer promises to pay the insured according to the terms of the policy if a loss occurs. <u>Loss</u> is defined as reduction in the value of an asset. To be paid for a loss, the insured must notify the insurer by making a <u>claim</u>.

<u>Risk</u> is the <u>possibility (uncertainty) that a loss might occur</u> and is the reason that people buy insurance. If a certain event happens -- accident, sickness, or death -- loss occurs. Insurance is designed to provide for such losses, while not providing the insured with the possibility of gain from the accident, sickness, or death.

<u>Speculative risk</u> (such as gambling) creates a risk situation and offers the <u>opportunity for gain as well as the possibility of loss</u>. It is this type of risk that <u>insurance won't cover</u>.

<u>Pure risk is the type of risk that insurers accept</u>. With pure risk, there is the possibility that a certain event will occur, for example, accident or sickness. However, it is the purpose of insurance <u>to restore the insured to his/her original position</u>, not to provide a person with the opportunity of making a profit on an accident or sickness.

## ELEMENTS OF INSURABLE RISK

Risk managers evaluate risks for loss frequency (probability of loss), severity, and potential dollar losses over time. Once the loss exposures are identified and analyzed, the best techniques for dealing with them must be examined.

There are <u>four ways to manage risk</u>. A risk may be retained, avoided, reduced, or transferred. A risk is <u>retained</u> when a person decides to assume financial responsibility for certain events. The deductible amount on a health insurance policy may be seen as a way the insured retains some portion of the risk.

In addition, his/her premium is reduced because of this assumption of risk. To <u>avoid</u> a risk, a person might stay home rather than drive somewhere. A risk is <u>reduced</u> when a person practices living a healthier lifestyle, thereby reducing the chance of major illness.

A risk may be <u>transferred in two ways</u>. If someone's negligence causes an injury, the person injured could sue the negligent party, <u>transferring the burden of the risk to the negligent party</u>.

The second method for transferring risk is accomplished through the <u>use of insurance</u>. The risk of loss is transferred to the insurance company. However, unlike the first instance of risk transfer, the entire burden is not merely transferred to one party; <u>it is shared among a number of insureds</u> who share the same chance and uncertainty of an event occurring. The characteristics for determining which group of individuals share a common risk are such things as age, sex, and occupation.

Insurance companies predict the potential losses of a large group by studying the past experiences of the group using the mathematical principles of probability and statistics. Looking at groups of individuals, rather than the individuals themselves, to make predictions is called the <u>pooling concept</u> and is an accurate way of predicting potential losses.

## LAW OF LARGE NUMBERS

The law of large numbers allows an insurance company to predict the expected losses of a group. The basic principle of this law is that <u>the larger the number</u> of separate risks of a like nature combined into one group, <u>the more predictable the number of future losses</u> of that group within a given time period. For the law of large numbers to operate, <u>it is essential that a large number of exposure units be combined</u>. The exposure unit in life and health insurance is the economic value of the individual person's life. In property and casualty insurance, it is the car, home, or other item to be insured. Insurance companies can only predict the number of losses expected for a group, not for each individual.

If large enough numbers of exposure units are combined, the degree of error in predicting future losses decreases as the number of individual exposure units in a group increases. The larger the group, the more closely the predicted experience will approach the actual loss experience.

Insurance companies collect premiums to cover expenses, profits, and the cost of expected losses. The expected losses are based upon the past experience of the average risk. The fact that some people never experience an automobile accident or that some live well beyond their life expectancy is immaterial, for they are balanced by other people who are involved in accidents or die prematurely. Those insureds who suffer loss are compensated, while many other insureds do not experience sizable losses.

## INSURABLE INTEREST

Individuals may not be able to purchase any kind of insurance they desire. To be insurable, a risk must involve the possibility of <u>loss only, and not gain</u>, and the applicant must have a legitimate <u>interest</u> in the preservation of the life or property insured. This requirement is called <u>insurable interest</u>.

A person is presumed to have an insurable interest in his/her own life. An individual is also considered to have an insurable interest in the life of a close relative or a spouse. Insurable interest can also be based on a <u>financial loss</u> that will take place if an insured individual dies. An example is two partners in a business, each of whom brings substantial expertise to that business. If one partner should die, the business could fail, resulting in a loss to the other partner.

For <u>life insurance</u>, insurable interest must exist at the <u>time of the application</u> for insurance, but it need not exist at the time of the insured's death. For <u>property and casualty insurance</u>, insurable interest must exist at the <u>time of loss</u>.

## INSURABLE RISKS

An insurance company must be able to predict future losses accurately. Also, the company must deal only with <u>insurable risks</u>. Not all risks are insurable, and it is important to outline those risks to which insurance concepts can be properly applied.

**Large Number of Homogeneous Units:** The expected loss experience of a group of exposure units cannot be predicted with any certainty unless there is a large number of exposure units in that group. Risks are not considered insurable unless the insurance company has a large enough number of similar risks and knows enough about its previous loss experience to be able to predict the future reliably.

**Loss Must Be Ascertainable:** Since the purpose of insurance is to reduce or eliminate the uncertainty of economic loss, it is essential that the insured's economic loss be ascertainable. In other words, the <u>insurer must be able to place a monetary value</u> on the loss. In <u>life</u> insurance, monetary value is placed on the insured's <u>income-earning capacity</u>. It is especially difficult to determine economic loss under <u>health</u> insurance. For this reason, economic loss is measured by <u>lost wages</u> or by <u>actual medical expenses</u> incurred. The potential loss must be measurable so that both parties can agree on the precise amount payable in the event the loss occurs.

**Loss Must Be Uncertain:** Since the purpose of insurance is to reduce or eliminate uncertainty, it is obviously not in the public interest to permit the writing of insurance for intentional acts, such as a person committing suicide two days after purchasing an insurance policy. Uncertainty arises out of NOT knowing what is going to happen, or being unable to predict what is going to happen to the individual exposure unit. If insurance is provided for other than uncertain losses, the element of chance is not a factor. Nor is there any element of uncertainty in losses occasioned by natural wear and tear or deterioration, depreciation, or defects in property covered under insurance. Losses are expected in these situations, therefore, such losses would not be uncertain.

**Economic Hardship:** The nature of the loss must be such that an economic hardship would occur should the loss occur. There would be little point in obtaining insurance to cover occurrences so minor that a loss would not produce economic hardship. For example, if a person loses one day's pay because of an injury, a loss occurs, but it is not significant enough to be covered by insurance.

The nature of the loss must be such that it is worthwhile to incur the premium cost to cover potential loss. It must be economically feasible to insure. A comparison of the potential loss with the cost of premium is a major consideration to the insurance buyer.

**Exclusion of Catastrophic Perils:** While the ability to predict future losses with a reasonable degree of accuracy is critical to the insuring function, certain types of perils do not lend themselves to prediction. Such perils, when they cause losses, do not establish a pattern of predictability that can be relied upon for future predictions of anticipated loss. These perils are usually <u>excluded from coverage</u>. Examples of excluded catastrophic perils are <u>war, nuclear risk and floods</u>.

# PRINCIPLE OF INDEMNITY

The principle of indemnity restores the insured person, in whole or in part, to the condition he/she enjoyed <u>prior to the loss</u>. Restoration may take the form of payment, repair, or replacement.

In life and health insurance, the principle of indemnity takes on a different meaning because value cannot be placed on a human life. With respect to life insurance, the "value" is assigned not to the person's life, but to the person's potential <u>earning power</u>. The intent of a life-insurance policy is to allow the family to continue financially as if the principal breadwinner were still alive.

# INSURERS

**Types of Insurers:** Insurance is provided to the public by <u>three major sources</u>: private commercial insurers, private commercial service organizations, and the United States Government. Other types of private insurers include reciprocals, fraternal insurers, Lloyd's of London, and re-insurers.

1. *Stock Insurers:* A stock insurance company, like other stock companies, consists of stockholders who own shares in the company. The individual stockholder provides capital for the insurer. In return, they share in any profits and any losses. Management control rests with the Board of Directors, selected by the stockholders. The Board of Directors elects the officers who conduct the daily operations of the business.

2. *Mutual Insurers*: In a mutual company, there are <u>no stockholders</u>. In a mutual company, <u>ownership rests with the policyholders</u>. They vote for a Board of Directors, which in turn elects or appoints the officers to operate the company. Funds not paid out after paying claims and not used in paying for other costs of operation may be returned to the policyholders in the form of <u>policy dividends</u>. Dividends from a mutual may <u>never be guaranteed and are not taxable</u>.

3. *Nonprofit Service Organization:* Service insurers are unique to the health insurance field, and technically they are not insurers. They are organizations providing <u>prepaid plans</u> for hospital, medical, and surgical expenses. They do not provide cash benefits to the plan subscriber, but instead <u>pay the provider of medical services directly</u> to the extent covered in the contract. Best known of the service insurers are the various <u>Health Maintenance Organizations or HMOs</u>.

4. *Reciprocal Insurers:* Reciprocal insurers are <u>unincorporated groups</u> of people providing insurance for one another through individual <u>indemnity agreements</u>. Each individual who is a member of the reciprocal is known as a <u>subscriber</u>. Administration, underwriting, sales promotion, and claims handling for the reciprocal insurance are handled by an <u>attorney-in-fact</u>.

5. *Fraternal Insurers:* Fraternal benefit societies are primarily life insurance carriers that exist as social organizations and usually engage in charitable and benevolent activities. Fraternal insurers are distinguished by the fact that their membership is usually drawn from those who are also members of a <u>lodge or fraternal organization</u>. One characteristic of fraternal life insurance is the open contract, which allows fraternal insurers to <u>assess their policyholders</u> in times of financial difficulty.

6. *Reinsurance:* Reinsurance is a form of insurance between insurers. It occurs when an insurer (the re-insurer) agrees to accept all or a portion of a risk covered by another insurer.

   Companies often use reinsurance <u>to reduce the risk of a catastrophic loss</u>. Insurance against loss by earthquakes and aviation accidents might not be available if a single carrier had to assume all

©*TesTeachers Publishing – www.testeacherspublishing.com*

of the risk. Reinsurance makes it possible for a carrier to issue a policy and then share the risk with a larger insurer or a group of insurers.

Reinsurance may be written on an <u>excess of loss</u> basis, which means the re-insurer will pay only the portion of loss that exceeds a threshold, or on a <u>quota share</u> basis, which means that the insurers will share loss on a pro rata or fixed-percentage basis or as <u>facultative</u>, where the insurer elects to reinsure certain risks, but not others.

7. *Captive Insurers:* Captive insurers are <u>formed to serve the insurance needs of their stockholders</u> while avoiding the uncertainties related to commercial insurance availability and costs. A captive insurer's stock is controlled <u>by one interest or a group of related interests</u> who have direct involvement and influence over the company's operations. For example, an association of self insured corporations may purchase reinsurance from a captive insurer that they control. Most captive insurers are <u>non-admitted alien corporations</u>.

8. *Excess and Surplus Lines:* Occasionally, it may be difficult to place a risk in the normal marketplace. If the risk is very large or unusual in nature, typical carriers may be unwilling to assume it. For some special risks, the only market may be with specialty carriers. Such business must be placed through a licensed excess or <u>surplus lines broker</u>, who will attempt to place it with an <u>unauthorized carrier</u> located in another state or out of the country (such as Lloyd's of London).

9. *Government Insurers:* The Federal government provides life and health insurance through various sources. The Federal government has offered a variety of military life insurance plans as well as Medicare for seniors, which is part of Social Security.

Because <u>private insurance policies exclude catastrophic risks</u>, the Federal government has stepped in to provide <u>National Flood Insurance</u>, Federal Crime Insurance, Federal Crop Insurance, and insurance on mortgage loans. At the state level, governments are involved in providing unemployment insurance, Workers' Compensation programs and secondary-injury funds, and state-run medical-expense insurance plans.

Federal, state, and local governments provide <u>social insurance</u> to a segment of the population who would otherwise be without disability income, retirement income or medical care.

**Domestic, Foreign, and Alien Insurers:** An insurer is defined not only by its corporate status, but also by its locality, or "domicile of incorporation." If an insurer is incorporated under the laws of the state in which it conducts business, that insurer is considered a <u>domestic insurer</u>. If an insurer conducts business in a state where it is not resident, the insurer is considered a <u>foreign insurer</u>. If an insurer is incorporated in a country other than the United States, it is considered an <u>alien insurer</u>.

Therefore, an insurer incorporated in California and conducting business in California is considered a domestic insurer. This same California-based insurer conducting business in Colorado would be considered a foreign insurer there. An insurer incorporated in Canada and conducting business anywhere in the United States or its territories is an alien insurer.

**Authorized vs. Unauthorized Insurers:** Before an insurance company can conduct business it must, by law, receive the authority to do so. Insurance statutes require a company to secure a license from the Department of Insurance to sell insurance in a particular state. Once the insurer receives the license, it is considered "<u>admitted</u>" into the state as a legal insurer, and is "<u>authorized</u>" to transact the business of insurance. This licensing power is used to regulate company activities. Licenses may be issued to domestic companies, foreign companies, or alien companies.

## FINANCIAL STATUS (INDEPENDENT RATING SERVICES)

In today's market, no matter what the type of insurance company, producers and clients are very concerned about financial stability. To determine the financial strength of a prospective carrier, producers and clients often turn to independent rating services such as Best's Guide, Standard & Poor's, and Moody's. These private publications may be purchased direct from the publishers or are available at most larger libraries. They rate insurance companies according to the amount of financial reserves the company has available to pay future claims and other liabilities, such as cash surrenders.

## MARKETING SYSTEMS

Insurance companies market their products generally by using producers to sell their products or by selling directly through mass marketing. The majority of policies are sold through producers.

Companies that sell through producers vary by whether their producers are their employees or independent businesspersons, and by who owns the policy expirations.

Independent insurance producers sell the insurance products of several companies and work for themselves or for other producers. They sell their clients the policies that fit the clients' needs best among the many insurers they represent, and are paid a commission for each sale. The independent producer owns the expirations of the policies sold, meaning that that individual may place that business with another insurer upon renewal if it is in the best interest of the client.

Exclusive or captive producers represent only one company, and may be paid a salary or compensated by commissions. Exclusive producers do not own the policy expirations. If the exclusive producer has a group of producers working for him/her, the employing producer then becomes a managing general agent. The managing general agent is paid by an overriding commission; which is in addition to the commission paid to the soliciting producer.

Managing General Agents (MGAs) may be required to obtain an MGA license from the state Department of Insurance. MGAs may be independent, representing several insurance companies, or they may have an exclusive agreement with just one carrier.

Direct writing companies pay salaries to employees whose job function is to sell their company's insurance products. In this case, the insurance company owns the expirations and the producers' business.

The franchise marketing system provides coverage to employees of small firms or to members of associations. Unlike group policies, in which benefits are standard for classes of individuals, persons insured under the franchise method receive individual policies that vary according to the individuals' needs.

Franchise plans are attractive to employers who do not, according to the laws of their state, meet the qualifications for a "true group." They allow the employers to offer individual insurance to their employees at a lower premium than for insurance purchased on an individual basis. Premiums may be deducted from the individual's paycheck.

Non-insurance sponsors are being used more and more. The most common are banks and companies that issue credit cards. This marketing system reaches a select group of individuals who have a history of periodic payments. Usually the sponsor is responsible for the billing of premium, which is added to the billing statement or deducted from checking accounts. <u>Vending-machine</u> sales usually consist of travel-accident policies sold from coin-operated machines at airports. A large amount of coverage is available at low premiums. The coverage is good only for the duration of a single trip and usually covers <u>accidental death only</u>.

## PRODUCERS

<u>Life and health insurance producers (or agents)</u> generally <u>do not have the authority to issue or modify insurance contracts</u>. Customarily, life and health insurance producers are authorized to solicit, receive, and forward applications for the contracts written by their companies. The producer may receive the first premium due with the application, but usually not subsequent premiums, except in industrial life insurance. The insurance company approves and issues the contract after receiving the application and premium from the applicant through the producer. <u>Life and health producers usually cannot bind coverage</u>.

<u>Property and Casualty producers</u> appointed by <u>property and casualty</u> insurance companies generally are granted more authority. These producers <u>may bind</u> or commit their companies by <u>oral or written</u> agreement. They sometimes inspect risks for the insurance company and collect premiums due. Producers <u>may also be licensed as brokers</u>, especially in the area of Surplus Lines.

Since most Surplus Lines insurers, such as Lloyds of London, are "unauthorized," they must conduct their business locally through a licensed representative known as a <u>Surplus Lines Broker</u>. Generally, Surplus Lines Brokers must first be licensed as Insurance Producers and are required to post a "license" bond with the state, since they are responsible for the collection of premium taxes on the Surplus coverages they place.

An understanding of the <u>Law of Agency</u> is important, as an insurance company, like other companies, must act through producers.

Agency is a relationship in which one person is authorized to represent and act for another person or for a corporation. Although a corporation is a legal "<u>person</u>," it cannot act for itself, so it must act through producers. <u>A producer is a person authorized to act on behalf of another person, who is called the principal</u>. When one is empowered to act as a producer for a principal, he/she is legally assumed to be the principal in matters covered by the grant of agency. Contracts made by the producer are the contracts of the principal. Payment to the producer, within the scope of his/her authority, is payment to the principal. The knowledge of the producer is assumed to be the knowledge of the principal. The <u>authority of a producer</u> is of three types: express, implied, and apparent.

<u>Express authority</u> is an explicit, definite agreement. It is the authority the principal gives the producer as set forth <u>in his/her contract</u>. It is very important for a producer to know the limitations of the contract and to operate within its limits. To do otherwise could place the producer in a position of personal liability for <u>Errors and Omissions</u> (E&O). The producer's actions and knowledge <u>are binding</u> on the insurance company, so he/she must be alert to the consequences of his/her actions and words.

<u>Implied authority</u> is <u>not expressly granted</u> under an agency contract, but it is actual authority that the producer has to transact the principal's business in accordance with general business practices. For example, if a producer's contract does not give him/her the express authority of collecting and submitting premium, but the producer does so on a regular basis and the company accepts the premium, then the producer is said to have implied authority. That is, it is a general business practice to collect premium, and <u>by accepting the premium from the producer</u>, the company <u>has implied</u> that the producer has the authority to conduct this practice.

Apparent authority is the authority a producer seems to have because of certain actions taken on his/her part. This action may mislead applicants or insureds, causing them to believe the producer has authority that he/she does not, in fact, have. The principal adds to this impression by acting in a manner that reinforces the impression of authority. For instance, a producer's contract usually does not grant him/her the authority to reinstate a lapsed policy by accepting past due premiums. If, in the past, the company has allowed the producer to accept late premiums for that purpose, a court would probably hold that the policyholder had the right to assume that the producer's acceptance of premium was within the scope of his/her authority.

All premiums received by a producer are funds received and held in trust. The producer must account for and pay the correct amount to the insured, insurer, or other producer entitled to the money.

A producer has a fiduciary duty to the insured or applicant. A fiduciary relationship is developed when a person relies on, or places confidence, faith, or trust in, another person's action or advice. A producer, as a "fiduciary," has accepted the obligation of acting in the insured's best interest. To do this, the producer must become familiar with not only the features of the various policies that he/she sells to the public, but also the many uses to which these policies can be put. The producer must also explain the features of each policy, including its provisions, riders, exclusions, and all possible options to the client.

The producer also owes certain general responsibilities to the company. First, a producer owes the duty of loyalty. Second, the producer owes a duty to obey the company and to perform in accordance with instructions given by the company. If the producer violates the instructions and causes the company a loss, he/she may be liable to the company for any breach of duty.

Third, a producer has a duty to act with that degree of care that a reasonable person would exercise under comparable circumstances. Fourth, a producer must account for all property or money belonging to the company that comes into the producer's possession. Fifth, a producer is required to inform his/her company of all facts that are pertinent to the agency relationship in order that the company will be best protected.

Since a producer acts in the place of his/her company, the act of the producer is, under the eyes of the law, considered to be the act of the company. Each producer should stress to a potential insured the importance of filling out the insurance application completely and honestly. The signed application often becomes a part of the policy and statements made therein may invalidate the insurance contract if they are not true.

Once the insurance company is satisfied that the applicant is a good candidate for insurance, and agreement has been reached as to coverage and premium, the policy will be delivered to the producer. It is important to remember that coverage usually does not begin until the policy is delivered to the insured by the producer, except when binding receipts are used.

Errors and Omissions (E&O) insurance is needed by professionals who give advice to their clients. It covers negligence, error, or omission by the insurer or the producer who is the insurer's representative. E&O policies protect producers from financial losses they might suffer if insureds sue to recover for their financial loss due to a producer giving them incorrect advice (error) or not informing them of an important issue (omission).

E&O policies cover only losses due to negligence, error or omission. For example, a producer can be sued if he/she replaces an existing policy and fails to mention that the probationary period starts over. E&O policies usually have a high deductible that provides an added incentive for a producer to minimize his/her errors. E&O policies <u>do not cover embezzlement or filing of false financial statements or bodily-injury or property-damage liability</u>.

## CONTRACTS

Insurance policies are contracts. In order to be enforceable in court, they must contain <u>four essential elements</u>, often given the acronym "COAL":

**Consideration:** The exchange of something of value between the parties. The client pays the premium and the insurance company promises to provide coverage. The consideration given between parties <u>does not necessarily have to be equal</u>.

**Offer:** This must be clearly communicated. Usually, the offer is made by the client when he/she completes and signs the application and writes out his/her check for the first premium payment.

**Acceptance of the Offer:** This is usually done when the underwriter approves the application and issues the policy for delivery.

**Legal Purpose and Legal Capacity:** Contracts for illegal purposes are unenforceable in court, and, of course, all parties to a contract <u>must be competent to contract</u>, meaning they must be of age, of sound mind, and not under the influence of drugs or alcohol.

Since insurance contracts are unique because the client must buy them <u>as written</u> without any chance to modify or clarify the contract language, the <u>Doctrine of Adhesion</u> states that if the insurance contract language is vague or unclear, <u>any ambiguity will be construed in favor of the insured</u>, since that person had no chance to change it when he/she bought it. This is why insurance companies don't like to go to court, since they usually lose! The Doctrine of Adhesion is also known as the Doctrine of Reasonable Expectations.

Of course, insurance companies issue most policies based on the answers contained in the application, which are considered to be <u>representations</u>, or the <u>truth to the best of the client's knowledge</u>. If everyone lied, the insurance industry would not be able to function. It is based on the <u>Doctrine of Utmost Good Faith</u>, which <u>applies to all parties</u> involved, including the applicant, the producer, and the insurer.

The legal doctrine of <u>Waiver and Estoppel</u> also relates directly to the responsibilities of insurance producers. <u>Waiver</u> is defined as the <u>voluntary giving up of a known right</u>. Once given up, it cannot be used as a defense in court. In other words, once a waiver of a known right has occurred, the party waiving those rights is stopped from asserting that right in the future. This is known as the <u>Doctrine of Estoppel</u>.

Of course, some clients do make misrepresentations on applications or attempt to conceal material facts from the producer and underwriter. <u>Concealment</u> is defined as the <u>deliberate omission</u> of a material fact. <u>Fraud</u> is defined as a <u>deliberate attempt to deceive</u> the producer or insurance company. Either could cause the policy or claim to be <u>voided</u> by the insurance company. However, since fraud is very hard to prove, most insurance companies are reluctant to use it as a defense, since if they fail to prove it, the other party may sue the insurance company for libel or slander and will probably win.

A <u>Warranty</u> is defined as an <u>absolute guarantee of truth</u>, and if written, such statements are usually required to be <u>notarized</u>. Life insurance companies usually don't ask the client to make any warranties on the application. Instead, the applicant is expected to furnish <u>representations</u>, which is the <u>truth to the best</u>

of his/her knowledge. When the application is attached at policy issue, representations become <u>part of the contract</u>.

However, on some Property & Casualty policies, the insured may be entitled to a premium discount if they "warrant" that they have installed certain safeguards, such as a burglar alarm or a sprinkler system. Breach of this type of warranty may void coverage.

Insurance contracts are also <u>unilateral</u>, in that only one party to the contract, <u>the insurer</u>, makes an enforceable promise to pay a covered claim if the premium has been paid.

Personal contracts of insurance are also <u>aleatory</u>, in that the outcome depends upon chance. Further, the consideration exchanged need not be equal. The insured may pay a premium, but never have a claim.

To help identify individual "loss exposures," producers should be able to identify the various hazards that increase the insurer's risk, or chance of loss. There are <u>three types of hazards</u>: 1) a "moral" hazard, which is presented by a dishonest client; 2) a "morale" hazard, which is presented by a careless client; and 3) a "physical" hazard, such as a dangerous occupation or hobby.

Life insurance polices are "valued" contracts, that pay the agreed policy limit to your beneficiary upon your death. If the insurer won't pay, the beneficiary could sue the insurer for "breach of contract."

However, most Health Insurance policies follow the <u>Principle of Indemnity</u>, which states that the purpose of insurance is to restore the insured financially. Such policies will pay the amount of the claim or the policy limit, whichever is less. No profit is allowed.

# General Insurance

# KEY FACTS

- <u>Insurance</u> is defined as the <u>transfer of PURE risk</u> to the insurance company in consideration for a premium.

- Domestic companies are incorporated (domiciled) in this state.

- Concealment is defined as the failure to disclose a material fact.

- Insurance companies seek to insure a large number of "homogeneous" (similar) risks.

- To be insurable, a risk must be "calculable" (measurable).

- Exclusions (such as self inflicted injury) are designed to prevent "adverse selection."

- Reinsurance is a form of insurance between insurers, designed to reduce the risk of catastrophic loss.

- Surplus Lines is hard to place insurance written by "unauthorized" insurers.

- An "alien" insurer has their home office in another country, such as Canada.

- Binders are temporary insurance containing all the terms of the policy to be issued.

- Conditional or "binding" receipts are used in L&H. Binders are used in P&C.

- A producer's "express" authority is written down in their producer's contract with the insurer.

- "Implied" authority is that which a producer has that is necessary to the transaction of business.

- "Apparent" authority is the authority that a client thinks that a producer has.

- The Law of Agency states that an insurer is responsible for the acts of their producers.

- Producers have "fiduciary" duties when handling premiums for the client or the insurer.

- If a producer discovers negative information about a client, they should notify the insurer.

- A representation is defined as telling the truth to the best of your knowledge.

- Insurance contracts are "unilateral" (one sided), since only the insurer makes an enforceable promise.

- Fraud is the deliberate attempt to deceive.

- Insurance contracts are "conditional," with conditions that apply to both the insured and insurer.

- Insurance contracts are based upon the Doctrine of Reasonable Expectations, which means that it is reasonable for the average person to believe that coverage applies.

- Conditions state the insured's duties in the event of a claim (for example, Notice of Claim).

- Errors & Omissions insurance protects professional persons such as insurance producers in case they are sued for negligent performance of their duties.

- A representation is defined as the truth to the best of your knowledge.  A warranty is defined as a sworn statement of truth, guaranteed to be true.

- Transacting insurance includes collecting premiums and handling claims.

- Stock insurance companies may pay dividends to stockholders.  (non-participating policy)

- A reciprocal is an unincorporated insurance company managed by an attorney-in-fact.

- Mutual insurers may pay dividends to policyholders.  Dividends may never be guaranteed.

- To obtain a Certificate of Authority, an insurer must file a financial statement, rates, and policy forms.

- A policy may be "modified" only by a company officer in writing.  (an endorsement or rider)

- A "foreign" company is incorporated in another state.

- Binders may start coverage.  Binding authority is in the producer's contract.

- Independent Producers own their own accounts and are not insurance company employees.

- The Doctrine of "Utmost Good Faith" states parties to the contract rely on the honesty of each other.

- Insurance laws are not required to be uniform from one state to another.

- It is legal to advertise honest differences in insurance contracts.

- Producers have E&O exposure when replacing one policy with another.

- Speculative risk has the possibility of gain or loss and is not insurable.

- The Law of Large Numbers allows insurers to predict claims more accurately.

- Direct writing insurance companies use salaried or "exclusive" producers.

- A producer's Express Authority is contained in their producer's contract.

- The chance of loss without any chance of gain is called <u>Pure Risk</u>.

- <u>Concealment</u> is defined as the failure to disclose a <u>material fact</u>.

- If policy language is vague, a court will rule in favor of the client under the <u>Doctrine of Adhesion</u>.

- <u>A waiver</u> is defined as the voluntary giving up of a legal right.

- Once a legal right is waived, it can no longer be asserted under the <u>Doctrine of Estoppel</u>.

- <u>A hazard</u> is something that increases the risk.

- An example of a <u>physical hazard</u> on L&H insurance is smoking.

- A <u>careless person</u> presents a "<u>morale</u>" hazard.

- A <u>dishonest person</u> presents a "<u>moral</u>" hazard.

- The Principle of Indemnity states that the purpose of insurance is to make you "<u>whole</u>" again.

- Risk is defined as the <u>chance or uncertainty of loss</u>.

- Insurance is defined as the <u>transfer of risk</u> in consideration of a premium paid.

- Consideration is defined as the <u>exchange of values</u>.

- <u>Consideration need not be equal</u>.

- Risk can be managed in four ways: <u>Transferred, Retained, Avoided or Reduced</u>.

- On L&H insurance, insurable interest must exist at the time of application, <u>but not at time of claim</u>.

- If you would benefit if a person <u>continues to live</u>, you have an insurable interest in that person.

- An "<u>Aleatory</u>" contract is one where the outcome depends on chance.

- Liability may be avoided by entering into a "<u>hold harmless</u>" agreement.

- An agent (producer) may <u>not</u> modify a policy.

- Group insurance "participation requirements" help to <u>avoid adverse selection</u>.

- An exposure is defined as a <u>condition that could result in a loss</u>.

- A client must initial any change that a producer makes on an application.

- A <u>Lloyd's association</u> is a syndicate formed to underwrite risks in the residual market.

- Agents (producers) are also known as "field underwriters."

- Parties to a contract must have legal capacity. A person who is considered to be "sane" has the capacity to enter into contracts.

- A proposal communicated from one party to another is known as an "offer."

- "Speculation" is not an element of an insurable risk.

- Self-insurance makes sense if future losses are "predictable."

- When a "ceding" insurer picks and chooses which risks to reinsure and the reinsurer picks and chooses which risks to accept, it is known as "facultative" reinsurance.

- The state insurance department looks at an insurer's legal reserves in order to determine "solvency."

- The Securities and Exchange Commission (SEC) enforces Federal securities laws.

- A misstatement of a material fact on the application could affect coverage.

- The insurer's expenses are a factor in determining the premium charged.

- A "conditional receipt" is not given to an applicant unless the initial premium has been paid.

- Sharing commissions with agents with like licenses is permitted.

- Insurers purchase reinsurance for a number of reasons, but not to stabilize profits.

- An insurer can legally pay a commission to a person who is no longer licensed, as long as that person was licensed when they sold the policy.

- The law of large numbers states that the more people an insurer insures, the easier it will be to predict future losses. It is used to predict future losses on the average, not individually.

- An "authorized" insurer is an insurer who is licensed to legally sell within a state.

- The requirement that both parties must bring something of value to a contact is "consideration."

- It is not a violation of the Federal Fraud and False Statements regulations to sell insurance in another state as long as the producer holds a valid non-resident license in that state.

- An individual who has been convicted of violating the Federal Fraud and False Statement regulations is known as a "prohibited" person, and may not engage in the business of insurance in a state without the prior approval of the Commissioner or Director of Insurance of that state.

# General Insurance Concepts

# PRACTICE EXAM

1. All of the following are true about "speculative risk," EXCEPT:

   A. Speculative risk involves an uncertainty of loss
   B. Speculative risk involves a possibility of gain
   C. Speculative risk is a feature of gambling
   D. Speculative risk is a feature of insurance

2. An insurer incorporated under the laws of the state in which it is operating is considered to be a(n):

   A. Foreign insurer
   B. Alien insurer
   C. Domestic insurer
   D. Reciprocal insurer

3. An insurance company owned by its policyholders, who receive a return of unused premiums in the form of policy dividends, is a(n):

   A. Stock company
   B. Assessment insurer
   C. Mutual company
   D. Fraternal insurer

4. Which of the following is not one of the available methods for dealing with an exposure to risk:

   A. Retain the risk
   B. Transfer the risk
   C. Avoid the risk
   D. Ascertain the risk

5. The authority of an insurance producer that is spelled out in the written words of the agency contract between the producer and the insurer is:

   A. Apparent authority
   B. Presumed authority
   C. Express authority
   D. Implied authority

6.  Under contract law, the actions by a party may intentionally and voluntarily give up a known right. When this occurs, it is known as:

    A.  Warranty
    B.  Waiver
    C.  Representation
    D.  Binding contract

7.  In the formation of a legal contract, each party must give something of value. Under contract law, this is referred to as:

    A.  Adhesion
    B.  Consideration
    C.  Indemnity
    D.  Agreement

8.  Because an insurer writes the policy language and the insured has little or no control over the content, any ambiguity in the wording is usually resolved in favor of the insured. Because the design and wording of a policy are in the hands of the insurer, insurance policies are said to be:

    A.  Aleatory contracts
    B.  Unilateral contracts
    C.  Contracts of adhesion
    D.  Contracts of indemnity

9.  When an insurance applicant makes a statement, to the best of his/her knowledge, on an application that becomes part of the contract, the statement is considered to be a:

    A.  Condition precedent
    B.  Waiver
    C.  Representation
    D.  Warranty

10. The uncertainty about loss that exists whenever more than one outcome is possible is called:

    A.  Insurable interest
    B.  Hazard
    C.  Indemnity
    D.  Risk

11. In property and casualty and in medical-expense insurance, the principle of making someone "whole" again after a loss by paying only for actual losses is called:

    A.  Subrogation
    B.  Warranty
    C.  Indemnity
    D.  Estoppel

12.    Which type of licensee may legally represent an "unauthorized" insurer, such as Lloyds of London:

       A.    Any insurance producer
       B.    An independent insurance producer
       C.    A Surplus Lines broker
       D.    A service representative

13.    The insurance business is regulated primarily by:

       A.    State laws
       B.    Federal laws
       C.    Individual insurance companies
       D.    The National Association of Insurance Commissioners

14.    In which company may stockholders share in the profits and losses of the insurer:

       A.    Stock
       B.    Service
       C.    Mutual
       D.    Assessment

15.    In which company may policyholders receive policy dividends when there is a profit:

       A.    Stock
       B.    Service
       C.    Mutual
       D.    Assessment

16.    A producer is a representative of:

       A.    The insured
       B.    The insurance company
       C.    The general agency system
       D.    The policyholder

17.    Which of the following terms means that an insurance contract may be of unequal benefit to one party or the other:

       A.    Valued
       B.    Unilateral
       C.    Aleatory
       D.    Adhesion

18.    Which of the following contractual elements consists of the "offer" and the "acceptance":

       A.    Consideration
       B.    Competent parties
       C.    Mutual Agreement
       D.    Legal object

19. Insurance is a means of:

   A. Eliminating risk
   B. Avoiding risk
   C. Transferring risk
   D. Retaining risk

20. A moral hazard:

   A. Arises through an individual's carelessness or irresponsible action
   B. Is the tendency to create a loss on purpose, to collect from the insurance company
   C. Arises from the condition, occupancy, or use of the property itself
   D. Is not a consideration in insurable risk

21. All of the following are required elements of a legal contract, EXCEPT:

   A. Offer and acceptance
   B. Legal purpose
   C. Competent parties
   D. Waiver and Estoppel

22. A binder:

   A. Is always a written agreement
   B. Guarantees that a policy will be issued
   C. May only be issued by the insurance company
   D. May be oral or written

23. An independent producer:

   A. Represents only direct writers
   B. Works for a solicitor
   C. Represents more than one insurance company
   D. Is a "captive" producer

24. All of the following choices are true about "insurance," EXCEPT:

   A. It is a social device for spreading loss over a large number of people
   B. A large, uncertain loss is traded for a small, certain loss
   C. Insurance is a mechanism for handling speculative risk
   D. Insurance transfers risk from one party to a group

25. Some producers supervise all of an insurance company's business within a specified territory. These producers appoint other producers, supervise their business, and receive an overriding commission on that business. What is the formal name for this type of producer?

   A. Managing General Agent
   B. Captive producer
   C. Exclusive producer
   D. Independent producer

# General Insurance Concepts

# PRACTICE EXAM ANSWERS AND RATIONALES

1. **D** Only pure risk is insurable, which is defined as the chance of loss without any possibility of gain. Speculative risk, like investing in the stock market that has the chance of gain or loss, is not insurable.

2. **C** A domestic company has their home office in this state. A foreign company is in another state and an alien company is in another country.

3. **C** A mutual company has no stock although it is a corporation. Ownership of the company rests with the policyholders, who might receive a dividend from accumulated surplus, if declared. Dividends are not guaranteed. Dividends paid by mutuals are not taxable. A stock company is owned by shareholders, who have "equity" in the company. The stockholders may also receive dividends, which are taxable. Stock companies issue "non-participating" policies. A fraternal insurer is non-profit with a lodge system that sells L&H insurance only to their own members.

4. **D** Once a risk is identified, it can be dealt with in several ways. Self insurance is risk retention. Insurance is defined as the transfer of risk. Avoiding risk is difficult.

5. **C** Express authority is written down or "expressed" in your producer's contract. Implied authority is the authority a producer has based on the reasonable expectations of his/her customers. Apparent authority is the authority created when the action or inaction of an insurer gives the impression that such authority exists.

6. **B** Waiver is defined as the voluntary giving up of a legal right. The doctrine of estoppel states that once you voluntarily waive a legal right, you can't get it back.

7. **B** Consideration is defined as the exchange of values. A client exchanges a small certain amount (the premium) for a large uncertain amount (the possibility of a claim). The Principle of Indemnity states that you cannot recover more than you lost.

8. **C** The Doctrine of Adhesion states that any ambiguity in an insurance contract is always construed against the party who wrote it, the insurer. This is why the insured often wins in court, since they have to buy the policy on a "take it or leave it" basis, without any negotiation.

9. **C** Representations are defined as the truth to the best of your knowledge and are required on insurance applications. Warranties are defined as something you guarantee to be true, and are usually not required, although some P&C policies ask that the customer "warrant" that a loss prevention device (such as a burglar alarm) has been installed in order to get a rate reduction.

10. **D**  Risk is the chance or uncertainty of loss. A hazard is something that increases the risk. The word indemnity means to pay or to reimburse the insured for covered losses. The principle of indemnity states that an insurance policy cannot pay you more than you actually lost.

11. **C**  The Principle of Indemnity states you cannot make a profit from insurance. Subrogation is a provision that allows your insurance company to stand in your place to recover moneys they have already paid you.

12. **C**  Surplus Lines Brokers represent "unauthorized" insurers, such as Lloyds of London. Producers represent the insurer. A service representative works for an insurance company in a marketing capacity. An independent producer may represent as many insurers as he/she wants and is paid on a straight commission basis.

13. **A**  Insurance is regulated by state law. The National Association of Insurance Commissioners (NAIC) works to provide some uniformity in state insurance laws, but there is a long way to go.

14. **A**  Stockholders may receive dividends from the shares of stock they own in a stock company. These dividends are not guaranteed, but if paid, are taxable as ordinary income.

15. **C**  A mutual company may pay dividends to policyholders since they issue a "participating policy." Dividends, if paid, are not taxable and are never guaranteed.

16. **B**  Producers represent the insurer. Under the Doctrine of Agency, insurers are responsible for what their producers do.

17. **C**  Aleatory means that the consideration is not necessarily equal. A valued contract is like life insurance, where the insurer agrees to pay a specified amount upon the death of the insured, regardless of his/her human life value. All insurance contracts are unilateral, meaning one-sided. The doctrine of adhesion states that any vague language in an insurance contract will be construed against the insurance company, since they wrote it.

18. **C**  Mutual agreement of the parties is also known as offer and acceptance. The client makes the offer when they sign the application and write the initial premium check. The underwriter accepts the risk by issuing the policy.

19. **C**  Insurance is defined as the transfer of risk in consideration of a premium paid. If you drive without auto insurance, you are retaining the risk by self-insuring. If you take the bus, you are avoiding the risk. If you sell your car, you are eliminating risk.

20. **B**  A moral hazard is created by a dishonest person, such as someone who may use arson to collect on their fire insurance. Moral hazards are best spotted by the producer, who is considered to be the "front line" underwriter.

21. **D**  Waiver and Estoppel are legal doctrines, but are not parts of the contract.

22. **D**  P&C producers often have the authority to make "binders" of coverage, which may be either oral or written. Although a binder creates temporary coverage while the application is being underwritten, it does not guarantee that the policy will be issued. L&H producers do not have binding authority. Instead, they utilize either a Conditional Receipt, which states that there is no coverage until all conditions are satisfied, or a Binding Receipt, which provides a limited amount of coverage while the application is in underwriting.

23. **C**   Captive or exclusive producers work for only one insurer and are often company employees. Independent producers are self-employed and usually represent more than one insurer on a straight commission basis.

24. **C**   Speculative risk, like the chance of winning the lottery, is not insurable.

25. **A**   A Managing General Agent (MGA) is like a sales manager who is responsible for recruiting and training producers on behalf of an insurer in a specific territory. They need a special MGA license and are compensated on a commission over-ride basis.

# SECTION 3

# Life Insurance Basics

## INSURABLE INTEREST

Life insurance is based upon the concept of <u>Insurable Interest</u>, which is based usually on a <u>family situation or economics</u>. Of course, everyone is considered to have an insurable interest in his/her own life, but, if you want to buy a life insurance policy on the life of another, you must prove insurable interest to the company underwriter <u>at the time of application</u>.

For example, if you want to buy life insurance on your spouse or child, you would have to prove that the family relationship exists and that you would suffer personally and/or financially upon the death of the family member. Another example is <u>Key Person</u> insurance, in which a business owner buys life insurance on a key employee, since the business would suffer if the key party died.

Both of the above are examples of <u>Third Party Ownership</u>, where the insured is the family member or key person and the policyholder is one of the other family members or a business owner. The <u>owner of the policy retains all rights of ownership</u>, including the right to name a beneficiary, pay the premium, take a loan or cash surrender, etc. If the third party insured is an adult, that person's <u>written consent</u> is also required.

The purpose of requiring insurable interest as a prerequisite to buying a life insurance policy on the life of another is to <u>prevent gambling</u>. Without this requirement, you could buy a policy on anyone with a dangerous life style and name yourself as beneficiary, hoping to profit from his/her death.

Historically, life insurance has been primarily <u>regulated by state law, not federal</u>. In the 1940s, Congress passed the <u>McCarran Act</u>, which states that the Federal government has the right to regulate the business of insurance, but only to the extent that it is not regulated by state law. This exempts the insurance industry from most of the provisions of the Federal antitrust laws.

However, if an insurance contract contains "variable" features, in which the client bears the investment risk, the contract will come under Federal securities laws. For example, both <u>variable annuities and variable life insurance</u> contracts place the client's funds in <u>separate accounts</u>, which are very similar to mutual funds. Since the client could possibly lose his/her invested dollars, these policies have been found to meet the definition of a security as defined under the Federal <u>Securities Act of 1933</u>.

Federal securities laws are enforced by the <u>Securities and Exchange Commission</u>. A producer selling these products must also have a Federal <u>Financial Industry Regulatory Authority (FINRA)</u> license (either Series 6 or Series 7) in addition to his/her state life insurance license. Due to the risk involved, the producer must also give his/her client a disclosure document commonly known as a <u>prospectus</u>.

## PERSONAL USES OF LIFE INSURANCE

The main purpose of life insurance is to offer protection to your survivors in the event of your death. Other personal uses of life insurance include the creation of an estate, cash accumulation, liquidity, estate conservation and viatical settlements.

If you buy a $1,000,000 life insurance policy and then die, it could be said that you have created an estate that will now go to your beneficiary income-tax free as life insurance proceeds.

If a client would like to have both protection and cash accumulation, Cash Value life insurance will satisfy both needs. Upon death, the policy will pay the face amount to the beneficiary. If the client lives, the accumulated cash value may be borrowed from the insurer or the client may elect to surrender his/her policy for its cash value at any time, providing instant liquidity.

Or, a wealthy client may purchase life insurance simply to pay estate taxes, thereby ensuring that their estate will pass on to their heirs intact and without further estate tax obligations.

Investors may find investment opportunities through viatical settlements. With this type of settlement, a terminally ill person may give up their rights to their policy, in exchange for advance payment of a portion of the death proceeds. The policy is assigned to the investor who names themselves as beneficiary to receive the face amount when the insured dies. The difference between what they paid and what they receive is their profit.

## DETERMINING AMOUNT OF PERSONAL LIFE INSURANCE

A producer usually uses one of two methods to calculate how much insurance coverage a client needs. The first is called the "needs approach." The other is the "human life value approach." Neither method takes "self maintenance" costs into consideration.

**Human Life Value Approach:** This is based on the earning potential of the insured projected over a period of future years. In this method, the producer calculates what a family would lose in income by the death of the principal wage earner and presents a plan that would reimburse that loss.

**Needs Approach:** The producer simply determines the needs of the individual client and presents a plan that will meet those needs. Needs would include burial expense, family maintenance, children's education and continuing income for the surviving spouse.

After your death, your family or estate could be responsible for various items including funeral expenses, estate taxes, mortgages, and other debts. In addition, your family will need both short-term and long-term income for day-to-day living and educational expenses. In addition to replacing the lost salary or services of the deceased, beneficiaries should take the Social Security "blackout" period into consideration when planning future income needs.

For example, a "currently insured" client dies, leaving a 35-year old spouse and a 10-year old child. Under Social Security survivors' benefits, the spouse and child are eligible for monthly benefits until the child turns age 16. After that, benefits stop for both the surviving spouse and child. The spouse is now 41, but will not be eligible for Social Security benefits until age 60, leaving a "blackout" period of no Social Security benefits of almost 20 years. The spouse will need income from the proceeds of the deceased's life insurance policy during this period. Also, certain settlement options selected by the beneficiary upon death of the insured may exhaust proceeds over a period of time. Beneficiaries should also understand the lifetime income features of annuities as a life insurance settlement option when planning for future income needs.

When <u>planning for income needs</u>, the beneficiary of life insurance proceeds may decide to either <u>liquidate</u> the death proceeds from an insurance policy <u>or</u> deposit the proceeds in an interest bearing account, drawing the interest only and <u>retaining the capital in the account</u>.

## BUSINESS USES OF LIFE INSURANCE

**Buy and Sell Agreements:** Cross Purchase Buy/Sell Agreements help with the orderly continuation of a business in the event that an owner dies prematurely. Based on legal contracts that set a value on each person's portion of ownership in the business, such agreements are commonly funded through life insurance. The proceeds allow another individual to purchase the deceased owner's interest so that the survivors can receive a fair cash settlement and the business can continue without disruption. Buy/Sell Agreements may be used in any form of business, whether it is a sole proprietorship, partnership or corporation. The premiums are not tax-deductible, but neither are the proceeds taxed.

**Key Person Life Insurance:** This type of coverage protects a business against loss of one of its most valuable assets - a key employee. This life insurance program would provide the corporation or employer with funds if a key employee were to die and his/her contribution to the company was terminated. Obviously, the loss of a key employee may not be recovered, but the proceeds of the policy will permit the employer to reduce his/her financial loss. Policy proceeds may be used to hire a new key person, hire temporary help or train new employees.

The primary purpose is to indemnify a business for financial losses caused by the death of a valuable employee. Key Person life insurance also receives favorable tax treatment, as the death proceeds are not taxable. However, premiums are not deductible for business income-tax purposes.

**Executive Bonuses:** Some employers use life insurance products to fund-deferred compensation plans which enable highly paid corporate employees to defer current income, such as an executive bonus, and have it paid at a later date when the employee may be in a lower tax bracket.

## CLASSES OF LIFE INSURANCE POLICIES

**Group Life Insurance:** The most inexpensive type of life insurance, since it is usually sold to employer groups on a payroll deduction plan, which lowers the cost of administration <u>compared to individual policies</u>. Also, since people who are working are usually younger and in better health than the population in general, the cost of mortality is generally lower. True Group Life plans usually require a <u>minimum of 10 people</u> be covered and they usually have participation requirements in order to prevent adverse selection. <u>The grace period is 31 days</u>. Most Group insurance is written as Annual Renewable Term. Group rates are based on past claims' history to some extent (experience rating).

**Ordinary Life Insurance:**

1. *Whole Life:* Sometimes called Cash Value life insurance and is considered to be <u>permanent</u>. It <u>covers</u> you <u>until you die or until the policy reaches maturity</u>, which is normally age 100. A Whole Life policy <u>cannot</u> be changed without the client's consent and it never has to be renewed, although the premium may be paid annually or even more frequently.

Whole Life is said to have a relatively low net cost, since it does develop a cash value after the third year that belongs to the policyholder while living. However, upon death of the insured, the policy will pay the "face amount" (policy limit), but the company will keep the accumulated cash value. This is how Whole Life policies are able to maintain a level premium as you get older. Actually, since they keep the cash value upon your death, the insurance company's risk diminishes over time, since at age 100, your cash value will equal the face amount of the policy.

Whole Life will pay the face amount at death or maturity, whichever comes first. So, if you live to 100, the company will pay you your accumulated cash value, which will be at least equal to the face amount of your policy. This is simply a return of your own money, plus interest.

2. *Term:* Considered to be temporary, in that it is usually purchased for a particular temporary need, such as to cover a bank loan or a mortgage. Although term is the most inexpensive type to buy at issue, over the long run, its net cost may be higher than Whole Life since there is no cash value to offset the cost. The word term means time, and a Term policy is written for a specific period of time, such as one year, five years, etc. When the term is over, the policy will expire. Most Term policies are renewable, but since you are now older, at a higher premium. Seldom will a Term policy cover you past age 65, since the chance of death (risk) is too great. There are several types of Term, including Annual Renewable Term, Level Term and Decreasing Term, all of which will be discussed later in this chapter.

3. *Endowment:* Policies that are similar to Whole Life, except they mature (endow) at a predetermined age that is selected by the client upon purchase. For example, an Endowment at 65 (E65) purchased with a face amount of $100,000 at original age 30, will pay $100,000 upon the death of the insured prior to age 65. However, if the client lives to age 65, the policy will endow and pay the client $100,000, which can be used for retirement purposes. An Endowment policy also has a cash value, but it accumulates much faster than it would in a Whole Life policy. This is because the policy matures at a predetermined age (65 in our example) instead of age 100. This means that the premium would have to be much higher, since the insurance company does not have the use of your money to age 100. Of course, if the premium is higher, the cash value would also accumulate much faster. Endowments are also often used for children's educational purposes.

All ordinary life insurance policies base their premiums and benefits on the 1980 CSO (Commissioner's Standard Ordinary) Mortality Table, which is based on the Law of Large Numbers. This table tracks the life spans of 10,000,000 people from newborns through age 100 and calculates the number of people that will die, on the average, at each age per 1,000 people. So, you can look at this table to find out how many people your age will die this year, but the table is unable to tell you which ones. According to this table, everyone dies by age 100.

All three types of ordinary life insurance have one thing in common: They have a grace period of at least 30 days, during which time coverage remains in force. If you die in the grace period, the insurance company will pay the face amount of the policy, but it will subtract the overdue premium from policy proceeds.

**Industrial (Home Service) Life Policies:** Very popular during the 1930s and 1940s and were sold by, so called, "debit" producers, who called on clients once a week. Since the premium was paid weekly and there are four weeks in a month, the grace period on Industrial Life policies is 28 days. Most Industrial policies had face amounts (policy limits) of $1,000 or less and did develop cash values. Producers usually don't sell this type of insurance anymore, but it is still sold by mail (Direct Response policies).

**Nonparticipating Policies:** Stock companies issue nonparticipating policies, meaning that company profits may be returned to the stockholders (who own the company) in the form of dividends. The policyholders are not entitled to share in company profits. Dividends paid to stockholders of a stock company are considered to be ordinary income and are taxable.

**Participating Policies:** Mutual companies do not have stock. Although they are corporations, they are owned by the policyholders. If the Board of Directors declares a dividend, it will be paid to the policyholders. The IRS has ruled that these dividends are a return of premium already paid, so they are not taxable. Mutual companies issue participating policies. Dividends may never be guaranteed.

**Fixed vs. Variable Life Insurance and Variable Annuities:** Fixed insurance products, such as Traditional Whole Life, have fixed guaranteed rates of return. Cash values are invested in the insurer's general account in a conservative fashion, since the insurer bears the investment risk.

For example, if a whole life product guarantees a 4% rate of return on the cash value accumulation but the general account only earns 3%, the insurer must make up the difference. In addition, the cash value is guaranteed to be a certain amount at a specified time in the future, assuming the insured pays all required premiums and does not take out any policy loans.

However, variable products do not have a guaranteed rate of return nor do they have a guaranteed cash value. The cash value in variable contracts is invested in the insurer's separate account, which is similar to a mutual fund. Since there are no guarantees, other than the minimum death benefit on a variable life policy, the insured bears the investment risk.

As a result, variable life insurance and variable annuities are considered to be securities and are regulated as such by the Federal Securities and Exchange Commission (SEC). Clients purchasing variable products are seeking to "hedge" against inflation, since most mutual funds have kept up with the rate of inflation in the economy over a period of time.

## PREMIUMS

Since insurance companies require that premiums be paid in advance, they have money to invest that earns interest. So, the cost of death (mortality) plus expenses minus interest equals the Gross Annual Premium.

Net Single Premium is an initial participating life insurance policy premium minus policy dividends when the insured applies such dividends to pay part of the policy premium.

The method and frequency with which a premium is paid to the insurer is called the Premium Payment Mode. This is simply how often the premium is paid - monthly, quarterly, semi-annual or annual installments.

## PRODUCER RESPONSIBILITIES

**Solicitation:** State law prohibits insurers and producers from engaging in untrue, deceptive or misleading advertising in connection with the solicitation of life insurance. When soliciting life insurance, producers may not refer to the Life and Disability Insurance Guaranty Fund.

In addition, insurers shall provide to all prospective life insurance purchasers, (except those buying annuities, credit life, group life or variable life) a Buyer's Guide and a Policy Summary (proposal) prior to accepting the applicant's initial premium, unless the policy contains an unconditional 10-day free look. In this case, the Buyer's Guide and Policy Summary must be delivered no later than the policy delivery date. A Buyer's Guide and Policy Summary must also be provided to any prospective purchaser upon request.

The purpose of the Buyer's Guide and Policy Summary is to improve the purchaser's ability to select the most appropriate plan of life insurance, to understand the basic features of life insurance and to evaluate the relative costs of similar plans of insurance.

If the purchaser is considering purchasing a policy where cash values, death benefits, dividends or premiums may vary based on events or situations the company does not guarantee (such as interest rates), he/she may get an illustration from the producer or company that explains how the policy works. The illustration will show how the benefits that are not guaranteed will change as interest rates and other factors change and what the company guarantees.

Purchasers may utilize one of two methods, as explained in the Buyers Guide, to compare the true cost of life insurance:

1. *Interest-adjusted Net Cost Method:* Also known as the Life Insurance Surrender Cost Index, this index is useful if you consider the level of cash values to be of primary importance. It helps you compare the costs of different policies that you are considering if at some future point in time, such as 10 or 20 years, you take cash surrender. An interest rate is used to reflect the time value of the accumulated cash values.

2. *Comparative Interest Rate Method:* Also known as the Life Insurance Net Payment Cost Index, this index is useful if your main concern is the benefits that are to be paid at your death and if the level of cash value accumulated is of secondary importance. It helps you evaluate the relative premium costs of the different policies you are considering at some future point in time, such as 10 or 20 years, if you continue paying premiums and do not take cash surrender. An interest rate is used to reflect the time value of the premiums paid rather than the accumulated cash values.

Regardless of the index used, it is important to remember that a policy with a small index number is generally a better buy than a comparable policy with a larger index number.

**Field Underwriting:** Under the Entire Contract Clause, the application is usually combined with the policy to form a legally enforceable contract. The application is the underwriter's main source of underwriting information and it will contain general information about the applicant, medical information about the applicant and statements made by the producer regarding the applicant. This last part, often called the Producer's Report, contains information regarding the producer's personal knowledge of the applicant, such as financial status, habits and character.

If the underwriter is going to order an investigative report from an independent investigating firm, the applicant must be given the proper Notice Regarding Insurance Information Practices as required by the Federal Fair Credit Reporting Act.

The application also permits the applicant to select the Mode of Payment (budget-plan options), how dividends are to be paid (if any), the manner in which policy proceeds would be paid upon the applicant's death and the designation of a beneficiary.

The application must be signed by the proposed insured, the applicant (if different from the insured) and the producer. Once completed, the producer may not change anything on the application without the written consent of the applicant.

Of course, the producer is also responsible for collecting the premium at the time the application is signed. Insurance companies employ actuaries who calculate the cost of mortality (death) based on the

Law of Large Numbers. To this cost is added (or loaded) certain insurance-company expenses such as acquisition costs (commissions, cost of physical exams, underwriters, etc.), general overhead expense (rent) and loading for unforeseen contingencies. Acquisition costs are usually highest the first year.

When accepting the initial premium from an applicant, a producer usually gives a <u>Conditional Receipt</u>, which makes the coverage effective on the date of application if the company finds the applicant to have been insurable on that date. Remember, the Conditional Receipt is never given unless you receive the premium. It is the producer's responsibility to advise the client which conditions must be met in order for coverage to apply, if any. Some companies use a <u>Binding Receipt</u> instead, which always makes coverage effective on the date of application. A Binding Receipt (or temporary insurance agreement) limits the maximum amount that the company is liable for until the policy is issued, which is known as the "Temporary Term of Coverage." A producer's binding authority, if any, is found in the producer's contract with the appointing insurance company.

When calculating the premium for a life insurance policy, most insurance companies require that the rate be figured based on the applicant's closest birthday. However, many companies will allow producers to <u>backdate coverage up to six months</u> in order to help the applicant obtain a younger original age.

Applicants must also indicate on the application, whether or not the new application for life insurance will <u>replace</u> a policy the applicant already owns. <u>If yes</u>, with certain exceptions, the producer must also give the applicant a <u>Notice Regarding Replacement</u> and a <u>Policy Proposal or Outline of Coverage</u>. The Notice explains to the applicant that replacement is not always in his/her best interest, since he/she is older and the premium may go up. The new policy will not likely develop a cash value until after the third year, the Suicide Clause and the Incontestability Clause period starts over, etc.

Although replacement is <u>not</u> illegal, the new insurer must notify the existing insurer when replacing coverage. Convincing a client to replace coverage to his/her detriment is called <u>twisting</u>, which is a violation of the State Insurance Code.

Insurance underwriters also rely heavily on the producer as <u>a front line underwriter</u>. Since the company underwriter never gets to meet the applicant, the decision is based mostly on the analysis of the various consumer reports on the applicant. The producer, as field underwriter, is in a better position to determine whether or not the applicant really fits the underwriting guidelines of the company.

**Delivery:** Once it is approved and issued, the producer <u>usually</u> will personally deliver the policy to the insured. This enables the producer to thoroughly explain all coverage provisions, exclusions and riders to the insured. Sometimes, the company will mail the policy directly to the insured. Whether the policy is personally delivered or mailed, most policies contain a <u>Free Look</u> provision that starts at the <u>time of policy delivery</u> to the insured. If the policy is mailed, the Free Look starts on the <u>date of mailing</u>. The Free Look enables the insured to return the policy within a certain number of days of policy delivery (<u>usually 10</u>) for a complete refund of all money paid. The client need not give any reason for his/her request. Of course, there is no coverage if the policy is returned.

In unusual situations, the producer may submit the application (without any premium payment) for underwriting consideration. For example, your client does not meet the underwriting standards outlined in your Producer's Manual. However, due to extenuating circumstances, you feel that the risk presented is acceptable. In this event, you could have the client complete and sign the application and submit it to underwriting for review. If the underwriter agrees with you, the policy will be issued COD (the premium to be collected on delivery). Of course, there is no coverage yet, since the premium has not been paid. Upon policy delivery, you will have to collect the first premium and have the client sign a

<u>Statement of Continued Good Health</u>, ascertaining that their health has not changed since the original application was completed. <u>Upon obtaining this statement and the appropriate premium</u>, coverage will begin.

## INDIVIDUAL UNDERWRITING BY THE INSURER

**Information Sources and Regulation:** Company underwriters rely heavily on the completed application, the <u>Producer's Report</u> within the application, <u>Investigative Consumer Reports</u>, <u>medical questionnaires and physical exams</u> and information supplied by the <u>Medical Information Bureau</u> (MIB). This is a nonprofit association that maintains medical data on applicants for life insurance. MIB information is reported by code to member insurance companies, but it does not indicate any action taken by other insurers, nor the amount of life insurance requested. An insurer may not refuse a risk based solely on data supplied by the MIB. There must also be other relevant underwriting factors.

Insurance company actions taken from reports and findings are not recorded anywhere in MIB files. Applicants have the <u>right to see any information</u> the MIB holds on them. Recourse against inaccurate information is prescribed under the <u>Fair Credit Reporting Act</u> or state privacy protection acts. MIB procedures require:

1. *Written Notice:* Issued to the applicant that the insurance company may report health findings to the MIB

2. *Authorization:* Issued by the applicant for the MIB to disclose information to member companies

3. *Disclosure:* Issued to the applicant, upon written request, of information contained in MIB files. The MIB will disclose medical information only to the applicant's physician, whom the applicant must then contact.

These disclosures are contained in a section of the application called the <u>MIB Notice</u>, which is usually located just above the signature line.

Most states have made efforts to pass legislation addressing the testing, non-discrimination and confidentiality of information relating to <u>Acquired Immune Deficiency Syndrome</u> (AIDS) or the <u>Human Immunodeficiency Virus</u> (HIV).

<u>No one</u> may require the performance of an HIV-related test without, first, receiving the specific written informed consent of the <u>applicant</u>. In addition, no one who obtains confidential HIV-related information, in the course of processing the insurance application, may disclose that information, <u>except</u> to the applicant or to persons to whom disclosure is authorized in writing. This includes, but is not limited to, a physician designated by the applicant or the MIB under procedures intended to ensure confidentiality.

HIV-related tests and application responses may be shared with those who are involved in <u>underwriting decisions</u>, excluding producers and brokers. However, it should be noted that a general authorization for the release of medical information is <u>not</u> a release of confidential HIV-related information, unless it specifically so states. Anyone making a disclosure of HIV-related information, in accordance with these regulations, shall keep a record of all such disclosures. Upon request, the <u>applicant</u> shall have access to such records.

**Selection Criteria:** Making any unfair discrimination between individuals of the same class and equal expectation of life in the rates charged or benefits payable for any contact of life insurance is considered to be an Unfair Trade Practice. The availability of any insurance contract, the amount of benefits payable or type of coverage shall not be restricted on the basis of sex or marital status. Further, <u>people who are blind may not</u> be unfairly discriminated against in any manner and <u>shall not</u> be considered to have a different life expectancy, unless such blindness is relevant to the expected risk of loss.

Underwriters are also expected to protect the insurance company from <u>adverse selection, poor risks and applicants with fraudulent intentions</u>. Adverse selection exists when clients, due to a particular company's underwriting standards, take advantage of a situation that ends up costing the insurance company money in excess claims.

For example, since Group Life insurance has few, if any, underwriting standards, a person might take a job just to qualify for the insurance that he/she would normally be unable to purchase due to health reasons. This would be adverse selection from the insurance company's viewpoint and may end up costing it money. To solve this problem, most companies have participation requirements on group contracts, such as requiring that at least <u>75%</u> of the eligible employees enroll in a <u>contributory group</u> (the employees pay part of the premium). By requiring 75%, the insurance company is assured of obtaining a high percentage of the healthy workers, thereby preventing adverse selection. In a <u>non-contributory group</u>, in which the employer pays the entire premium, <u>100%</u> must enroll.

Underwriters are also very concerned with applicants who present a <u>moral hazard</u>, by misrepresenting health, financial status, occupation or dangerous hobbies. Generally, a moral hazard is presented by a dishonest applicant and is often very difficult to detect, which is why the producer's personal evaluation of the client as a front line underwriter is so important.

Whether or not a producer is a good front line underwriter will become evident over a period of time by examination of the producer's <u>loss ratio</u>. A loss ratio is determined by dividing losses by total premiums received. If a particular producer's loss ratio is higher than the company average, it may be that the producer is failing as a front line underwriter. Remember underwriters have four choices: <u>issue the policy</u>, <u>issue with a surcharge</u>, <u>issue with an exclusion</u> or <u>reject the application entirely</u>.

**Classification of Risks:** Underwriters also classify risks based on the categories of <u>standard, substandard or preferred</u>.

1. *Standard Risk:* The average risk with no special health problems and no dangerous hobbies or occupation. The Producer's Manual contains standard rates for applicants by age and gender.

2. *Substandard Risk:* If the applicant is substandard (high exposure), companies have several methods of determining what the surcharged rate should be, including:

   A. Rated-Up Age: This plan assumes the applicant is older than he/she really is. For example, the company might charge a 30-year-old person with a health problem a rate based on age 40 instead.

   B. Flat Additional Premium: A specific additional premium is added to the standard rate. For example, if the standard rate for a 30-year old client is $10 per $1,000, the company might charge an additional $5 per $1,000 surcharge, for a total of $15 per $1,000.

   C. Tabular Rating: Here the company actuary determines what the exact surcharge should be for a client with a particular impairment based on claims history of similar clients.

D. Graded Death Benefits: The company charges the client a premium for $100,000 face amount, but only writes the policy for $75,000 instead. After a period of time without claim, the company may gradually increase coverage up to $100,000.

3. *Preferred:* Most surcharges are based on a percentage table that is applied to the standard rate. <u>Most clients are insurable</u>. It's just a question of how much it will cost. If the client is truly preferred, that is, one who does not smoke and who keeps fit by regular exercise, many companies will offer special policies with rates even lower than the standard.

<u>Most applicants for Life insurance are able to purchase insurance at standard rates</u> (those published in the rate manual). If the applicant has a dangerous hobby, the insurance company may still issue the policy by <u>rating</u> the policy higher (a surcharged premium) or by issuing the policy at standard rates but with an exclusion for the dangerous hobby. If excluded, the insured would not be covered if he/she died as a result of the dangerous hobby.

# Life Insurance Basics

# KEY FACTS

- The applicant's <u>Consideration</u> is both the <u>answers</u> on the application and the <u>premium</u>. In return, the insurance company promises <u>coverage</u>. Consideration does not have to be equal.

- Coverage can NEVER begin unless the <u>premium</u> has been paid.

- The earliest that coverage COULD start would be the day of application, assuming the client paid the first premium, had no conditions to fulfill, and had not lied on the application.

- <u>Surcharges</u> (Rate-Ups) may be accomplished by basing rates on an older age, a different gender, a flat fee, or as percentage adjustment to the Manual Rate.

- A Surcharge is an example of a <u>Counteroffer</u>. There is no coverage until the client accepts the policy at the higher rate and pays the increased premium.

- A Rate-Up or <u>Surcharge</u> may be charged every year for a dangerous hobby or health problem.

- An <u>incomplete application</u> is usually returned. However, should the underwriter approve it, coverage begins and the company has waived its ability to <u>contest a claim</u>.

- <u>Insurable Interest</u> must exist at the time of application, but not necessarily at the time of a claim.

- The <u>less</u> frequent the <u>Mode</u> of payment, the <u>lower</u> the total annual premium will be, and vice versa. There is no service charge or fee if you elect the Annual Mode of payment.

- <u>Variable Life</u> producers do NOT have to be registered with the New York Stock Exchange (NYSE). They DO have to be registered with the Financial Industry Regulatory Authority (FINRA).

- Client funds invested in a <u>Variable Life</u> contract or <u>Variable Annuity</u> must be kept in the insurance company's <u>Separate Account</u>, which is similar to a mutual fund.

- Client funds used to purchase <u>Whole Life</u> and <u>Fixed Annuities</u> are kept in the insurance company's <u>General Account</u>, which is invested more conservatively.

- Stockholders in small, privately held <u>closed corporations</u> often enter into <u>Buy/Sell agreements</u> with the corporation that are funded by Life policies.

- <u>Insurable interest</u> may be based on economics or family relationships.

- The SEC (Securities Exchange Commission) is a <u>Federal agency</u> that regulates securities.

- FINRA (Financial Industry Regulatory Authority) is an association that regulates its <u>own members</u>.

- The company underwriter determines the <u>final rating classification</u>, not the producer.

- Life insurance premiums are based on <u>mortality (death) plus company expenses minus interest</u> earned on company investments.

- Third Party Administrators (TPAs) are more common due to the growth of <u>self-funded plans</u>.

- A "<u>standard risk</u>" is one with an average life span. Most clients' are "standard."

- A "<u>rated</u>" policy is one issued to a sub-standard risk with dangerous hobbies or health problems.

- Life insurers may discriminate based upon <u>physical hazards</u> (age and health) of the client.

- The "needs approach" to life insurance <u>does not consider</u> future earnings.

- Life insurance advertising <u>may stress</u> honest contract differences.

- Acquisition costs of life insurance companies are highest the <u>first policy year</u>.

- <u>Policy modifications</u> must be in writing and signed by a company officer.

- A 60 year old male has a higher mortality rate than a 60 year old female.

- A brother and sister have an insurable interest in each other based upon genetics.

- You have an insurable interest in another person if you would benefit if they continue to live.

- A "preferred risk" need not have a high income.

- A policy that provides for business continuation in the event that a business partner dies is based upon a "cross-purchase buy/sell" agreement.

- A corporation may buy a policy on a shareholder to provide for "stock redemption" in the event of the shareholder's death.

- A "stock redemption" plan is an agreement whereby a corporation agrees to buy back the stock of a deceased shareholder.

- When life insurance is purchased as an "executive bonus" for a corporate employee, the policy belongs to the employee.

- Life insurance covers death due to either sickness or accident.

- The total cost of premiums that the insured pays over a 12 month period is known as the "gross annual premium."

- Insurers must provide to all prospective life insurance purchasers both a Buyer's Guide and a Policy Summary.

- The HIV consent form states that the results of an HIV test will only be shared with certain individuals, such as the underwriter.

- A parent does not need their minor child's consent in order to purchase life insurance on them.

# Life Insurance Basics

# PRACTICE EXAM

1.  A prospect's statements made in the application for insurance, constitute a part of which of the following:

    A.  Consideration Clause
    B.  Incontestability Clause
    C.  Subrogation Clause
    D.  Coinsurance Clause

2.  An insurable interest must exist when:

    A.  A life insurance policy is issued
    B.  Death proceeds become payable
    C.  Policy ownership is transferred
    D.  Cash values are borrowed

3.  If an applicant for a life insurance policy is found to be a substandard risk, the insurance company is most likely to:

    A.  Refuse to issue the policy
    B.  Charge an extra premium
    C.  Require a yearly medical exam
    D.  Lower its insurability standards

4.  If an applicant for a life insurance policy is a student pilot, which of the following is true:

    A.  They will receive a discounted premium
    B.  The insurer would consider them to be a standard risk
    C.  The insurer would consider them to be a preferred risk
    D.  They would have to pay more than a standard risk for their coverage.

5.  On May 8, a prospect filled out an application for a life insurance policy but paid no premium. The insurance company approved the application on May 14 and issued the policy on May 15. The producer delivered the policy on May 26 and collected the first premium. The coverage became effective on:

    A.  May 8
    B.  May 14
    C.  May 15
    D.  May 26

6. Statements made by an applicant for a life insurance policy that are supposed to be true are referred to as:

   A. Representations
   B. Facts
   C. Warranties
   D. Information

7. A producer takes an application from a proposed insured without receiving payment of the first premium. The insurance company issues the policy and, when the producer visits the proposed insured to deliver it, the producer realizes that the health of the applicant has deteriorated significantly since the application was taken. The producer should:

   A. Obtain the premium from the prospect and send it to the company immediately
   B. Rate the policy and obtain any additional premium required
   C. Deliver the policy as it was issued
   D. Refuse to deliver the policy or to accept any premium offered

8. In the formation of a life insurance contract, the special significance of a Conditional Receipt is that it:

   A. Guarantees the applicant that a policy will be issued in the amount applied for in the application
   B. Serves as proof that the producer has determined the applicant to be fully insurable for coverage by the insurance company
   C. Is given by the producer only to applicants who fully prepay all scheduled premiums in advance of policy issue
   D. Is intended to provide coverage on a date earlier than the date of the issuance of the policy

9. An applicant has been denied insurance coverage because of information contained in a consumer report. According to the Fair Credit Reporting Act, all of the following statements are true about this situation, EXCEPT:

   A. The applicant has the right to obtain a copy of the consumer report directly from an insurance company that used the report
   B. The applicant has the right to obtain disclosure of the substance of the information in the consumer report from the reporting agency
   C. The applicant has the right to obtain the identity of other inquirers who have obtained consumer reports on him/her within the past six months from the reporting agency
   D. The reporting agency cannot issue any report containing adverse information about the applicant that predates the report by more than seven years, except in the case of a bankruptcy, which may be reported for a 10-year period

10. Fixed life insurance products are guaranteed by the insurance companies:

    A. Separate account
    B. General account
    C. Primary account
    D. Secure account

11.  Which of the following is true of the duties of the Financial Industry Regulatory Authority (FINRA):

     A.  They are responsible for making sure that their members follow Federal laws and rules
     B.  They are responsible for creating Federal securities laws
     C.  They are responsible for administering state insurance licensing exams
     D.  They are responsible for regulating insurance agencies

12.  Which of the following is true of the duties of the Securities and Exchange Commission (SEC):

     A.  They are responsible for administering Federal securities examinations
     B.  They are responsible for enforcing Federal securities laws
     C.  They are responsible for enforcing Federal regulation of fixed insurance products
     D.  They are responsible for regulation of non-resident insurance agents

13.  When insuring substandard life-insurance risks, provision is usually made for the expected higher death rate by:

     A.  Charging an extra premium
     B.  Reducing the Death benefit
     C.  Establishing special risk groups
     D.  Reducing the producer's commission

14.  If a proposed insured has a hazardous occupation, the insurance company may:

     A.  Remove the Family Plan benefit
     B.  Cancel the application
     C.  Rate the insured
     D.  Reduce the dividends

15.  A plan, usually funded by Life insurance, to purchase a deceased partner's share of a business is known as a:

     A.  Deferred Compensation plan
     B.  Qualified Retirement plan
     C.  Key Employee Life policy
     D.  Buy and Sell Agreement

16.  The Fair Credit Reporting Act provides:

     A.  That the applicant for insurance be informed that a consumer report may be requested
     B.  Protection to debtors against harassment by lending institutions in the event of default
     C.  For the availability of Credit Life insurance on a fair and impartial basis
     D.  The funding for a national clearinghouse of credit information for life-insurance companies' underwriting operations

17. Insurance may be considered to be in force when the:

    A.    Producer completes the application and the proposed insured signs it
    B.    Proposed insured signs an application and a medical examiner acceptable to the insurance company completes an examination of the proposed insured
    C.    Agency manager deposits the initial premium check into an escrow account
    D.    Insurance company mails a policy to the producer and the producer delivers it to the proposed insured and collects the first premium

18. Which of the following applicants for Life insurance is most likely to obtain coverage as a standard risk?

    A.    An obese office worker
    B.    A student pilot
    C.    A person who skydives
    D.    A traveling heavy-equipment salesperson

19. All of the following are true about Social Security benefits, EXCEPT:

    A.    Monthly payments must remain the same once benefits commence
    B.    Benefits may include a lump-sum Death benefit and a monthly income to survivors
    C.    Virtually all employed persons are covered
    D.    Benefits are financed through taxes

20. All of the following statements about Life insurance and the risk it covers are true, EXCEPT:

    A.    Life insurance is a mechanism for pooling and sharing risks
    B.    As the number of separate risks of the same type increases, the amount of loss within a given period becomes more certain
    C.    The probability of an individual insured's death increases each year until it becomes a certainty
    D.    Life insurance is like a mutual fund in that a certain sum of money must be set aside each year to meet the contractual obligations of the insured

21. In life insurance, insurable interest must exist at which point in time:

    A.    The time of loss only
    B.    The time of application only
    C.    The time of application and the time of loss
    D.    Insurable interest is not required in life insurance, only health insurance

22. An insurer with a Certificate of Authority in this State is known as a(n):

    A.    Certified insurer
    B.    Licensed insurer
    C.    Authorized insurer
    D.    Non-admitted insurer

23. In order to avoid unfair discrimination, life and health insurance rates must be the same:

    A. Regardless of gender
    B. For those who present essentially the same hazard
    C. Regardless of age
    D. Regardless of health

24. Which of the following presents the highest mortality risk:

    A. 40 year old male
    B. 40 year old female
    C. 50 year old male
    D. 50 year old female

25. Insurance underwriters may check an applicant's records with all EXCEPT:

    A. The Medical Information Bureau (MIB)
    B. Consumer reporting agencies
    C. The Internal Revenue Service (IRS)
    D. Credit bureaus

26. Those convicted of making fraudulent or false statements under Federal law may be subject to all of the following penalties EXCEPT:

    A. Jail
    B. Fine
    C. License revocation
    D. Community service

27. All of the following are true about insurable interest on life insurance EXCEPT:

    A. It must exist at the time of death
    B. It may be based upon genetic relationships
    C. It may be based upon economics
    D. It may be based upon love and affection

28. A life insurance preferred risk has all of the following characteristics EXCEPT:

    A. Non-smoker
    B. Exercises regularly
    C. High income
    D. Not overweight

29. All of the following are true about Life insurance "inspection reports" EXCEPT:

    A. They relate to an applicant's medical history
    B. They are also known as investigative consumer reports
    C. They are often ordered by underwriters
    D. They relate to an applicant's credit, character and habits

30. Regarding Social Security survivors benefits, the period of time between when the youngest child turns age 16 and a surviving spouse becomes eligible for Social Security benefits is called the:

   A. Waiting period
   B. Black-out period
   C. Elimination period
   D. Accumulation period

# Life Insurance Basics

# PRACTICE EXAM ANSWERS AND RATIONALES

1. **A** The Consideration Clause states, "In consideration of the premium paid and the statements and answers contained herein, I hereby apply for life insurance with ........" The Incontestability Clause states that the insurance company may not contest a claim for any reason after the policy has been in force for two consecutive years. The Subrogation Clause has to do with Liability insurance and the Co-Insurance Clause has to do with Major Medical (Health) insurance.

2. **A** Insurable interest is based upon love, devotion, economics or a family relationship. An insurable interest must exist at the time of application for one person to buy a policy on the life of another. It need not exist at the time of claim. This requirement prevents gambling or the possibility of murder.

3. **B** Most clients are insurable, it's just a matter of selecting the proper premium to match the risk being undertaken. When the client completes the application and writes a check for the first premium, he/she is making an offer to buy insurance from the company. If the company declines to write coverage at the premium quoted, they may offer to do so at a higher price. This would constitute a counteroffer by the company. The applicant would then have the right to accept or reject the new offer.

4. **D** A standard risk is an average person. A preferred risk is a person who is in exceptional health, and would receive a discount from the standard rate. A person who is a student pilot would have to pay a higher premium than the standard risk. However, if the insurance company wanted to exclude coverage while the insured was learning to fly, and the applicant agreed, the premium would be reduced. But if the insured died in a plane crash while learning how to fly there would be no coverage.

5. **D** No valid contract can exist without consideration, which in this case, was not offered until the policy was delivered on May 26. Had the initial premium been collected when the application was first completed on May 8, coverage **could** have been effective at that time assuming the applicant met all the requirements contained in the company's Conditional Receipt. All contracts must contain these four essential elements: 1) Consideration, 2) Offer, 3) Acceptance and 4) Legal Purpose and Capacity. (*Remember: C-O-A-L*)

6. **A** Insurance law only requires that applicants answer questions by stating the **truth to the best of their knowledge**. These answers are called representations. Warranties, which are sworn statements of truth, are not required.

7. **D** Remember, due to lack of consideration, no valid contract exists yet. Therefore, the producer, who is bound to protect the company, should refuse to deliver the policy or accept any premium offered.

8. **D** The Conditional Receipt is just that, conditional. This means that coverage is conditional upon the applicant meeting all of the underwriting requirements of the company and paying the premium. If the applicant does meet all the conditions, then it is possible that coverage could begin as early as the date of application.

9. **A** The Fair Credit Reporting Act is a Federal law that is designed to protect individuals who are being investigated by consumer reporting agencies or credit bureaus. The law requires <u>pre</u>-notification of any possible investigation and <u>post</u>-notification if any adverse underwriting action is taken by the company as a result of the information received from a credit bureau. An applicant for insurance also has the right to request a copy of the credit report that the company obtained. However, this report may not be obtained directly from the insurance company, but only from the credit bureau that made the report.

   In addition to this Federal law, many states have their own Privacy Protection Act, which states basically the same things. Remember, pre-notification must be **in writing** and when the applicant signs an application, this disclosure by the company that it may order an investigative type report is usually located right above the applicant's signature line.

10. **B** All fixed insurance policies are guaranteed by the insurance company's general account. The portfolio of the general account is invested in medium-term fixed-income-producing debt securities such as bonds and real estate mortgages. The insurer assumes the risk in a fixed product since it guarantees a minimum amount of interest in the contract. If the earnings in the general account are not sufficient to equal the minimum interest due the insurer must make up the difference. Variable products are funded by the insurer's separate account.

11. **A** The Financial Industry Regulatory Authority (FINRA) is a nonprofit self regulatory organization that is responsible for oversight of its members (broker/dealers and registered representatives). The main objective of FINRA is to self regulate the over-the-counter securities market. Since variable insurance products are considered to be securities under Federal law, insurance producers must also obtain a FINRA license in order to sell them.

   Although FINRA is responsible for Securities Licensing exams, the state Department or Division of Insurance is responsible for insurance licensing and administering licensing exams, in addition to regulating insurance agencies.

12. **B** The Securities and Exchange Commission (SEC) is responsible for enforcing Federal securities laws, such as the Securities Exchange Act of 1934. Securities licensing is administered by the Financial Industry Regulatory Authority (FINRA). The statutes administered by the SEC are designed to promote full public disclosure and protect the investing public against malpractice in the securities markets.

   Insurance is regulated at the state level by the Director or Commissioner, who is the head of the Department or Division of Insurance in the state. Fixed insurance products are regulated by the Department of Insurance, NOT the SEC. The same goes for the non- resident insurance agents.

13. **A** A substandard risk in Life insurance is a client with a history of health problems, or a dangerous hobby or occupation. Most of these clients are insurable if they are willing to pay a higher premium or surcharge to the "standard" rate tables.

14. **C** The underwriting department can offer Life insurance to nearly everyone who is willing to pay the premium. To "rate" or "surcharge" the policy means that the underwriter offers coverage at rates

higher than the "standard" or rate published in the producer's manual. It's then up to the applicant to decide if they still want to purchase the policy at the higher price.

15. **D**    A Buy/Sell Agreement is usually set up by an attorney in an effort to reach a predetermined decision on who will own the business in the event one of the partners dies. Without life-insurance policies to fund the agreement, it would be of little value, since no funds would be available to purchase the share of the business owned by the spouse or estate of the deceased business partner.

A Deferred Compensation plan is a fringe benefit some companies offer to key executives as a way to defer income from one tax year to another. A "Qualified" Retirement Plan is one in which the contributions paid in are not subject to current taxation, meaning it meets IRS qualifications. A Key Employee Life insurance policy is usually purchased by a business, naming the business as beneficiary, in the event a key person dies. The policy proceeds would be used to train a new Key Employee.

16. **A**    The Fair Credit Reporting Act is a Federal law that is designed to protect applicants from unfair investigative reporting. It requires that an investigative reporting agency have the applicant's written consent prior to ordering a report (pre-notification) and it also requires that if adverse underwriting action is taken based on the information found in this report, the applicant has the right to obtain a copy of the report from the reporting agency involved (post-notification).

17. **D**    This policy was ordered on a COD (collect-on-delivery), or "submittal" basis, meaning that there is no coverage until the company issues the policy AND the first premium is paid.

18. **D**    Applicants with dangerous hobbies, health problems, or dangerous occupations are most likely to be surcharged when buying life insurance. Of the choices here, only the traveling salesperson is likely to be able to buy insurance at standard rates.

19. **A**    Social Security is a type of social insurance. Social Security actually covers Old Age (retirement), Survivors Benefits, Health Insurance (Medicare), and Disability Income insurance. There is a lump-sum death benefit, but it is only $255.00. Since Social Security benefits are tied to the Consumer Price Index, the amounts of monthly benefits will usually go up over a period of time.

20. **D**    Life insurance is based upon the Law of Large Numbers. A life insurance Mortality Table starts with 10,000,000 lives. By age 100, all have died, making death a certainty. All the responses to this question are correct except D, and it is correct also, EXCEPT for the reference to Mutual Funds. Remember, any part of a question that is false makes the entire question false. Life insurance has nothing in common with Mutual Funds, which are regulated under Federal securities laws. It is true, however, that life-insurance companies do have to set aside a certain sum of money each year to meet the future contractual obligations they have to the insured.

21. **B**    In order to purchase life insurance on another person you have to prove insurable interest at the time of application. If you would benefit from the continued life of an individual, you have an insurable interest in their life. In life insurance, insurable interest only has to be present at the time of application, NOT at the time of loss. Insurable interest is generally based on blood (family) or money (business partner or key employee). For example, an individual would not be able to purchase life insurance on their best friend, since they do not have insurable interest. Insurable interest was created to prevent people from profiting from the death of others.

22. **C** Virtually all insurers doing business in this state must obtain a Certificate of Authority from the Commissioner authorizing them to do business in this State. An "authorized" insurer is also known as an "admitted" insurer.

23. **B** L&H insurers will vary their rates based upon gender, age and/or health. Such discrimination is considered to be fair, since it is based upon verifiable statistical data filed with the Commissioner. However, it would be unfair discrimination to charge different rates for those who present essentially the same hazard.

24. **C** According to the Commissioner's Standard Ordinary Mortality Table, which is based upon the law of large numbers, the average 50 year old male will not live as long as the average 50 year old female, which means they will pay more for life insurance.

25. **C** IRS records are confidential and are not available to insurance underwriters.

26. **D** Under Federal law, those who are convicted of making fraudulent or false statements to regulators, filing false financial statements with regulators or writing threatening letters to regulators are known as "prohibited persons," since they are prohibited from engaging in the insurance business without the prior consent of the Commissioner. Prohibited persons may also be jailed, fined and are subject to license revocation.

27. **A** Although insurable interest must exist at the time of application, it need not continue to exist at the time of death.

28. **C** There are 3 main risk classifications: 1) The standard risk, which is presented by the average person; 2) the non-standard risk, which is presented by a person who may be over-weight, smokes or has health problems; and 3) the preferred risk, which is presented by a person who does not drink or smoke and exercises regularly. A person's income level has nothing to do with their risk classification.

29. **A** A Life insurance "inspection report" is also known as an investigative consumer report. It is usually ordered by the underwriter to verify an applicant's credit, character and habits. Inspection reports fall under the provisions of the Federal Fair Credit Reporting Act.

30. **B** Under Social Security, survivors benefits are only paid to surviving spouses who have children under age 16. For example, a 30 year old widow's youngest child is age 10 when her husband dies. Social Security will pay the widow survivor's benefits until that child reaches age 16, or in this case, 6 years, at which time the widow will be age 36. After that, survivor's benefits will stop until the widow reaches retirement age, which is age 60 for widows whose retirement is based upon their deceased husband's social security contributions. This period of time, which in this example is 24 years, is known as the "black-out" period.

# SECTION 4

# Life Insurance Policies

## TERM LIFE INSURANCE

### Level Term:

1. *Annual Renewable Term:* A policy in which the face amount stays level, but as the insured gets older, the premium increases each year. For example, a 30-year old male in good health could buy a $100,000 ART policy for an annual premium of about $100. However, he would have to renew the policy next year (no physical exam is required to renew it) and the premium would increase to about $110. The year after he would have to renew it again and the premium would increase to about $125. Every year the premium will increase and eventually the policy may lapse, since the insured can no longer afford it. Even if he could afford it, most ART policies are only renewable to age 65 or so. Plus, there is no cash value on term.

2. *Level Premium Term:* Since most clients do not like their premiums to increase each year, most insurers also offer level premium term, where both the premium and the face amount (policy limit) stay level for a period of time, such as five years, 10 years or even 20 years. If a 30-year old male bought a $100,000 five-year level term policy, the premium would stay the same (approximately $125) every year since it is based on the insured's average age during the five-year period. However, at the end of the five-year period, the policy would have to be renewed for the next five years and the premium would increase substantially since it is based on the insured's age for the next five years.

Remember, the word term means time and term insurance is written for temporary periods of time. It is not permanent insurance. In order to be covered, you must die in the term. Plus, since there is no cash value to offset the cost of your insurance, term insurance is the most expensive in the long run. However, term insurance is very popular with clients who have temporary needs, such as an outstanding loan or mortgage responsibility.

Re-entry option: A common feature on many term policies, this option gives the insured the opportunity to pass a physical exam at the end of the term in order to qualify to renew the policy at a lower premium rate than the guaranteed rate available. Of course, if the insured fails the physical, he/she can always renew at the rate guaranteed in the policy.

**Decreasing Term:** A policy in which the <u>premium stays the same</u> each year, but the amount of <u>coverage decreases</u>, usually on a straight-line basis. These policies are usually written to protect a mortgage balance or to fill a business need. They are usually written for periods of 10, 20 or 30 years and expire at the end of the policy period with no option to renew. Although the premium stays the same throughout the policy period, since the amount of coverage goes down, the cost really increases.

For example, if a client bought a 20-year Decreasing Term policy with a face amount of $100,000 and a premium of $250 per year. After 10 years, the premium would still be $250 per year, but the amount of coverage would have decreased to $50,000, so you could say that the cost had doubled. Decreasing term is often attached as a rider or endorsement to a Whole Life policy to enable the insured to purchase a large amount of coverage at a minimal price. As with all Term insurance, Decreasing Term has no cash-value accumulation. It is often used as <u>mortgage protection insurance</u>.

**Convertible Term:** Most Level and Decreasing Term policies are <u>convertible at any time to Whole Life insurance without a physical exam</u>. Again, this option is not required by law, but most companies offer it, since without it, most people would not buy Term insurance. If it is convertible, the insured may convert his/her Term policy to Whole Life (never another Term policy) without proof of insurability. The premium will increase, but only because Whole Life is more expensive than term. Conversions are done <u>at the client's "attained" age</u> at the time of conversion.

After conversion, the client has a new Whole Life policy that can never be changed as long as he/she continues to pay his/her premiums. The new Whole Life policy will also accumulate cash values. Obviously, a client who became sick and thought he/she might die within a few years would want to convert, since his/her Term policy would eventually reach a point at which he/she would be unable to renew it.

## WHOLE LIFE INSURANCE

**Continuous Premium (Straight Life):** Premium payments are based upon client's (original) age at issue and <u>can never be changed</u>. Whole Life policies must accumulate a cash value <u>after the third year</u> in force. A Whole Life policy can never be canceled or changed by the insurance company. Premium rates are based on the assumption that the client will continue to pay premium <u>until age 100</u>. The policy reaches maturity at age 100 and, if the client has continued to pay, the insurance company will then pay the client the face amount (policy limit) or the cash value, <u>whichever is more</u>. The client may take a policy loan or surrender the policy for cash at any time during the policy period after cash values have accumulated. This type of coverage is the <u>least-expensive permanent type of life insurance</u>, if kept in force for a number of years, since the accumulation of cash value lowers the net cost over a period of time. Conversely, Whole Life is the most expensive type of insurance in the short run.

**Limited Payment and Single Premium:** These policies are exactly like Ordinary or Straight Life policies, except, the <u>premium is paid over a shorter period of time</u>. A single premium policy requires the client to pay his/her entire premium (to age 100) up front. It has an <u>immediate cash value</u>, but the policy does not mature until age 100. There are several types of limited pay life contracts:

1. *Life Paid Up at 65 (LP65):* This policy requires the client to pay all of his/her premiums <u>by age 65</u>, so the <u>premiums are much higher</u> than a traditional Whole Life policy that assumes you will pay to age 100. If a client, age 30, took out a regular Whole Life policy, he/she would have to pay premiums until age 100 (a total of 70 years). However, if a client took out a LP65 at age 30, he/she would only have to pay premiums until age 65. At age 65, the cash value would be higher than it would have been if the client had purchased the Whole Life policy, but the premiums would also have been approximately <u>twice as much</u>. In addition, an <u>LP65 does not reach maturity until age 100</u>. At which time, the company will pay, to the insured, either the cash value or the face amount, whichever is more, if the insured is still living. This type of policy is a form of Whole Life. The only difference is the <u>premium-paying period has been shortened</u>. Whenever the premium-paying period is shortened, the insured has to pay the same amount of premiums he/she would have paid by age 100, but in a shorter period of time, so the <u>premium is always higher</u>.

*Truism:* The <u>shorter the premium-paying period, the higher the premium, and vice versa</u>, assuming everything else is equal.

2. *20-Pay Life/30-Pay Life:* Like an LP65, these contracts require the client to pay over a shorter period of time. For example, a client, age 30, who bought a 20-pay life contract would have to pay all the premiums in just 20 years, instead of paying over the 70-year period to age 100, so the <u>premium would be much higher</u>. Again, this is a variation of Whole Life, and the policy does not mature until age 100, although the cash value does build very rapidly.

3. *Single Premium Life:* This policy becomes <u>fully paid up by paying a single premium at policy inception</u>. This is sometimes called a One-Pay Life policy. This policy would have an <u>immediate cash value</u>, but would be very expensive. **Remember the truism:** *The shorter the premium-paying period, the higher the premium and the faster the cash values build.* An insurance company would offer a discount to anyone buying this type of policy based on the present value of money.

**Modified Premium and Graded Premium Whole Life**: Since level premium whole life insurance is expensive, many insurers offer premium discounts during the early years of a policy to make it easier to sell.

For example, a **modified premium whole life policy** may be offered with initial level premiums that are substantially lower than straight whole life. The insured would pay the reduced premiums for a specified period of time, such as 5 years, during which the cash values would build very slowly.

However, after 5 years, the premiums would increase to be substantially more than they would have been if the insured had purchased traditional whole life in the first place. The premium will remain level at this higher amount for the duration of the policy. Remember, <u>it is the premium that is modified, not the face amount. The face amount remains level throughout</u>.

A **"graded" premium whole life policy** also starts out with much lower premiums for the first 5 years, but <u>the premiums will increase gradually</u> each year for 5 years until they reach a point at which they will remain level at an amount that would be higher than they would have been if the insured had purchased traditional whole life in the first place. <u>Again, it is the premium that is graded, not the face amount, which remains level</u>.

To summarize, a modified premium whole life policy starts out with a low (or discounted) level premium for the first 5 years, which increases at the end of the 5 year period to a much higher level premium for the duration of the policy. A graded premium whole life policy also starts out with a low premium that gradually increases each year for 5 years, after which it remains level.

**Endowment Policies:** An Endowment policy is exactly the same as a Whole Life policy, except maturity occurs at a predetermined time selected by the insured. Most Endowment policies are written for retirement purposes or for educational purposes (children's college fund). For example, if an insured bought an Endowment to age 65 (E65) at age 25, with a face amount of $50,000, the beneficiary would receive $50,000 if he/she died anytime between age 25 and 65. If the insured were still alive at age 65, they would be paid the $50,000 by the insurance company and could use it for retirement purposes. Of course, in the meantime, the policy would have accumulated a cash value and the insured could take loans on it. In this example, the policy reaches maturity at age 65 and "endows."

**Remember**: *The endowment is always the most expensive type of life insurance.* It can be written for any length of time or to mature at any age, but age 65 is typical. Pure Endowment policies, without any life insurance protection, are also available, but seldom sold.

**Enhanced Ordinary Life (Economatic):** This is a type of whole life with a term insurance rider which uses dividends to buy additional paid-up insurance.

For example, assume that a client needs $100,000 of whole life insurance, but can't afford to buy that much, so he/she buys $75,000 of whole life and attaches a $25,000 decreasing term rider, which is cheaper.

As dividends are declared by the mutual insurer, they are used to buy additional paid-up insurance. In theory, the amount of paid-up insurance purchased will increase as the amount of the term rider decreases. Eventually the paid-up additions will replace the coverage provided by the decreasing term rider and the client is left with $100,000 of whole life insurance, while only paying an "economical" premium on a $75,000 policy.

## FLEXIBLE PREMIUM POLICIES

**Adjustable Whole Life Insurance:** This policy is marketed to meet the insured's changing needs and ability to pay premiums in an uncertain economic climate. With an Adjustable Life policy, an insured may adjust the face amount of the policy, the amount and/or frequency of premium payments or the period of protection, generally without any underwriting.

Naturally, an adjustment made to one policy provision will also affect other provisions. For example, increasing the premium will cause the face amount and cash values to increase as well.

**Universal Life:** This is an adjustable benefit life insurance contract that accumulates cash values and has a flexible premium. A Universal Life policyholder may increase the death benefit without buying another policy, although they may have to prove insurability to do so. Also, the policyholder has the flexibility to reduce the death benefit as well.

Generally, after deducting expenses (load), the insurance company will deposit the remainder of the premium paid into a cash value account. From this cash value account, the company will deduct the amount needed to pay for the death benefit selected by the policyholder. If the policyholder pays more premium than what is required to provide the desired death benefit plus other administrative costs, the cash value will increase.

Some forms of Universal Life contracts have adopted a "back end" load instead. By postponing sales loads until later (when withdrawals are made), the policy might show a more attractive return than one using the more traditional "front end" load.

Each month, the accumulated cash value of the Universal Life contract will also be credited with interest at the current rate. The current rate actually consists of two parts:

1. *The Minimum Guaranteed Interest Rate:* Usually around 4%.

2. *Excess Interest:* Once a year, the insurer projects its current interest rate, which combines the minimum guaranteed rate and any excess interest they anticipate earning above the minimum. For example, if the guaranteed minimum rate is 4% and the insurer anticipates earning 3% above that, then the current rate would be 7%. The current rate is guaranteed only for one year. If the insurer earns less than 7% for that year, they lose money. If they earn more than 7%, they make money.

There are two options concerning death benefits under Universal Life: Option A, which provides a <u>level death benefit</u>, and Option B, which provides an <u>increasing death benefit</u>. Under either option, the <u>death benefit is received tax-free</u> by the beneficiary.

1. *Option A (level death benefit):* The death benefit is the policy's stated face amount, which is actually made up of the sum of the accumulated cash value, <u>plus</u> the amount of risk (insurance protection). <u>As cash value increases, the amount the insurance company has at risk decreases</u> (they offset). The premium, which remains level, is used to purchase a decreasing amount of protection over a period of time. This is the same concept utilized in Straight Whole Life contracts.

   However, there is a limit as to how far replacement of the amount at risk by cash value accumulation can go. Under present tax law, in order to qualify as life insurance and continue to exclude the death benefit from Federal income tax, <u>the Universal Life policy must always include an amount at risk until age 95</u>, when the accumulated cash value may equal the death benefit. This means that the insurance company would no longer have any risk. To assure compliance with these tax regulations, if the cash value (prior to age 95) approaches the face amount of the policy, the insurance company <u>must automatically increase the death benefit</u> to continue to provide for an amount of risk.

2. *Option B:* The policy provides for an increasing death benefit that is made up of the <u>policy face</u> amount <u>plus</u> the <u>cash value</u> account. The amount of pure risk for the insurance company is a <u>level</u> amount <u>equal</u> to the <u>policy face</u> amount.

   For example, your client buys a Universal Life (Option B) policy with $100,000 face amount. At first, there would be no cash value, so if the client died, the beneficiary would just receive the face amount of $100,000. Later on, as the cash value increases, the death benefit would be more than the face amount, since <u>the death benefit equals the face amount plus the cash value</u>. Let's say the client who has a face amount of $100,000 also had a cash value (after a number of years, depending on the size of the premiums paid) of $25,000. If the insured dies, the policy would pay the beneficiary $125,000. However, when comparing Option B to Option A, you can see that the insured always has more "pure" protection with Option B than with Option A. For this reason, Option B would be the more expensive policy.

The featured benefit most preferred by Universal life policyholders is the <u>flexibility of premium payments</u>. It is not necessary to make a premium payment each year as long as there is sufficient cash value available to pay for the pure insurance protection. Thus, all a policyholder needs to do is make one large payment (a single premium) and the accumulated cash value will continue the policy in force without any further premium payments until the cash value is exhausted. At this point, another premium payment must be made or the coverage will expire.

Other provisions found in most Universal life policies, such as a 30 day grace period, loan provisions and non-forfeiture provisions remain the same as those found in most Whole Life policies. ***Remember***: *Universal life is simply a type of whole life.* It is commonly called "<u>Interest Sensitive</u>" Whole Life, since the current interest paid will fluctuate periodically with changes in the economy.

While the benefits provided by a traditional whole life policy are "bundled" or packaged together, Universal Life policies are considered "transparent" in that benefits (such as the cash value and the death benefit) may be viewed separately.

## SPECIALIZED POLICIES

**Joint Life (First-to-Die) Policies:** These are Whole Life contracts written with <u>two or more persons as the named insured</u>. Most commonly, the policy is issued on two lives, with the insured amount payable on the death of the <u>first insured to die</u>.

A variation of the Joint Life policy is the <u>Last Survivor policy</u>. It pays the insured amount not to the beneficiaries of the first insured to die, but to those of the last. Proceeds are often used to pay estate taxes, which are due when the second spouse dies.

**Juvenile Life Policies:** Juvenile Life insurance is any form written on the life of a minor. One type of policy is commonly called the "<u>Jumping Juvenile</u>" because it automatically increases in face amount at a given age, usually 21, but the <u>premium remains level</u>. The usual jump is from $1,000 to $5,000.

A payor benefit rider may be <u>added on a Juvenile Life policy for an extra premium</u>. It waives the premiums on the child's policy if the applicant (usually a parent) <u>dies or becomes disabled</u> before the child attains a stated age (usually 21).

<u>Juvenile Endowments</u> are written on children at very young ages, down to birth with some companies. Usually the endowment period is to age 18 or age 21 and the money often is used for college expenses.

## GROUP LIFE INSURANCE

**Characteristics of Group Plans:** Most group life insurance plans share six basic characteristics:

1. True group plans usually require a minimum of at least 10 persons to be covered under one master contract, although minimums are less in some states.

2. Coverage is usually written without requiring a physical examination.

3. The master policy is issued to an employer, trust, association or union. The contract is between the employer and the insurer. Certificates of insurance are issued to the individuals covered stating the amount of coverage and their designated beneficiary.

4. The coverage must be written to benefit the employee and their dependents.

5. Premiums are based on the past claims history of the group, which is known as experience rating. Group premiums may be shared by the employer and the employee, which is called a "contributory group," or the premiums may all be paid by the employer (a non-contributory group).

   If contributory, at least 75% of those eligible must enroll. If non-contributory, 100% must join. These percentage requirements are called "participation requirements" and are designed to prevent adverse selection. If it wasn't for participation requirements then only the employees in poor health would enroll and the insurer would lose money.

6. Amounts of coverage are usually determined based upon salary level, job title or time on the job. Some employers may allow dependents to enroll as well.

**Group Eligibility:** The following groups are authorized for Group Life Insurance:

1. *Employees:* The amount of insurance must be based upon some plan, such as a job description or salary, that precludes individual selection by the employer.

2. *Debtors:* Groups may be established if the amount of insurance on the life of the debtor does not exceed the amount owed to the creditor. Policy proceeds are payable to the master policyholder to extinguish debt.

3. *Multiple Employer Trusts:* Groups covering employees of small companies in the same industry. The trust is the policyholder.

**Group Life Standard Provisions:**

1. Coverage for a dependent spouse or child may be offered, at the discretion of the employer.

2. Dependent's coverage has the same rights of conversion as the insurance on the life of the insured person (31 days).

3. If a Group Life policy is other than Term Insurance, it shall have non-forfeiture provisions.

4. Group Life Insurance shall have a grace period of 31 days, during which the death benefit coverage shall continue in force.

5. Group life shall be incontestable after two years.

6. Group life insurers will issue individual certificates of insurance protection to insureds stating the amount of coverage, beneficiary and conditions.

7. Group Life coverage shall be convertible to any form of insurance, EXCEPT Term Insurance, without a physical examination within 31 days of termination of employment. The face amount of the new policy issued shall not be in excess of the group coverage. The premium on the new policy shall be based on the insured's age at conversion.

8. Death occurring during the 31 day conversion period is covered on a Group Life policy, whether or not the insured had yet applied for an individual policy.

9. Group Annuities contain a grace period of 30 days and Entire Contract Clause, a Misstatement of Age Provision and Non-Forfeiture Benefits.

10. Most group life policies contain a "Facility of Payment" clause that states that if there is no beneficiary at the time the group insured dies, the insurer may make payment to anyone who appears to be entitled to the death benefit due to their willingness to assume the insured party's medical bills or burial expenses, even though they may not be a direct insurable interest in the insured.

## CREDIT LIFE INSURANCE

This is usually a type of Decreasing Term insurance written on the life of the debtor. The coverage may be Individual or Group, but it is usually written on a group basis and proceeds are payable to the creditor to extinguish the debt. This is often sold by car dealers, banks and other creditors.

The maximum policy period <u>cannot exceed the life of loan</u>, and the <u>policy limit cannot exceed the amount owed</u>. To prevent excess profits in this area, a Credit Life insurance company must pay out a certain percentage of its premiums in claims. If it doesn't, its rates will be considered <u>unreasonable in relation to benefits</u>, and it will have to lower them.

# Life Insurance Policies

# KEY FACTS

- A real-estate producer, because of fluctuating income, might purchase <u>Adjustable Whole Life</u>.

- On <u>Modified Whole Life</u>, the premiums are lower than normal for the first five years, but then increase to a higher-than-normal fixed premium thereafter. The face amount is level.

- On <u>Graded Premium Whole Life</u>, the premiums <u>gradually</u> increase for the first five years, then remain level at a higher-than-normal amount thereafter. The face amount is level.

- <u>Variable Whole Life</u> must include a method to enable a client to calculate his/her cash value.

- The client may skip, reduce, or increase premiums on a <u>Variable/Universal Life</u> policy. The policy will not lapse as long as there is enough cash value to cover expense deductions.

- <u>Variable Whole Life</u> allows the client to <u>self-direct</u> his/her cash-value investment.

- <u>Variable products</u> have no guarantees and are not backed by the <u>Guaranty Fund</u>.

- An <u>Increasing Term</u> policy's limits increase each year. An Increasing Term policy is sometimes called a <u>Return-of-Premium</u> policy.

- <u>Term insurance</u> is renewable without a physical examination, up to a certain age.

- <u>Term</u> insurance may be converted to <u>Whole Life</u>, but not the reverse. <u>Conversion</u> is based on the client's <u>current age</u>.

- A <u>Credit Life</u> policy is a type of <u>Decreasing Term</u>. Benefits are paid directly to the creditor.

- Although it is a type of Decreasing Term, Credit Life is usually NOT used for Mortgage Protection.

- The policy limits on Credit Life cannot exceed the amount of the loan.

- On group credit life, the creditor is both the policy holder and the beneficiary.

- <u>Conversion</u> from a Group Life policy to an Individual policy when you terminate employment is permitted for 31 days, <u>regardless</u> of health.

- <u>Limited-Pay Whole Life</u> policies, though paid up earlier, do not mature until the client's age 100.

- <u>Universal Life</u> offers flexible premiums and a minimum guaranteed rate of return.

- Investing in <u>Variable products</u> is considered a <u>hedge</u> against inflation.

- In a <u>Contributory</u> Group Life plan (employee pays part of premium), 75% of those eligible must participate. In a <u>Non-contributory</u> plan (employer pays total premium), 100% must participate.

- <u>Experience rating</u> is for large groups only. Rates are based on claims experience of the group.

- An <u>Endowment policy</u> is just like Whole Life, except that they reach maturity prior to age 100. An Endowment is always the <u>most expensive</u> Life policy.

- If a client wants to be sure of having a certain amount of money at a certain time in the future, he/she should purchase an <u>Endowment</u>.

- <u>Whole Life</u> policies must contain a table showing their Guaranteed Cash Value at the end of each year (Anniversary Date) for the first 20 years. It is shown per unit (per thousand).

- A combination policy with <u>Level Term plus Whole Life</u>, both written on the Primary Insured, is called a <u>Family Maintenance policy</u>. It does not cover dependents.

- A combination policy with <u>Decreasing Term plus Whole Life</u>, both written on the Primary Insured, is called a <u>Family Income policy</u>. It does not cover dependents.

- On a <u>Family Income</u> or <u>Family Maintenance</u> policy, the lump-sum Whole Life proceeds are paid out AFTER all of the monthly payments have been paid.

- A combination policy that automatically covers all family members, including <u>newborn children</u> (after a short waiting period) at no extra premium charge is called a <u>Family policy</u>.

- Whole life benefits are "<u>bundled</u>" (packaged). Universal life benefits are "<u>transparent</u>" (stand-alone).

- Individual policies are usually <u>more expensive</u> than group.

- You can't form a group <u>just to buy</u> insurance.

- Group life is <u>convertible for 31 days</u> after job termination.

- On a 20-pay life, the cash value will equal the face amount <u>at maturity</u> (age 100).

- Whole life and Limited Pay life both <u>reach maturity</u> at the same time (age 100).

- A single premium may buy a policy that is <u>paid up for life</u> (age 100).

- A single premium policy has an immediate cash value.

- On group life, the employer may require an employee to pay the premium for dependent's coverage.

- If an employer pays all of the premiums to cover his/her employees, 100% of the eligible employees must enroll in the group plan.

- Employees covered by a group insurance plan receive Certificates of Insurance.

- The face amount of a mortgage protection life insurance policy will decrease at the same rate as the mortgage balance declines.

- Loans are not prohibited on Universal Life policies.

- Life settlement contacts are between the life insurance policy owner and a third party.

- The term rider added to a parent's life insurance policy to cover a child is "level" term.

- Buying life insurance on the life of a child does not provide income to the child in the event that a parent dies.

- A "whole life" insurance policy purchased today may provide retirement income later.

- A loan may be taken from a "whole life" policy as soon as it develops a cash value.

- On "adjustable" life insurance, the insured may have to pass a physical exam in order to increase coverage.

- A person who seeks to sell their life insurance policy in a viatical settlement is known as a "viator."

- Adjusting the premium paid on an "adjustable" whole life policy will affect the face amount, and vice-versa.

- Universal life is a type of whole life insurance and has many of the same features.

- A "joint life" policy only pays when the first party dies.

- A "joint life survivorship" policy pays when the last party dies.

- It is the face amount that decreases on a decreasing term policy, not the premium.

- On an annual renewable level term policy, the premium will increase every year, although the face amount will remain the same.

- Convertible term is convertible based upon the current or attained age of the client.

- A policy written on the life of a child does not pay benefits when a parent dies.

- On term life insurance, the "re-entry" option is contingent upon the insured passing a physical exam.

- Decreasing term is the type of life insurance provided in mortgage redemption insurance.

- Industrial life insurance policies are written with low policy limits or face amounts.

- Whole life insurance will pay the face amount upon death or age 100, whichever comes first.

- A juvenile life insurance policy is a life insurance policy written on the life of a minor.

# Life Insurance Policies

# PRACTICE EXAM

1. Mr. Shulkin owns a 30-Pay life policy that he purchased at the age of 30. The cash value will equal the face amount of the policy when he reaches the age of:

    A. 60
    B. 65
    C. 70
    D. 100

2. At age 30, Clark Peterson wishes to purchase a Whole Life policy. His producer explains that he can pay for the policy in several ways. One method is called 20-Pay Life, and another, Straight Life. Clark wishes to know which plan will accumulate cash value at a faster rate in the early years of the policy. Which of the following would be the producer's most appropriate response:

    A. "Straight Life will accumulate cash value faster."
    B. "20-Pay Life will accumulate cash value faster."
    C. "Both plans will accumulate cash value at the same rate."
    D. "The rate of cash-value accumulation depends on the profitability of the insurance company."

3. A single premium used to buy a Whole Life policy will pay up the policy:

    A. For one year
    B. For three years
    C. To age 65
    D. For the life of the policy

4. Which of the following is an example of a Limited-Pay life policy:

    A. Whole Life
    B. Life Paid-Up at age 65
    C. Renewable Term to age 70
    D. Endowment maturing at age 65

5. Which policy provides the greatest amount of protection for an insured's premium dollar as well as some cash accumulation:

    A. Term
    B. Annuity
    C. Limited-Pay Life
    D. Whole Life

6. Which type of insurance policy would provide the greatest amount of protection for a temporary period during which an insured will have limited financial resources:

   A. Term
   B. Whole Life
   C. Annuity
   D. Endowment

7. Which statement about a Renewable Term policy is true:

   A. It is renewable at the option of the insurance company
   B. It is renewable at the option of the insured
   C. It is renewable at the option of the insurance company, with proof of insurability
   D. It is renewable at the option of the insured, with proof of insurability

8. Which policy is generally used to accumulate funds for education:

   A. Endowment
   B. Term
   C. Life Paid-Up at age 65
   D. 20-Pay Life

9. All of the following is true about Universal Life EXCEPT:

   A. Taking out a loan will affect cash value accumulation
   B. Insurance company administrative costs are subtracted from the cash value
   C. The death benefit paid to the beneficiary is taxable as ordinary income
   D. Loans are permitted

10. An insurance prospect wants to purchase a policy that will accumulate the largest amount of cash by the age of 65. Which policy would be most likely to satisfy the prospect's needs:

    A. Yearly Renewable Term
    B. Endowment at age 65
    C. Life Paid-Up at age 65
    D. A combination Term and Whole Life

11. Cheryl Schultze, age 27, is advised by her producer to purchase life insurance to cover a 20-year-amortized $50,000 business-improvement loan. Which plan would adequately protect Ms. Schultze at the minimum premium outlay:

    A. A $50,000 Whole Life policy
    B. A $50,000 20-Year Endowment policy
    C. A $50,000 Level Term policy for 20 years
    D. A $50,000 Decreasing Term policy for 20 years

©TesTeachers Publishing – www.testeacherspublishing.com

12.   Which statement is true about the premium payment schedule for a Whole Life policy:

A.   Premiums are payable throughout the insured's lifetime, and coverage continues until the insured's death

B.   Premiums are payable for a designated period of time only, after which coverage is no longer provided

C.   Premiums are payable until the insured's retirement only, after which coverage is continued automatically until the insured's death

D.   One premium, in the amount of the insured's choice, is payable at the time of application, and the balance of the premiums is deducted from the face amount of the policy at the time of the insured's death

13.   Which of the following, if any, is the basic coverage issued to an eligible member under the Servicemen's Group Life Insurance (SGLI) program:

A.   Whole Life insurance
B.   Term insurance
C.   Endowment insurance
D.   None of the above

14.   An employee becomes ineligible for the group plan. The employee has the option to convert their $10,000 of group coverage to individual coverage within 31 days. Which of the following is true:

A.   The employee can convert to a new individual term policy with a face amount of $50,000
B.   The employee is subject to underwriting for the individual policy
C.   The employee can convert to a maximum of $10,000 of whole life coverage without a physical exam, with the premium based on the insured's age at conversion
D.   The employee can convert to a maximum of $10,000 of whole life coverage without a physical exam, with the premium based on the insured's age when they enrolled in the group plan

15.   When a corporation establishes a contributory Group Term contract, what percentage test must be met for participation:

A.   100%
B.   75%
C.   67%
D.   50%

16.   The plan of Permanent Life insurance that offers cash value at the lowest premium is:

A.   A Whole Life policy
B.   A Limited-Pay Life policy
C.   A Term policy
D.   An Annuity contract

17. Which of the following policies provides only a Death benefit that declines over a definite and limited period of time:

    A.  Joint Life
    B.  Annuity
    C.  Endowment
    D.  Decreasing Term

18. All of the following statements about Credit Life insurance are true EXCEPT:

    A.  It is often sold by car dealers, banks and other creditors
    B.  The maximum policy period cannot exceed the life of the loan
    C.  The coverage is unlimited
    D.  It is a type of decreasing term

19. Darla Jenkins purchased a $100,000 individual Whole Life policy January 1, 2010 and paid an initial annual premium of $1,000. After her policy is issued Darla becomes interested in hang gliding and dies in a hang gliding accident on January 15, 2011, without paying her annual premium. What will the insurer pay to her beneficiary:

    A.  $99,000
    B.  Zero, since she died hang gliding
    C.  $100,000
    D.  Zero, since she did not pay her premium

20. An employee's evidence of participation in a Group Life plan is the:

    A.  Certificate of Insurance
    B.  Policy
    C.  Master contract
    D.  Proof of Employment

21. When an insured purchases a Decreasing Term policy, which of the following decreases each year:

    A.  The reserve
    B.  The premium
    C.  The face amount
    D.  The cash value

22. A Whole Life policy furnishes a form of Permanent protection because it never has to be:

    A.  Reinstated
    B.  Reduced
    C.  Renewed or converted
    D.  Used for a loan

23.	The insured can receive the face amount of an Endowment policy if they are still living when the policy's:

    A.	Cash value equals the face amount
    B.	Cash value equals the premiums paid
    C.	Cash value exceeds the premiums paid
    D.	Premiums paid exceed the face amount

24.	Which of the following best describes the normal Conversion benefit available to terminated employees under a Group Life insurance policy?

    A.	The employee may convert to an individual Term policy within 31 days by submitting evidence of insurability
    B.	The employee may convert to an individual Permanent Life policy within 31 days by submitting evidence of insurability
    C.	The employee may convert to an individual Term policy within 31 days without submitting evidence of insurability
    D.	The employee may convert to an individual Permanent Life policy within 31 days without submitting evidence of insurability

25.	Which of the following statements about Adjustable Whole Life is true:

    A.	Adjusting the premium will also adjust the face amount
    B.	Reducing the premium will increase the face amount
    C.	Increasing the premium will lengthen the premium payment period
    D.	In order to increase the face amount of coverage a physical exam is required

26.	Which of the following is NOT true regarding employer group life insurance:

    A.	The employees receive Certificates of Insurance
    B.	If the employer pays all of the premium, 100% of eligible employees must enroll
    C.	The employer may require employees to pay the premium for dependents
    D.	The employer is the beneficiary

27.	If a client buys a new $50,000 life insurance policy and dies 1 month later:

    A.	There is no coverage, but the premium will be refunded
    B.	Only 1/12th of the face amount will be paid
    C.	There is no coverage since the claim occurred in the contestability period
    D.	The insurer must pay the claim

28.	Which of the following is NOT true regarding Universal Life insurance policies:

    A.	The cash value is debited to pay for the increased cost of mortality
    B.	Loans are prohibited
    C.	They have a guaranteed minimum cash value
    D.	They have a guaranteed minimum interest rate

29. Which type of Life insurance is written as whole life:

    A.  Credit
    B.  Group
    C.  Single premium
    D.  Mortgage redemption

30. Which of the following is true when Life insurance is used to fund an Executive Bonus plan:

    A.  The employer owns the policy
    B.  The employee pays the premium
    C.  The employee owns the policy
    D.  The policy is usually written as level term

31. What type of Life insurance has a rate of return that may keep up with inflation, but will never fall below the minimum guaranteed in the policy:

    A.  Variable life
    B.  Whole life
    C.  Equity indexed life
    D.  Adjustable life

32. All of the following are true regarding graded premium whole life policies EXCEPT:

    A.  They are also known as adjustable whole life
    B.  They are purchased by those who expect their future income to increase
    C.  The premium increases gradually, then levels off
    D.  The face amount remains level

33. All of the following are true about Universal Life insurance EXCEPT:

    A.  Expense charges must be stated separately in the policy
    B.  A policy that has a cash value cannot lapse for non-payment
    C.  Once a cash value develops, loans may be taken
    D.  Proceeds payable to a beneficiary are taxable

# Life Insurance Policies

# PRACTICE EXAM ANSWERS AND RATIONALES

1. **D** Limited pay life insurance policies such as Life Paid Up at 65 or 20-Pay Life are simply variations of Whole Life policies. The cash value will equal the face amount of the policy (at least) at the maturity of the policy, which is always age 100 on Whole Life policies. These limited-pay policies are designed so that the insured may pay his/her premiums faster and be "paid up" at a certain age. However, just because the premiums are paid up doesn't mean the policy has matured.

2. **B** With the exception of the Endowment policy, which is always the most expensive and always builds cash values the fastest, you can simply remember this truism: The shorter the premium-paying period, the more expensive the premiums and the faster the cash value builds. Since all the policies mentioned are forms of Whole Life, reaching their maturity at age 100, the only thing different is the premium-paying period. A 20-Pay Life requires that all the premiums be paid within 20 years from the day it is purchased. A Whole Life (or Straight Life) policy requires the premiums to be paid to age 100. If Clark is now 30, the assumption is that he would have to pay premium to age 100, or 70 years. Obviously, 20-Pay Life, which would require the premiums to be paid in over three times as fast, would be much more expensive and would also build cash values much faster.

3. **D** If a single premium is used to purchase a whole life policy the policy will be paid up for the life of the policy. No further premiums need be paid. Whole Life policies can be purchased and paid for a number of different ways. Continuous premium traditional Whole Life policies were originally purchased with periodic premiums that were paid for the life of the insured. However, many people did not want to pay their life insurance premiums over their entire life, so the insurance company created a number of variations of premium payment. The insured can now select to pay their Whole Life policy premium for a specified number of years (Pay Life), or to a certain age (Life Paid-up). The insured can also select to pay the full premium on day one (Single Premium). Remember, the shorter the premium paying period the higher the premium and the faster the cash value will build.

4. **B** There are three basic types of life insurance: 1) Whole Life, 2) Term and 3) Endowment. Limited Pay Life policies, such as LP 65 and 20-Pay Life, are variations of Whole Life or Straight Life. The premium-paying period has been shortened, but the policy still does not mature until age 100.

5. **D** If we had not mentioned cash accumulation, the answer would have been Term. However, Term has no cash value, so the answer is Whole Life, which is the most inexpensive type of permanent insurance and is required to have a cash value after the third policy year. Although Limited Pay Life is a type of Whole Life, it is incorrect since it is usually quite expensive due to the shortened pay-in period. Annuities have no cash value except the money the annuitant paid in. Since there is no death benefit, no protection is offered.

6. **A**  The word "term" means time. Time is temporary. A Term policy, since it is the most inexpensive type of insurance, would provide an applicant the greatest amount of protection (face amount) on a temporary basis. However, in the long run, Term may be the most expensive type of insurance.

7. **B**  If most Term policies (except Decreasing Term) were not renewable, no one would buy them. This option allows the insured to renew the policy for another term without proving good health. Of course, the insured does not have to renew, it is at his/her option. Annual Renewable Term (ART) is a good example. It must be renewed every year. The rate goes up as the insured gets older, but no proof of good health is required. However, most Term policies are renewable only up to a certain age, usually age 60 or 65, depending on the company.

8. **A**  Endowment policies are usually sold either for retirement purposes at age 65 or to children to fund their college education. This type of policy reaches maturity at a predetermined time selected by the insured or policyholder. An E 65 would reach maturity at 65 and the cash value would equal the face amount. A 15-year Endowment covering a three-year-old would endow at the child's age of 18 and the funds could be used for his/her college education. Of course, if the insured dies during the policy period (before the policy endows) then the company would pay the face amount to the beneficiary. Endowments are always the most expensive type of life insurance. Endowment policies also contain the three non-forfeiture options, since they do have a cash value.

9. **C**  Remember, Universal Life is a type of Whole Life insurance and is sometimes referred to on the exam as "interest sensitive" whole life. Universal Life policies have a cash value with a minimum guaranteed interest rate and an excess current interest rate. The return the insured receives on the cash value will vary and is interest rate sensitive. Loans are permitted, and if taken will definitely have an effect on the cash value accumulation. However, death benefit proceeds are not taxable.

10. **B**  Since an Endowment at age 65 reaches maturity at age 65, rather than age 100, it will be much more expensive than an LP 65. Since it is more expensive, it will also build cash values much faster, since the face amount and the cash value must be at least equal by age 65.

11. **D**  The key words here are "minimum premium." Term is the most inexpensive type of coverage. Since Cheryl's $50,000 loan will be paid off over 20 years and the loan balance will decrease each year, Decreasing Term makes sense. Decreasing Term is not renewable or convertible.

12. **A**  Whole Life insurance assumes that the insured will pay the premiums until death or until age 100, whichever comes first. If the insured is still alive at age 100, the policy will reach maturity and pay the insured the face amount or cash value, whichever is more. This is because the insurance company's Mortality Table states that everyone has died by their 100th birthday.

An insured who would like to retire at age 65, keeping the life insurance in force but discontinuing premium payments, should consider buying an LP 65, which is a Whole Life policy with a limited payment period. Of course, the shorter the premium paying period, the higher the premium.

An insured buying Straight Whole Life, which matures at age 100, could also stop paying his/her premiums at age 65 by selecting the Reduced Paid Up Non-forfeiture option. This would result in the insured having a new Whole Life policy paid up to age 100 with a cash value and a death benefit somewhat reduced from his/her original policy, but no further premiums would be due.

13. **B**  Eligible servicemen and servicewomen are offered Servicemen's Group Life Insurance (SGLI) on a payroll-deduction plan while on active duty. The rates are subsidized by the government and the plan is underwritten by private insurance companies. This type of insurance is Level Term,

but it is convertible to Whole Life insurance without proof of insurability when the insured is discharged from the service.

14. **C**   The insured is eligible to convert from the group policy to an individual policy issued by the same insurer within 31 days of ineligibility. The insured CANNOT convert to term, but they can convert to a more expensive type of life insurance, such as whole life. There is no underwriting to convert to an individual policy, however the ex-employee would be responsible for paying the entire premium, which is based on their age at conversion (attained age), not age of enrollment in the group. When converting from a group policy the individual can only convert to a face amount that is no higher than that of the group policy.

15. **B**   All Group Life insurance is Term insurance. Actually it is Annual Renewable Term and it is rated on the average age and claims experience of the entire group, which is called "experience rating." Remember, this type of insurance has a 31-day Grace Period and is convertible to Whole Life upon leaving employment. A Contributory Group plan requires that both the employer and the employees pay part of the premium. At least 75% of those eligible must participate, so the group is sure to get most of the healthy employees as well as those that are sick.

In a Noncontributory plan, the employer pays 100% of the premiums and 100% of those eligible must participate. In most states, there must be at least 10 persons eligible to form a Group plan. If only the sick employees were to enroll, the insurance company would be the victim of "adverse selection" and their loss ratio (claims ratio) could suffer, causing the rates to go up.

16. **A**   Since Whole Life has the longest premium payment period (to age 100), it also has the lowest premium of any policy with a cash value. Limited Pay policies are more expensive, since the premium-payment period has been shortened. Term policies have no cash value. Annuities are the opposite of insurance. There is no Death benefit. They only pay you if you live.

17. **D**   Often used to protect home mortgages or for temporary needs, Decreasing Term insurance has no cash values. Usually written for 5, 10, 15, or 20 years, the premium remains the same each year. However, since the amount of insurance decreases, you could say that the cost actually is going up each year. Decreasing Term is not renewable but it is usually convertible to Whole Life at the option of the insured without proof of good health.

18. **C**   Credit life is a type of decreasing term insurance written on the life of the debtor. Proceeds from the policy are payable to the creditor to extinguish the debtor's debt. The maximum policy period cannot exceed the life of the loan, and the policy limit cannot exceed the amount owed. It is not unlimited!

19. **A**   Since Darla died during the grace period, the insurer will pay the face amount minus the overdue premium she should have paid ($100,000-$1,000=$99,000). If Darla had died after the 30 day grace period without paying her premium there would be no coverage. There are three grace periods you must know for Life insurance: 28 days on industrial life, 30 days for all other types of life insurance including annuities, and 31 for group life. Although Darla died while participating in a dangerous hobby, the question makes no mention of hang gliding being excluded in the policy, so you have to assume that it is covered. Since Darla picked up this dangerous hobby after the policy had already been issued it will not affect her coverage.

20. **A**   On Group Life, the Employer is the Master policyholder and the Employee merely receives a Certificate of Insurance indicating how much coverage he/she has, who his/her beneficiary is, and whether or not he has dependents' coverage.

21. **C** Although the premium remains the same each year on Decreasing Term insurance, the face amount decreases, usually straight line each year. So, if you bought a 20-year Decreasing Term policy, after 10 years your face amount would be reduced by half. However, since the premium remains the same, you could say the cost of your insurance had doubled! Decreasing Term has no cash value. It is usually convertible, but not renewable.

22. **C** The terms Whole Life and Straight Life are interchangeable. As used, either term means "continuous, level-premium Ordinary Life" insurance. A Whole Life policy may never be changed by the company. The premium can never go up. It never has to be renewed or converted. Therefore, it is known as "permanent protection."

23. **A** On an Endowment policy, the insured's cash value will equal the face amount of the policy at maturity, which is a predetermined time, say age 65, set by the insured when they buy the policy. Whole Life policies always reach maturity at age 100. You could say that a Whole Life policy endows at age 100. A true Endowment policy will always mature earlier than age 100. Endowments are just like Whole Life, except that the maturity is always earlier.

24. **D** The conversion privilege on Group Life extends for 31 days after the insured terminates from the job. He/she can convert only to a Whole Life (Permanent insurance) policy written by the same company without submitting evidence of insurability. He/she cannot convert to more coverage than he/she had on the Group Life policy. He/she cannot convert to Term, only to Whole Life.

25. **A** Adjustable Whole Life is marketed to meet an insured's changing needs and ability to pay premiums in an uncertain economic climate. It is the most flexible type of Whole Life insurance. The insured can adjust the premium, face amount or the length of coverage. If the insured increases the premium they pay, the cash value will build faster and the face amount of coverage will increase. However, no physical exam is required unless the insured wants to increase the face amount above that which he/she originally purchased.

26. **D** In order for an employer to tax deduct the premiums they pay for group life insurance, the coverage must be written to benefit someone other than the employer. Employees covered by group life policies may designate anyone they choose as beneficiary.

27. **D** Assuming the premium has been paid, life insurance coverage becomes effective once the underwriter approves the application and issues the policy, and coverage will apply unless the insured lied about a material fact on his/her application or died as a result of suicide in the first 2 years.

28. **B** Universal Life (UL) policies are actually just a variation of whole life policies. They have minimum guaranteed cash values and rates of return and policy owners may take loans by using the cash value as collateral. The main advantage of UL is that premiums are flexible, meaning that once the cash value is sufficient, the policy owner may stop making premium payments and allow the insurer to debit the cash value to pay for the increasing cost of mortality as the insured grows older.

29. **C** Whole life insurance can be purchased with an annual premium for life, or as limited pay whole life, such as 20-pay life, life paid-up at age 65 or even with a large, single premium. Single premium policies would have an immediate cash value and are subject to the seven-pay test to determine if they are Modified Endowment Contracts. All of the other policies listed are types of term life insurance.

30. **C**  Although Life insurance may not be considered to be a retirement plan, some employers utilize it to fund Executive Bonus plans. Although the employer pays the premium, the policy belongs to the employee, who may surrender it for cash upon retirement.

31. **C**  Equity Indexed life insurance or annuities have a guaranteed rate of return, but can earn excess interest above the guaranteed rate since performance is calculated using an indexing method that is usually linked to the S&P 500 stock index. The stock market generally keeps pace with inflation over a period of time.

32. **A**  Graded premium whole life is sold initially at a discount, but the premium gradually increases over a period of time, although the face amount or policy limit stays the same. It is designed to attract customers who cannot afford whole life right now, but expect their future income to increase. Adjustable whole life is sold to people with fluctuating incomes who want a policy whose premium and/or face amount may be adjusted to meet their changing needs.

33. **D**  An advantage of UL is the flexibility of premium payments, meaning that if there is adequate cash value in the policy, the customer may skip premium payments and the policy won't lapse. UL policies are also considered to be "transparent," meaning that the expenses, such as the cost of insurance protection, must be clearly shown. Policy loans are permitted, but proceeds payable to a beneficiary are not taxable.

# SECTION 5

# Life Insurance Policy Provisions, Options and Riders

## STANDARD PROVISIONS

**Ownership:** Remember, the policyholder is not required to be the insured. For example, you may buy a policy on the life of your minor child. You are the policyholder and your child is the insured. Who owns the cash value? Who can designate the beneficiary? Who can take a loan? You can! You are the policyholder, and as such, all the owner's rights accrue to you.

**Assignment:** Two types of assignments can be made on life-insurance policies:

1. *Absolute Assignment:* This is common when you have purchased a life-insurance policy on the life of another (third-party ownership). You are the policyholder and the other person is the insured. You are the one who pays the premiums and you also own all rights to the policy, including the right to take a loan or take cash surrender.

   However, at some future point, you may wish to transfer all of your interests in this policy to the insured. You may do this by executing an <u>Absolute Assignment</u> and sending it to your producer or company. This <u>irrevocably transfers all of your rights of ownership</u> to the insured, who may now change the beneficiary, take a loan, or take cash surrender. Of course, the insured now has to pay the premium, as well.

2. *Collateral Assignment:* This is a <u>temporary type of assignment</u> in which you pledge the proceeds of your life-insurance policy to the bank as collateral for a loan or to enhance your credit standing.

   The bank temporarily controls the policy and during this time you cannot make any changes to your policy. If you die during this time, the insurance company will pay your policy proceeds to the bank to pay off your loan. Of course, any excess proceeds above what is owed to the bank would be paid to your beneficiary or estate.

<u>Neither type of assignment is binding upon the insurance company unless it is notified in writing</u>. Normally, the insurance company will provide you with the proper forms and you simply return the signed form to the company. After your bank loan is paid off, the bank releases you from your <u>Collateral Assignment</u> and the policy stands as it was prior to the assignment.

**Entire Contract:** Only the Entire Contract <u>is admissible in court</u> under the rules of evidence. Since the answers to the insured's questions regarding his/her health, occupation, and hobbies are located on the application for insurance, most insurance companies will attach the completed application (or a certified copy of it) to the policy contract at issue. By doing so, it becomes part of the Entire Contract. Nothing else may modify the contract once it is issued, unless both parties mutually assent.

**Modifications:** Once issued, the policy may not be modified (changed) in any way without the mutual consent of the parties, as stated in the <u>Entire Contract clause</u>. This prevents the insurance company from attaching exclusions or limiting endorsements to the policy later on, unless, of course, the client agrees to the modification.

In addition, <u>a producer may not modify an application</u> for insurance without the written consent of the applicant. For example, your client completes the application at your office. Later on, he/she calls you from home, requesting that you change it. You must have your client's <u>written consent</u> to make this change, meaning you would have him/her fill out a new application or initial the change.

**Right to Examine (Free Look):** This provision allows the client to take a specified number of days to examine a new life-insurance contract, during which the contract <u>may be canceled with the entire premium refunded</u>. From state to state, Free Look provisions vary from 10 to 30 days. The Free Look period <u>starts when the policy is delivered</u>. No reason need be given.

**Payment of Premiums:** "<u>Mode</u>" simply means how often you pay your premium. Life-insurance companies offer several different modes of payment, such as monthly, quarterly, semi-annual, annual, and check-o-matic. Since they often charge you a service fee for processing payments made other than on an annual basis, <u>the more often you pay, the higher your premium</u>. It is always cheaper to pay annually in advance. If you pay quarterly, and they charge you $2.00 per payment more for processing, than you are actually paying $8.00 a year more than you would pay on an annual basis.

**Grace Period:** There are three grace periods to remember:

1. *28 days:* Industrial Life (a type of whole life in which the premium is collected weekly and the face amount is usually $1,000 or less)

2. *30 days:* All other types of life insurance (<u>including annuities</u>)

3. *31 days:* Group Life

The purpose of the Grace Period is to protect the policyholder who forgot to mail a premium on time. If you should die in the Grace Period, it is assumed that you would have made your payment had you lived and the policy proceeds are paid in full <u>less the overdue premium</u>, which is subtracted from proceeds.

Remember, any outstanding policy loans, plus interest on those loans, would also be subtracted from policy proceeds any time you died, including during the Grace Period.

**Reinstatement:** The right to apply for reinstatement of lapsed policies is built into most Life insurance policies. However, just because you have the right to apply does not mean that the company will accept you. Most companies will allow you to apply for reinstatement up to five years from the time your original policy lapsed. In order to be accepted, <u>you must take a physical exam</u>, meet all company underwriting requirements, <u>pay all back premiums</u> and interest on those premiums, and <u>complete a reinstatement application</u>. The main advantages of reinstatement are: 1) since you get your original policy back, you will still be paying future premiums <u>based on your original age</u>, and 2) your original policy may have had loan interest rates much lower than a new policy may currently offer. <u>You cannot reinstate a policy after taking cash surrender.</u>

**Incontestability:** On an application for Life insurance, the applicant is obligated to answer all the questions with the <u>truth to the best of his/her knowledge</u>. This is called a <u>representation</u>. A representation on the application becomes part of the Entire Contract, if the company attaches the application to the new policy at issue.

When an applicant intentionally lies on his/her application, this is known as a <u>misrepresentation or fraud</u>. In order to protect the insurance company from lying applicants, new life-insurance policies are <u>contestable</u> for the first two years of the policy.

This means that if an applicant lies about anything that is <u>material</u> to the risk assumed by the insurance company and dies within the first two years of the policy, the insurance company may "contest" the claim and <u>void or rescind</u> the contract. <u>No coverage would exist.</u>

However, after two years have elapsed, the policy becomes <u>incontestable</u>. This means that after two years, <u>regardless of any false answers</u> the applicant may have made on his/her initial application, the <u>policy may not be voided and all claims must be paid</u>, even if the insurance company can prove the client lied. The balanced purpose of this clause is to protect the company for the first two years and, thereafter, to protect the policyholder. It is assumed that two years is long enough for the company to discover any false information the applicant may have given (either inadvertently or on purpose) on his/her application, so after two years have passed, the policyholder can quit worrying. <u>He/she is now covered regardless.</u>

**Misstatement of Age:** This clause protects the insurance company against an applicant who lies about his/her age, stating it to be either more or less than it really is. Usually, a client will state he/she is younger than he/she really is in order to receive a lower rate.

Misstating your age is never grounds for voiding the policy. However, the insurance company does have the right to adjust your face amount <u>up or down</u> to coincide with the <u>face amount or policy limit the correct premium would have purchased</u> if you had not lied about your age.

Remember, upon death, Proof of Loss (a death certificate) must be filed with the insurance company. A death certificate contains your date of birth, so the company can verify your age at that point.

There is <u>no time limit</u> on this clause, so you could have been paying the incorrect premium for years, but your face amount will still be reduced if you said you were younger than you really were when you purchased the policy. Conversely, your face amount would be increased if you had said you were older than you really were.

Remember, this is a <u>separate clause</u> from the Incontestability Clause and will not ever cause the policy to be voided.

**Exclusions:** Exclusions on a life insurance policy may be added by the company if the applicant has a dangerous hobby (such as being a student pilot) or has a health condition (for example, a history of heart problems) that they do not want to cover.

Exclusions may only be added at the time the new policy is first underwritten. Remember, once a Whole Life or Endowment policy is issued, <u>it can never be changed</u>, so if someone with an existing policy takes flying lessons, he/she is automatically covered since the insurance company cannot add an exclusion at that point. Renewable Term policies may not be changed either, except the rates will go up as the insured gets older.

Of course, any policy may be changed at any time with the <u>mutual consent</u> of both the insurer and the insured. All changes must be <u>signed by a company officer</u> before they become effective.

If an insured gives up the dangerous hobby, the company may be willing to remove the exclusion on the policy or remove the premium surcharge on the <u>rated</u> policy.

**Suicide Exclusion:**  Although life insurers may cover suicide right away, to do so would constitute "<u>adverse selection</u>" from the insurer's viewpoint, meaning that people contemplating suicide would buy a policy from them, knowing that they would be covered immediately.

To solve this problem, most states permit insurers to <u>exclude death by suicide up to two years</u> from the inception of the policy.  However, after two years, suicide is covered!  If an insured dies by suicide during the first two years, most companies will refund the premiums paid to the beneficiary as a matter of goodwill.

## BENEFICIARIES

**Designation Options:** Various beneficiary designation options available include:

1. *Individuals (Per Capita and Per Stirpes):* These designations are often used to benefit children. Under a Per Capita designation (individual), each child shares <u>equally in the death benefit</u>.  Under a Per Stirpes designation, each child, grandchild, etc., <u>moves up as necessary to replace beneficiaries</u> ahead of them who have died.

2. *Classes:* Class Designations, often used when your children are the beneficiaries, should be used when you want a specific group to share the proceeds <u>equally</u>, such as "all my children," rather than naming them individually.

3. *Estates:* Individual designations are always available if you wish to name a specific person as beneficiary, but if you fail to name anyone or if all of your named beneficiaries have died before you do, your <u>final beneficiary</u> is considered to be your <u>estate</u>.

4. *Minors:* A minor may be named as beneficiary as long as a <u>guardian is appointed</u> to receive the funds on his/her behalf.

5. *Trusts:* A trust, either <u>inter vivos</u> (that is, set up while the insured is still alive), or <u>testamentary</u> (created upon the insured's death according to his/her will), may also be designated as beneficiary. A trustee (often a bank) will administer the funds in accordance with the instructions set forth in the trust agreement.

**Succession:** A life insurance policy can have up to three categories of beneficiaries:

1. *Primary Beneficiary:* The first one named by the policy owner to receive the policy proceeds in the event of the insured's death.

2. *Contingent Beneficiary:* The second one named to receive the policy proceeds in the event that the primary beneficiary has predeceased the insured.

3. *Final Beneficiary:* The insured's estate.  If no primary or contingent beneficiary is named, the policy proceeds will automatically go to the insured's estate and could be subject to estate taxes.  If a beneficiary is named, the insured's creditors are prohibited from attaching the policy proceeds upon his/her death, thereby ensuring that his/her designated beneficiary receives the proceeds.  Therefore, it is always a good idea to name a beneficiary for life-insurance proceeds.

**Revocable vs. Irrevocable:** The policyholder, even if not the insured, has the right to designate any beneficiary he/she wants and to change it anytime he/she wishes. This is called appointing a revocable beneficiary. Remember, it is not necessary for the beneficiary to have an insurable interest in the insured in order to be the beneficiary. For example, you buy a policy on yourself appointing your spouse as primary beneficiary. You divorce, but you forget to change your beneficiary designation. If you die, your ex-spouse would still receive the policy proceeds.

Rarely, a beneficiary designation is made irrevocable. This means the beneficiary can NEVER be changed without his/her consent. Nor could a policy loan be taken without his/her consent, since it would affect the amount payable in the event of the insured's death. An Irrevocable Beneficiary designation is sometimes required by a court in relationship to a divorce proceeding in which the cash values may come under the Community Property laws of the state.

**Common Disaster Clause:** It is also important to understand the Uniform Simultaneous Death provision, which states that if both the insured and the primary beneficiary die as a result of the same accident, then it is always assumed that the insured died last. This provision ensures that the insured's contingent beneficiary would receive the policy proceeds, rather than the heirs of the primary beneficiary. *Remember: Under this provision, even if the primary beneficiary lives longer than the insured, it is assumed that the insured died last.* Many states place a time limit on Common Disaster, such as 10 days or 30 days. If the primary beneficiary outlives the insured by more than the time limit, this clause is voided.

**Spendthrift Clause:** The Spendthrift Clause protects life-insurance proceeds that have not yet been paid out to a named beneficiary from the claims of the beneficiary's creditors. This clause does not apply to proceeds that are payable in one lump sum. Generally, the clause states that the policy distributions payable to the beneficiary after the insured dies are not assignable or transferable and may not be attached in any way. This keeps the beneficiary from losing the proceeds to his/her creditors or from spending the money immediately himself.

## SETTLEMENT OPTIONS

There are several optional methods of paying out the policy proceeds to the beneficiary upon the death of the insured. Although the policyholder can pre-select the Settlement Option, usually the beneficiary is the party making the selection. There are five different settlement options available to the beneficiary:

**Cash:** Most beneficiaries select this option and receive a lump-sum payment from the insurance company. This is not taxable to the beneficiary.

**Interest Only:** If the beneficiary selects this option, the money remains with the insurance company to accumulate additional interest over a period of time. Of course, the beneficiary can change his/her mind and elect to take the money as cash whenever he/she desires. While the proceeds of a Life insurance policy left to a beneficiary are not subject to tax, the interest earned is taxable in the year earned, even if not paid out.

**Fixed-Period Installments:** Here, the beneficiary advises the company to pay out the policy proceeds to him/her over a set period of time, say 10 or 20 years. The company simply divides the amount available by the number of payments to be paid out. When the period is up, the principal amount is depleted. Of course, the unpaid balance continues to earn interest during this fixed period.

**Fixed-Amount Installments:** If the beneficiary wants a certain amount, say $1,000, to be paid to him/her monthly, the company will be happy to do so. However, payment of a fixed amount to the beneficiary over a period of time will eventually deplete the principal balance, if the amount paid exceeds the interest earned on the unpaid balance.

**Annuity:** If the beneficiary wants a <u>lifetime income</u> with a high degree of safety, he/she can use the proceeds to purchase a fixed annuity from the insurance company. Buying an annuity with the lump-sum proceeds would be an <u>Immediate annuity</u>, and the insurance company could start paying the annuitant monthly payments based on his/her age, sex, and life expectancy right away.

Instead of choosing one of the other settlement options, the beneficiary uses the money to buy an annuity, thereby becoming the <u>annuitant</u>. Although all annuities will pay the annuitant a <u>monthly income for life</u>, the type of annuity pay-out option selected will be a factor in determining the amount of the payments, since some options are riskier than others.

## NONFORFEITURE OPTIONS (GUARANTEED VALUES)

<u>Three non-forfeiture options</u> are required in all life-insurance policies that have or will have a cash value. This includes Whole Life, Limited Pay Life such as 20-Pay Life and Life Paid Up at 65, and Endowments. Even annuities are required to have Non-forfeiture options.

The purpose of these options is to <u>protect the money</u> you have saved in your cash-value account. After all, it is your money! What happens when you forget to pay your premium and your policy lapses? Can the company keep the money? Absolutely not! By law, the policyholder may select any one of the following three non-forfeiture options or provisions any time there is a cash value. If you do not pay your premium when due and your policy does lapse, the company will <u>wait 60 days</u> from your due date to hear from you regarding the option you prefer. For example, you bought a $100,000 whole life policy with an annual premium of $1,000 when you were age 30. You are now age 65 and your policy has a cash value of $40,000. If your policy lapses, either unintentionally or on purpose, the company must allow you to select any one of the following three non-forfeiture options:

**Cash Surrender Value:** You don't want your policy anymore. You're now age 65, your kids are grown up and your house is paid for, and it's time to retire. You can surrender your original policy by sending it back to the company anytime and the company is obligated to send your $40,000 accumulated cash value to you <u>within six months of your request</u>. Of course, you do not have any further insurance coverage, since you have "surrendered" your policy for cash, but you don't need any!

**Extended Term:** This is the <u>automatic option</u>. If the insurance company does not hear from you within 60 days of your due date, it must automatically give you this option, since it is not allowed to keep your money. Assuming the same facts as above, you, instead, give your $40,000 cash value to the insurance company. Your original policy has lapsed. In exchange, the company will give you a <u>new Term insurance policy with the same face amount</u> as your original policy had, which in the example was $100,000.

<u>No physical exam is required</u>. The new policy does not have any cash value since it is Term insurance. However, no additional payments are due. The Term policy is paid for until the expiration of the term. The company has internally purchased you a new Term policy with a face amount of $100,000.

The question is, how long will the term policy last? You gave the insurance company your $40,000 cash value (or they just took it, since they didn't hear from you within 60 days) and they used it to buy you a new $100,000 Term policy <u>for as long as the money will last</u>, based on your attained age at the time this option goes into effect.

Assuming you were age 65 (as in the example), your $40,000 may buy a new Term policy with a face amount of $100,000 for 23 years, 8 months, and 13 days. If you die within that term, your beneficiary will get $100,000. If you die one day later, the term has expired, and your beneficiary will get nothing. This Term policy has no cash value, so no loans may be taken.

**Reduced Paid-Up Insurance:** Instead of cashing in your policy, you would like to exchange it internally with the company for a new policy that has a "<u>reduced</u>" face amount (reduced from your original policy) but is <u>fully paid for</u> until you reach age 100 or die.

In effect, you are giving the insurance company all of your accumulated cash value to that point in exchange for your new Reduced Paid-Up policy. The new policy is issued <u>regardless of your health</u> (no physical required) and its immediate cash value will approximate the cash value you gave up. The new policy is still Whole Life, and the cash value will continue to accumulate until it equals the face amount of the policy at age 100. You may still take out policy loans or take cash surrender if you so desire.

In our example, you had bought a Whole Life policy at age 30 with a Face Amount of $100,000. You are now age 65 and your accumulated cash value is $40,000 after paying your premium for 35 years. You could take the $40,000 and retire by choosing the Cash Surrender option shown above. But you could, instead, give this $40,000 to the company as a single premium for a new Whole Life policy with a reduced face amount. In exchange, the company will "buy" you a new Whole Life policy Paid-Up to age 100, but the Face Amount will be less than the $100,000 you had on your original policy. No physical exam is required. In this example, the new Face Amount would be approximately $75,000.

This new $75,000 policy is fully paid-for until you die or turn age 100. No further payments are ever due. Your cash value would be immediately high, since you just gave the company $40,000 from your original cash value account. If you die at age 68, your beneficiary will receive the face amount of the new policy, which is $75,000. If you live to 100, your $40,000 cash value will have grown to be $75,000 by then and the company will write you a check.

This option is designed for people who want to continue their Life insurance in later years but do not want any further payments after they retire. This option may be selected at any age, not just age 65.

All three of these options are present in all policies with a cash value since they are required by law. As you can see, <u>Extended Term option would give you the most insurance protection</u> (face amount), while <u>Reduced Paid-Up will give you the longest period of protection</u> (to age 100).

## POLICY LOANS AND WITHDRAWAL OPTIONS

**Cash Loans:** Most policies are required to have a cash value <u>after the third full year</u> that premiums have been paid. Since the cash value belongs to the policyholder, he/she can borrow nearly all of it any time he/she wishes. However, the company has up to <u>six months to defer</u> a request for a policy loan.

Since the insurance company planned on having your cash-value funds to invest, and since its rate level was based on that fact, your taking of a policy loan upsets its actuarial calculations. The company counted on having your money to invest at a higher rate of interest than it was going to pay you on your cash-value account. The fact that the company might "profit" from this difference in interest rates was a factor in determining what your premium should be. If you borrow the money, the company doesn't have it to invest, and since it cannot change your rate, the company is at a disadvantage.

To make up for this, the company is permitted to charge you interest on the money you borrow. The maximum interest rate they can charge on a new policy is <u>8% fixed simple annual interest</u>. However, once a policy is issued, nothing can be changed, including the interest rate. Therefore, if you have a policy still in force that was written 20 years ago, the rate of interest on policy loans may still very well be just 5% or so.

Policy loans and accrued interest do not have to be paid back, at least while you are still alive. <u>At your death, any outstanding loans plus interest will be subtracted from policy proceeds</u>.

Insurance companies many also utilize an <u>adjustable interest rate feature that is based on the Moody's Monthly Corporate Bond Index</u>. As bond interest rates go up and down, so does your "floating" interest rate. Very few insurance companies choose this feature, since, in order to change rates, a company must file a significant amount of supporting data with the State Department of Insurance, which is time-consuming and expensive. The adjustable rate could be more or less than 8%, based on the Moody's Index. Adjustments may be made at intervals as specified in the policy.

**Automatic Premium Loans:** This option is available on any life-insurance policy that has or will have a cash value. Although usually free, the policy owner <u>must select</u> this option by checking the proper block on the application. If selected, this rider <u>will keep your life-insurance policy from lapsing due to nonpayment of premium</u>. If you do not pay your premium when due, on the last day of the Grace Period the policy will automatically borrow from its own cash value to pay it for you. Of course, this creates a policy loan that must eventually be paid back, plus interest. If you die with this loan outstanding, then the loan and accrued interest will be subtracted from policy proceeds.

*Remember:* *Automatic Premium Loan is an option that must be selected by the policy owner.* It is not attached automatically and <u>it is not a non-forfeiture option</u>. This rider <u>cannot be attached to a term policy</u>, since there is no cash value.

**Withdrawals:** Of course, as previously discussed, clients with cash-value policies may withdraw their money at any time, although most companies have the right to <u>defer a request for a loan or a cash surrender up to six months</u>. Most companies will not allow you to borrow 100% of your cash value, since if you do not pay your interest charges as they accrue, your <u>policy will lapse when the amount owed plus interest equals the cash value</u>. This is especially true on Variable Life, where the cash value will fluctuate based upon the performance of the separate account.

**Partial Surrenders:** Many companies selling Annuities, Universal, or Variable Life will charge you a <u>penalty</u> for early surrender, usually during the first seven years of a policy. These penalty charges must be stated clearly in the policy and/or the prospectus. They are usually written on a <u>declining basis</u>, so if you have maintained your policy for a certain number of years, they no longer apply.

## DIVIDEND OPTIONS

Many companies are corporations owned by stockholders. When you own stock in a "stock" insurance company, you may receive a dividend as declared by the company's Board of Directors. This type of dividend is considered to be ordinary income and <u>is subject to income tax</u>. You do not have to be a policyholder to buy stock in a stock insurance company. You merely call your stockbroker and ask him/her to purchase the stock on your behalf. Stock insurance companies issue <u>nonparticipating</u> (non-par) policies.

Mutual Insurance Companies are corporations, but <u>they do not issue stock</u>. To own part of a Mutual, you must buy a policy and become a policyholder. Mutual companies issue what is known as <u>Participating</u>

policies, sometimes called <u>Par</u> policies. The Board of Directors of a Mutual company may also declare a dividend to be paid to the policyholders. If paid, the IRS considers this type of dividend to be a return of an overpayment of premium and, therefore, <u>not subject to taxation</u>.

<u>Dividends may not be guaranteed</u>. It would be illegal to do so. You may cite the company's past record of paying dividends when making a proposal, but you cannot guarantee future dividends, since there is no way to be certain that they will be paid out. If a Mutual company does declare a dividend, the policyholder selects from the following <u>six methods of dividend payment</u>:

**Cash:** The insurance company simply sends the policyholder a check. If the dividend declared was $1.00, the client would receive $1.00 per thousand of face amount ($100 on a $100,000 policy).

**Reduction of Premium Payments:** The company keeps the dividend and uses it to offset the client's next premium, when it becomes payable. The client pays the difference.

**Accumulation at Interest:** The company keeps the dividends, which then accumulate additional interest. While the dividends are not taxable, <u>the interest is</u>. Of course, the client may instruct the company to pay them his/her accumulated funds at any time in the future.

**One-Year Term Option:** The client may instruct the company to buy him/her one-year Term insurance with his/her dividend serving as the premium. This would provide the client with additional short-term coverage, but when the year was up, the Term policy would expire.

**Paid-Up Additions:** The client may instruct the insurance company to use his/her dividends to purchase him/her <u>additional small Whole Life policies</u> each year with whatever dividends he/she may receive. These new policies will also have a cash value and will be issued <u>regardless of health</u>. For this reason, this option is often selected by a client in poor health. Over a period of time, a client may obtain a substantial amount of additional insurance without a physical by selecting this option.

**Paid-Up Option:** If dividends are used to purchase paid-up additions or left to accumulate at interest, then the Paid-Up option may also be selected. When the cash value of the original policy plus the accumulated interest and/or accumulated cash value of the paid-up addition equal the single premium due on the original policy, then the policyholder may elect to use these accumulated amounts to pay up the original policy.

| Six Methods of Dividend Payment | |
| --- | --- |
| **Cash** | Company sends check to policy owner |
| **Reduction of Premium Payments** | Company retains dividend and applies it toward next premium due |
| **Accumulation at Interest** | Company retains dividends and pays interest to policy owner (interest is taxable) |
| **Paid-Up Addition** | Company uses dividend to create new, small paid-up Whole Life policy for policy owner |
| **Paid-Up Option** | Company uses interest accumulated and/or cash values of additional Whole Life policies to pay-up original policy |
| **One-Year Term Option** | Company creates new, one-year Term policy for policyholder (nonrenewable) |

Do not confuse these six dividend options with the settlement options that were covered earlier. These options only apply to participating policies as issued by a mutual company. There are many mutual insurance companies. Of course, you may change from one dividend option to another at any time.

## DISABILITY RIDERS

**Waiver of Premium Rider:** This is actually a form of disability insurance attached to a life-insurance policy to pay the premium on behalf of the insured in case he/she becomes totally disabled. The insured's sickness or disability must last for at least six months, during which time the insured must pay his/her premium themselves. After six months, the premium is paid retroactively for the insured by the insurance company under the provisions of this rider. This rider costs extra (but not much), and the extra premium paid does not go towards cash value accumulation. This rider, as do most, drops off the policy automatically when the insured reaches a certain age, usually 60 or 65, and the overall policy premium is then reduced. This is sometimes abbreviated WP.

**Disability Income Benefit:** Although disability income insurance is usually sold as a separate policy, it can also be added to a life insurance policy as a rider for an additional premium. If purchased, this rider will pay your loss of net earned income if you are totally disabled as per the definition in the rider. There is usually a short waiting period before monthly benefits start.

**Payor Benefit Life/Disability:** As discussed previously, this rider is very similar to Waiver of Premium rider, except it is added to a policy written on the life of a child. It will pay the premium on the child's policy if the payor (usually a parent) becomes disabled or dies. Premiums will be paid by the insurer until the child reaches either age 18 or age 21, depending upon the company, at which time the child must assume the payments.

## ACCELERATED (LIVING) BENEFIT PROVISION/RIDER

This rider allows a policy owner to "accelerate" receipt of a portion of the policy's death benefit upon the insured's occurrence of a terminal illness, a catastrophic illness, or eligibility for long-term care.

Living benefits may be included on new policies as a provision or added to existing policies as a rider, generally with no additional premium charge. All insureds are eligible, regardless of age or health status, and there are no restrictions on use of the funds. However, the rider must be applied for before it can be exercised. This rider provides clients with additional means of accessing cash under a life policy, although it is not the only way of doing so. Clients may elect to take a policy loan or surrender the policy for cash instead.

Accelerated benefits are not taxable, although receipt of these funds may affect Medicaid and Supplemental Security Income (SSI) eligibility. This rider is not Health, Nursing Home or Long Term Care Insurance (LTC), and is not intended to eliminate the need for such coverage. Of course, future benefits payable upon death will be reduced by any amounts paid out under the terms of this rider. Without this rider or provision, a policyholder with a terminal illness may be forced instead to make a "viatical settlement," whereby they assign their life insurance policy to an investor. The investor buys the policy at a discount for cash and names himself as beneficiary. When the insured dies, the investor profits based upon the difference in the face amount of the policy and the amount they paid the policyholder.

## RIDERS COVERING ADDITIONAL INSUREDS

The **Family policy** is a combination of Whole Life on the breadwinner and a Level Term Rider on the spouse and children. After a short waiting period, newborn children are automatically covered with no increase in premium. The term coverage for both the spouse and children is renewable up to a certain age and convertible to Whole Life. The conversion privilege is offered if the primary insured dies. The **Other Insured rider** is used to add coverage to your whole life policy for a new spouse, subject to insurability.

A **Family Maintenance Policy** is also a policy that combines Whole Life insurance and a Level Term Rider, but <u>both cover the same person</u>. The insured buys a combination of Whole Life insurance, which provides permanent insurance coverage to age 100, and Level Term insurance, which is designed to provide the beneficiary with a monthly income for a specific period of time if the insured dies during the term of the Level Term Rider.

For example, a 30 year old insured buys a $100,000 Whole Life policy and adds a 10 year Level Term Rider with a face amount of $120,000 to the policy. The Level Term Rider is structured to pay the beneficiary $1,000 a month for 10 years (or a total of $120,000) if the insured dies prior to age 40, in addition to the $100,000 lump sum from the Whole Life policy. Remember, there are 120 months in 10 years! If the insured dies after age 40, the Level Term Rider has expired, but the Whole Life policy still covers the insured to age 100 or death, whichever comes first.

So, if the insured died at age 35, the beneficiary would receive $1,000 a month for 10 years, which is a total of $120,000 from the Level Term Rider **plus** the $100,000 lump sum from the Whole Life policy. Remember, the rider is Level Term, so the face amount will not decrease.

A **Family Income Policy** is similar, except that it <u>combines Whole Life insurance with a Decreasing Term Rider also written on the same person</u>, so it is cheaper to buy since decreasing term costs less than level term.

For example, a 30 year old insured buys a $100,000 Whole Life policy and adds a 10 year Decreasing Term Rider with a face amount of $120,000 to the policy. Although the Decreasing Term Rider is also structured to pay the beneficiary $1,000 a month if the insured dies prior to age 40, <u>the face amount of the rider is decreasing, not level</u>. The face amount of a 10 year Decreasing Term Rider will decrease 10% each year until it expires.

So, if the insured died after 5 years, the face amount of the 10 year rider would have decreased to $60,000, so the beneficiary will only receive $1,000 a month for 5 years, or 60 months. If the insured died after 9 years, the face amount of the rider would have decreased to $12,000, so the beneficiary would only receive $1,000 a month for one year. Of course, if the insured died after age 40, there would be no coverage under the rider since it expired, but the permanent Whole Life coverage would still apply. Remember, the rider is term insurance and <u>there is no coverage on term insurance unless you die within the term.</u>

## RIDERS AFFECTING THE DEATH BENEFIT AMOUNT

**Accidental Death:** Known as double or triple indemnity, the Accidental Death Benefit (ADB) rider may be purchased for around $1.00 per $1,000 of coverage. It will pay your beneficiary double or triple only in the event you die as a result of an accident. Also, you must die within 90 days of the accident or the insurance company does not consider it to be accidental death. This rider also drops off the policy automatically at age 60 or 65, since the chance of accidental death increases drastically at older ages. Technically, ADB is a form of health insurance attached as a rider to a life insurance policy.

**Guaranteed Insurability Rider:** The Guaranteed Insurability rider (GIR) protects the <u>insured's right to buy more coverage in the future without the need to prove good health</u>. It costs extra. The extra premium does not go toward cash value accumulation. As with WP above, the premiums charged for this and all riders on the policy must be shown separately from the actual life-insurance premium. GIR usually offers the insured five future dates at which he/she can purchase more insurance. If the insured started out with $10,000 face amount, after exercising all five of these options, he/she would have a face amount of $60,000. Of course, the premium charged for these extra amounts of insurance is based on the insured's age at the time the option is exercised (attained age), but is no more than it would be for a healthy person the same age. Extra options may also be offered for marriage and the birth of a child. If an option is not exercised, it is lost. All option dates must be used by the time specified in the rider.

**Cost of Living:** The Cost of Living rider increases the face amount of your policy to coincide with the rate of inflation, to assure the policyholder that the Death benefit will be adequate to cover family expenses at all times.

**Return of Premium Rider:** With the Return of Premium rider, you buy an increasing amount of Term insurance that always equals the total amount of premiums paid to date. This rider really doesn't actually return your premiums paid; it pays an additional amount of insurance equal to your premiums paid at death. You are simply buying additional term insurance.

**Return of Cash Value Rider:** Since some clients object to the fact that Whole Life companies keep your cash value upon your death, many producers offer the Return of Cash Value rider. This is actually a form of Increasing Term coverage that will pay an amount equal to your cash value along with your face amount if you die.

**Remember:** *Riders modify the policy, usually by making it better.* They can be added at any time with mutual consent of the parties. Most riders cost extra, but none of the extra premium goes toward cash value accumulation. Most riders drop off the policy around age 65 due to adverse selection. The extra premium charged would also drop off. Riders are sometimes called endorsements. Some riders are free, such as APL (Automatic Premium Loan), but still must be selected by the policyholder.

# Life Insurance Policy Provisions, Options and Riders

# KEY FACTS

- Although producers must sign the application, they are not a party to the contract. It is the responsibility of the producer to explain the policy provisions, riders, and exclusions to the client.

- On Graded Premium Whole Life, the premiums gradually increase for the first five years, then remain level at a higher-than-normal amount thereafter. The face amount is level.

- When you make an Absolute Assignment, you are the assignor. The party you assign your policy to is the assignee. Absolute assignments may not be revoked.

- Insurance companies have six months to defer a request for a loan or cash surrender.

- Your policy is the sole collateral for a policy loan. Policy loans are not taxable.

- In most states, Suicide is covered after two years. If you commit suicide within the first two years, no benefit is payable but all premiums are refunded to the beneficiary.

- An Irrevocable Beneficiary has a vested interest in the policy.

- Under the Common Disaster provision, it is assumed that the insured died last.

- On Reinstatement, the Incontestability and Suicide clauses start over.

- The Misstatement of Age provision runs for the duration of the policy. Discovery of a misstated age results in adjustment of benefits, not cancellation of the policy.

- If the Interest settlement option is selected, the interest paid is subject to taxes.

- Proceeds of a life insurance policy, left with an insurer, for the benefit of a beneficiary, may NOT be attached by creditors.

- A client may exercise the Free Look provision without giving any reason.

- The Free Look (usually 10 days) starts upon policy delivery. If the policy is mailed to the client by the company, the Free Look starts on the date of mailing. This is called Constructive Delivery.

- The Owner's Rights section of a Life policy states who has the right to change the beneficiary, who can take a loan, and who can take cash surrender.

- When a beneficiary selects the <u>Interest Only settlement option</u>, interest payments (which are taxable) will vary, but the beneficiary may withdraw the principal at any time.

- Examples of <u>third-party policy ownership</u> include Key Person and Partnership insurance, as well as a policy written on the life of a spouse or minor child.

- The beneficiary does NOT have to be of age in order to receive policy proceeds.

- If a policy with a cash value lapses for nonpayment, the client has 60 days from the Premium Due date to select a <u>Non-forfeiture option</u>. <u>Extended Term</u> is the Automatic Non-forfeiture option.

- Proceeds cannot be directly paid to a minor child since they <u>can't sign a release</u>.

- The Accelerated Benefits Rider will pay proceeds <u>prior to death</u> for those with a terminal illness.

- A "revocable" beneficiary may be <u>changed at any time</u> by the policy owner.

- The "fixed period" settlement option <u>does not</u> guarantee payments for the life of the beneficiary.

- The "reduced paid-up" non-forfeiture option may be <u>taken any time</u> there is a cash value.

- Failure to repay a loan will have a <u>permanent effect</u> on cash value accumulation.

- The "Entire Contract" includes the policy and anything else <u>attached at issue</u>, such as the application.

- If an insured misstates their age, upon their death the insurer will adjust the benefits based upon the amount of insurance the premium paid would have purchased if the correct age was known.

- Life insurance policies exclude suicide for the first two years.

- If an insured buys a life insurance policy and dies one month later, the insurer must pay the claim.

- The owner of a life insurance policy may transfer their ownership to another policy by making an "absolute" assignment.

- A life insurance beneficiary who elects to take the proceeds payable upon the death of the insured over a period of time has selected the "fixed period" settlement option.

- Premiums paid on behalf of a disabled insured under the "waiver of premium" rider are not considered to be a loan against the policy's cash value. If the insured satisfies the waiting period, the rider will pay the premiums retroactively to the date of disability.

- The "guaranteed insurability rider" allows the insured to increase coverage periodically without a physical exam.

- The Change of Insured Rider may be utilized by an employer who wants to transfer a Key Person life insurance policy from one key person to another.

- On a participating life insurance policy, if the policy owner selects the one year term dividend option, the dividend may be used to buy term insurance equal to the policy's death benefit.

- Life insurance proceeds create an "immediate estate" for the beneficiary.

- For "estate conservation" purposes, a beneficiary should select the "interest only" settlement option.

- The "reduced paid-up" non-forfeiture option will provide coverage for life.

- When an insured dies in the grace period without paying the premium due, the face amount will be paid to the beneficiary, less the overdue premium.

- The annual interest on a life insurance loan is added to the amount of the loan as it accrues.

- Under the "misstatement of age" clause, if the client understates their age, it is the face amount that is reduced.

- When a policy owner lists a group of people as beneficiaries, it is known as a "class designation."

- "Waiver of Premium" is a rider that will pay the premium on behalf of a disabled insured, after a short waiting period, until they either recover or die.

- When adding a "children's term rider" to a life insurance policy, all of the insured's children are covered for a single, flat premium charge, no matter how many.

- If the insured/owner of a life policy does not designate a settlement option prior to death, the beneficiary may choose whichever option they want. Most choose cash, which is not taxable.

- If a person purchases a whole life policy and adds a "return of premium" rider, they will have level coverage from the whole life policy, and increasing coverage from the rider.

- The "return of premium" rider and the "return of cash value" rider are both types of increasing term coverage.

- A "viatical settlement" is an agreement where a terminally ill insured (a "viator") sells their life insurance policy to an investor for less than its face amount, but for more than its cash value.

- The "waiver of premium" rider does not pay a cash benefit to the insured. If the insured becomes disabled for a certain period of time, this rider will pay the insured's premium until he/she recovers.

- If an outstanding policy loan, plus interest, exceeds the cash value of the policy, the policy will lapse.

- If a beneficiary takes the policy proceeds in a lump sum, the "spendthrift" clause will not apply.

- A contingent beneficiary will receive the policy proceeds if the primary beneficiary dies before the insured.

- New life insurance policies are "contestable" for material misrepresentation for the first two years.

- An "irrevocable" beneficiary cannot be changed without the consent of both the policy owner and the irrevocable beneficiary.

- Surrender charges levied by some insurers on annuities and universal life will reduce the amount a policy owner will receive upon cash surrender.

- A life insurance policy that has been surrendered for cash may not be reinstated.

# Life Insurance Policy Provisions, Options and Riders

# PRACTICE EXAM

1.  Dividend projections may be included in a proposal for life insurance when which of the following is true:

    A.  The applicant has requested that they be included
    B.  There is a clear statement that payment of future dividends is not guaranteed
    C.  The projected amounts are calculated on the basis of the Commissioner's Standard Ordinary Mortality Tables
    D.  The projected amounts do not exceed the dividends previously paid by the same insurance company

2.  In a policy insuring the life of a child, which of the following allows the premiums to be waived in the event of the death or disability of the person responsible for premium payments:

    A.  Waiver of Premium Provision
    B.  Reduction of Premium Option
    C.  Payor Provision
    D.  Reduced Paid-Up Option

3.  Which statement about the Reinstatement Provision is true:

    A.  It provides for reinstatement of a policy regardless of the insured's health
    B.  It guarantees the reinstatement of a policy that has been surrendered for cash
    C.  It requires the policyholder to pay, with interest, all premiums that are in arrears in order for the policy to be reinstated
    D.  It permits reinstatement within 10 years after a policy has lapsed

4.  A parent who wishes to have complete control of a son's life insurance policy until the son reaches age 25 can do so through the use of:

    A.  Insuring Clause
    B.  Consideration Clause
    C.  Payor Provision
    D.  Ownership Provision

5. An insured died during the grace period of his/her life insurance policy and had not paid the required annual premium. The insurance company is obligated to pay which of the following to the beneficiary:

   A. The cash value of the policy, if any
   B. The full face amount of the policy
   C. The face amount of the policy less any earned premiums
   D. A refund of any premiums paid

6. The life insurance policy clause that prevents an insurance company from denying payment of a death claim after a specified period of time is known as the:

   A. Misstatement of Age Clause
   B. Incontestability Clause
   C. Reinstatement Clause
   D. Insuring Clause

7. Which of the following statements is true about a policy assignment:

   A. It permits the beneficiary to designate the person or persons to receive the benefits
   B. It is valid during the insured's lifetime only because the death benefit is payable to the named beneficiary
   C. It transfers the owner's rights under the policy to the extent expressed in the assignment form
   D. It is the same as a beneficiary designation

8. A $10,000 life insurance policy with a Triple Indemnity Clause has been in force for three years. The insured is injured in a train wreck and dies in a hospital five months later. The death proceeds payable under the policy would be:

   A. $30,000
   B. $20,000
   C. $10,000
   D. $     0

9. The time period covered by the 10-Day Free Look Provision of a life insurance contract starts:

   A. When the contract is issued and mailed to the agency office from the home office of the insurance company
   B. When the contract is received in the agency office and given to the producer
   C. When the insured receives the contract and makes the first premium payment, if needed
   D. When the insured receives the contract and a Right to Look receipt

10. Which of the following is a non-forfeiture option that provides continuing cash-value build up:

    A. Extended Term
    B. Cash Surrender
    C. Reduced Paid-Up
    D. Deferred Annuity

11.  Which statement about a typical Suicide Clause in a life insurance policy is true:

     A.  Suicide is excluded as long as the policy is in force
     B.  Suicide is excluded for a specific period of years and covered thereafter
     C.  Suicide is covered for a specific period of years and excluded thereafter
     D.  Suicide is covered as long as the policy is in force

12.  Which individual policy conversion is usually permitted without any evidence of insurability:

     A.  Conversion from a Term policy to a Whole Life policy
     B.  Conversion from a Whole Life policy to a Term policy
     C.  Conversion to a larger amount of insurance
     D.  Conversion to a lower premium plan

13.  The provision in a life insurance policy that provides protection against unintentional policy lapse is known as the:

     A.  Reduction of Premium Option
     B.  Waiver of Premium Benefit
     C.  Payor Clause
     D.  Automatic Premium Loan Provision

14.  Which settlement option might provide payments that exceed the proceeds of the policy and the interest earned:

     A.  Life Annuity
     B.  Fixed Period
     C.  Fixed Amount
     D.  Interest Only

15.  The owner of a business is insured under a $100,000 Key Employee Life policy that contains a Double Indemnity clause and a Suicide Clause. The business has paid the annual premium of $2,000. Six months after the inception date of the policy, the insured commits suicide. The insurance company's liability for payment is:

     A.  $200,000
     B.  $100,000
     C.  $  2,000
     D.  $      0

16.  If the beneficiary's main objective for the death benefit proceeds is estate conservation, they would most likely select which settlement option upon death of the insured:

     A.  Cash
     B.  Fixed period
     C.  Fixed amount
     D.  Interest

17. Seth Brown, whose wife is his business partner, buys a life insurance policy on his wife's life. Because of this third-party ownership, the beneficiary should be the:

   A.   Policyholder
   B.   Policyholder's wife
   C.   Policyholder's estate
   D.   Policyholder's children

18. Which statement about the Misstatement of Age Provision in a life insurance policy is true:

   A.   If the insured's age has been overstated, it provides that a premium refund and the face amount of the policy will be payable
   B.   If the insured's age has been understated, it provides that a death benefit smaller than the face amount of the policy will be payable
   C.   It becomes inoperative after the expiration of the policy's contestable period
   D.   It is an optional provision

19. All of the following are a part of a life insurance policy, EXCEPT the:

   A.   Insuring Clause
   B.   Conditional Receipt
   C.   Copy of the application
   D.   Incontestability Clause

20. When someone other than the insured is the owner of a life insurance policy, the owner may do all of the following without the insured's consent, EXCEPT:

   A.   Surrender the policy for its cash value
   B.   Increase the amount of insurance
   C.   Make a policy loan
   D.   Change the beneficiary

21. An insured has a Whole Life policy with a $100,000 face amount and a $40,000 cash value. The insured's policy lapses, which non-forfeiture option should they select to provide lifetime coverage:

   A.   Reduced Paid-up
   B.   Cash Surrender
   C.   Extender Term
   D.   Paid-up Additions

22. If a parent purchases life insurance on their child all of the following are true EXCEPT:

   A.   The parent is the owner of the policy
   B.   The child is the insured
   C.   The parent is responsible for the premium
   D.   The parent is the insured

23. If a life-insurance policy does not permit the policyholder to change the beneficiary, the beneficiary is:

    A. Subsequent
    B. Irrevocable
    C. Contingent
    D. Guaranteed

24. Which of the following statements about the Automatic Premium Loan provision in a life-insurance policy is true:

    A. A loan taken under the provision is not interest-bearing
    B. The provision must be elected by the policyholder
    C. The provision applies only to Whole or Limited-Pay Life policies
    D. The provision cannot be revoked by the policyholder

25. When the primary beneficiary predeceases the insured, the proceeds are paid to the:

    A. Tertiary beneficiary
    B. Alternate beneficiary
    C. Contingent beneficiary
    D. Collateral beneficiary

26. If the insured understated his/her age and the error is discovered after the insured's death, the insurance company will:

    A. Refuse to pay the death claim
    B. Refund all past premiums paid with any accumulated interest
    C. Pay the face amount of the policy with a deduction for the amount of the underpayment of premium
    D. Pay the amount the premium would have purchased at the correct age

27. The purpose of a Grace Period provision is to:

    A. Protect the insurance company against adverse selection by policyholders
    B. Protect the policyholder against unintentional lapse
    C. Permit the beneficiary to establish an insurable interest
    D. Permit the insurance company to determine the cause of death

28. When the insured lists a group of beneficiaries it is known as a:

    A. Class designation
    B. Individual designation
    C. Minor designation
    D. Trust designation

29. Which of the following best describes the Waiver of Premium rider:

   A.   It is a rider that can only be added to a cash value life insurance policy which creates a loan against the cash value in order to pay the premium for the insured
   B.   It is a rider that can only be added to a cash value life insurance policy that will pay the insured's premium if they become totally disabled
   C.   It is a rider that can be added to any policy, that will pay the insured's premium after a waiting period if the insured becomes totally disabled
   D.   It is a non-forfeiture option that will provide the insured with term life insurance for a limited period of time if their original policy lapses

30. On term life insurance, the re-entry option is contingent upon:

   A.   Paying an increased premium
   B.   Being able to pass a physical exam
   C.   Buying another policy
   D.   Adding an accidental death benefit rider

31. Which of the following is true if the insured/owner of the policy does not pre-designate a settlement option for the beneficiary prior to death:

   A.   The beneficiary may select the settlement option upon death of the insured
   B.   The insurer may select the settlement option upon death of the insured
   C.   The insurer will keep the death benefit since no settlement option was designated
   D.   The insurer will automatically pay out a fixed dollar amount to the beneficiary, since it is the automatic option

32. An insurance company has which of the following options when an insured wishes to cash in his/her policy:

   A.   It must pay him/her within two weeks
   B.   It must pay him/her within 90 days
   C.   It may delay payment for one month
   D.   It may defer payment for as long as six months

33. Most collateral assignments of life-insurance policies are made in order to protect the:

   A.   Insured's insurability
   B.   Insured's personal or business credit
   C.   Beneficiary from the claims of creditors
   D.   Insurance company from fraudulent claims

34. If the insured's age was overstated at the time a life-insurance policy was purchased and the error is discovered upon the death of the insured, the insurance company will:

   A.   Void the policy
   B.   Be prevented from taking any action according to the provisions of the Incontestability clause
   C.   Refund the overcharge in premiums to the beneficiary
   D.   Provide the additional insurance in the amount that has been purchased by the additional premium

35. Which of the following Settlement Options provides for payments to be made in regular installments of a specified amount until the principal and interest are exhausted?

    A.   Fixed Amount
    B.   Fixed Period
    C.   Interest
    D.   Life Income

36. Protection against unintentional lapse of a Life policy is afforded by:

    A.   A policy loan
    B.   An automatic-premium loan
    C.   A non-forfeiture option
    D.   A Dividend option

37. A life insurance company may contest a policy during the Contestable period for which of the following reasons:

    A.   Nonpayment of premiums
    B.   Material misrepresentation
    C.   Change of occupation
    D.   Misstatement of age

38. An employer may transfer a Key Person life insurance policy from one key person to another by making a(n):

    A.   Absolute assignment
    B.   Change of insured
    C.   Life settlement transaction
    D.   Irrevocable beneficiary designation

39. If an insured with a participating whole life policy elects the one year term dividend option, the amount of term life insurance purchased by the dividend will equal:

    A.   All premiums paid to date
    B.   The annual premium due
    C.   The cash value
    D.   The death benefit

40. A person who enters into a viatical settlement is known as a:

    A.   Viatical settlement provider
    B.   Viator
    C.   Viatical settlement broker
    D.   Viatical settlement agent

41. Life settlement contracts are between the:

    A.   Policy holder and the insurer
    B.   Agent and the policy holder
    C.   Policy holder and the beneficiary
    D.   Policy holder and a third party

42. All of the following are true about the Accidental Death Benefit rider EXCEPT:

    A.   Death must be accidental
    B.   Death must be occupational
    C.   Death must occur within a certain period of time after the accident
    D.   Death must be related to an accident that occurs prior to a specified age

43. All of the following are true when the beneficiary of a life insurance policy selects the fixed period settlement option EXCEPT:

    A.   Each monthly payment is partly interest and partly principal
    B.   The amount of each monthly payment depends upon the total number of monthly payments remaining
    C.   At the end of the fixed period, the proceeds will be exhausted
    D.   Monthly payments will continue for a fixed period of time, or for life, whichever is longer

44. If the beneficiary of a $100,000 life insurance policy elects a 10 year fixed period settlement option and the annual payout is $13,000, including 6% interest, how much of the payout is excluded from income tax each year:

    A.   $ 1,300
    B.   $ 6,000
    C.   $10,000
    D.   $13,000

45. The clause in a life insurance policy that states "….a beneficiary cannot assign or encumber the policy proceeds prior to receipt…" is known as the _____ clause:

    A.   Incontestability
    B.   Entire contract
    C.   Spendthrift
    D.   Non-forfeiture

46. A life insurance dividend option that would result in cash value that is in excess of that guaranteed in the policy is:

    A.   Paid-up additions
    B.   Interest
    C.   Reduced paid-up
    D.   Apply to premium when due

47. If a life insurance policy contains a "war clause" and an insured dies as a result of war, the insurer will:

    A.  Pay nothing
    B.  Refund the premiums
    C.  Pay 50% of the death benefit
    D.  Pay the face amount of the policy

1.  **B**  Dividends **may** be paid to policyholders of a mutual insurance company, such as Mutual of New York. Dividends are considered to be a return of an overpayment by the IRS and, therefore, not taxable. Although a company may state its past dividend history in a proposal, it is illegal to guarantee future dividends, since they might not occur.

2.  **C**  The Payor Provision (sometimes called Payor Waiver of Premium) is an optional provision (or rider) often added to a policy insuring the life of a minor. The adult (usually the parent) may become sick or disabled and become incapable of paying the premium. This rider will then pay the premium on behalf of the sick or disabled payor. However, it is exactly like the Waiver of Premium Rider you would see on your own life insurance policy in that both riders have a six-month waiting period before premiums are retroactively paid. Both riders cost extra and will automatically drop off at age 60 or 65 at which time the premium would be reduced. The extra premium for these riders must be shown separately from the premium charged for the life insurance. None of the extra premium charge goes toward cash-value accumulation.

3.  **C**  Most companies will offer the right to apply for reinstatement for up to three (sometimes five) years after a policy has lapsed. Although the client may have the right to apply, the company does not have to take him/her. The client must prove continued good health and pay back premiums plus interest. The company has nothing to lose by offering Reinstatement. The client's only reasons to apply for reinstatement, rather than applying for a new policy, are that, if accepted, the reinstated policy would have the same original age and perhaps a lower interest rate on policy loans than a new policy may have. Policies that have been surrendered for cash may not be reinstated.

4.  **D**  Although you may not be the insured, you can still be the policyholder. If you buy a policy on your minor child, you own the policy and your child is the insured. You control the cash values and may designate the beneficiary. This is called the Ownership Provision. At a certain age, say age 25, you may assign your ownership of the policy to your child, giving up all rights to the policy. This is called an Absolute Assignment, meaning that it may never be revoked.

5.  **C**  There are three grace periods to remember: 28 days on Industrial Life, 30 days on all other life except group, and 31 days on group life. The purpose of the grace period is to protect the insured who honestly forgot to pay on the due date. The policy will not actually lapse until the end of the grace period. If a client dies within the grace period, it is assumed he/she would have paid the premium, so the company will pay the face amount to the beneficiary, less any overdue premiums.

6.  **B**  The Incontestability Clause protects the client who may have lied (misrepresentation) on the original application for life insurance. The company has two years to investigate the insured from the original date of application. If the client dies within the first two years and the insurance company can prove that he/she lied about a material fact on the original application, they can deny

the claim. However, after the two-year period has elapsed, they must pay the claim even if the client lied. So, those who lied can quit worrying after two years!

7.  **C**  There are two types of assignment: Absolute and Collateral. An Absolute Assignment transfers all of the policyholder's rights to another party, such as when a parent assigns the policy to the child who is also the insured. A Collateral Assignment occurs when the insured pledges his/her policy proceeds to the bank for a loan. This is seldom done anymore, since interest rates on life insurance loans are generally lower than those on bank loans.

8.  **C**  Accidental Death Benefit (ADB), sometimes called Double or Triple Indemnity, is a rider that may be attached to any life insurance policy for an extra premium charge. The additional benefits are paid only if the insured dies within 90 days of an accident. If the insured lingers beyond 90 days, the policy reverts back to single indemnity only, and the face amount without the rider is paid, since it is assumed that death resulted more from natural causes than as a result of the accident.

9.  **C**  The 10-day Free Look never begins until the policy is actually delivered. Even if the premium had been paid previously, the 10-day Free Look would not have begun until policy delivery. The client then has 10 days to rescind the policy and get all of the money back.

10. **C**  There are only three non-forfeiture options: 1) Cash Surrender, 2) Reduced Paid-Up and the automatic option, 3) Extended Term. Their purpose is to protect the insured's accumulated cash values in case the Whole Life or Endowment policy lapses. A client has 60 days from the policy's premium-due date to select the option he/she prefers. If none is selected, the company will give the client the automatic option, Extended Term. Here, the face amount of the new policy is the same as on the initial policy. The accumulated cash value is used internally by the company to pay the premium for a new Term policy at the insured's attained age. The policy term is, however, as long as that amount of money will buy. There is no cash value, and at the expiration of the term, the policy expires and the insured has no further coverage.

If the client selects the Reduced Paid-Up option, the company then uses all of the accumulated cash value to buy the client internally a new Whole Life policy paid up to age 100. It would have an immediate cash value, but no further premiums would ever be due. The face amount would be more than the accumulated cash value, but less than the original face amount of the initial policy, so it is called Reduced Paid-Up. Cash value would continue to accumulate, and at maturity (age 100) the cash value would equal the face amount. No physical exam is required. Of course, if the client takes Cash Surrender, there is no further coverage.

11. **B**  The Suicide Clause, which is completely separate from the Incontestability Clause, excludes coverage for death resulting from suicide during the first two years of a policy. After that, suicide is covered. If the insured dies by suicide during the first two years, there is no coverage, but the insurance company will refund the premiums paid in to date to the beneficiary.

12. **A**  The conversion privilege is simply a marketing tool that allows insureds who buy Term insurance to convert to Whole Life without proving continued good health. Without this privilege, few would buy Term insurance. You cannot convert Term-to-Term or convert to a higher or lower face amount, and you cannot convert Whole Life-to-Term.

13. **D**  Automatic Premium Loan (APL) is a rider that can be added to any life insurance policy that has or will have a cash value. It cannot be added to Term insurance. It is usually free, but the producer or client must check this option on the application. If the policy has a cash value and the insured forgets to pay the premium when due, the policy will not lapse, since it will borrow

from itself to pay the overdue premium. ***Remember:*** *This is a rider, not a non-forfeiture option.* However, when the insured dies, all loans are subtracted from policy proceeds, so the beneficiary's pay-out may be reduced.

14. **A**   There are five settlement options from which a beneficiary may select upon death of the insured. 1) <u>Cash</u>, 2) <u>Fixed Period</u> (proceeds, plus interest, are all paid out over a fixed period of time, say 10 years), 3) <u>Fixed Amount</u> (the beneficiary elects to receive $1,000 per month, plus interest, for as long as the money lasts), 4) <u>Interest</u> (the proceeds are left with the company to accumulate additional interest) and 5) <u>Life Annuity</u> (paid as long as the beneficiary/annuitant lives).

15. **C**   If an insured dies by suicide within the first two years of a new life insurance policy, there is no coverage. However, the insurance company will refund the premium paid to the beneficiary.

16. **D**   Life insurance proceeds create an immediate estate upon death of the insured. If the beneficiary is mainly interested in conserving that money for the future, they should select the interest settlement option. If the interest settlement option is selected the insurer keeps the death benefit and pays the beneficiary interest, usually monthly, which is taxable to the beneficiary as ordinary income. The beneficiary can obtain the death benefit from the insurer at anytime. When the beneficiary does decide to access the death benefit in the future it is tax free.

17. **A**   This is an example of Key Person insurance. The beneficiary is Mr. Brown, the policyholder. His wife, the key person, is the insured. Mr. Brown apparently feels that if his wife should die, he would need the funds from the policy proceeds to retrain someone capable of assuming her business duties. This type of policy is often written with the business as the beneficiary as well.

18. **B**   The Misstatement of Age Provision is separate from the Incontestability Clause. Lying about age cannot void the policy. However, it can reduce the amount of benefits paid at the time of your death. The formula to calculate this is as follows: The client is 40, but states 30, to get a lower rate. The client buys a $100,000 policy. The premium paid is $200 per year. At the correct age, the client should have paid $400 per year.

$$\frac{\textit{Client Did Pay} \quad \$200}{\textit{Client Should Pay} \quad \$400} \quad \text{x} \quad \$100,000 \textit{ Face Amount} \quad = \quad \$50,000 \textit{ Paid At Death}$$

The formula is: "Did" ÷ "Should" x Face Amount = Amount Paid. In the above example, the insurance company will pay 200/400, or ½ of the face amount the client thought he/she was buying.

19. **B**   Under the Entire Contract Provision, a copy of the insured's application for life insurance is attached to the policy. If it weren't, any false answers (misrepresentations) by the insured would not be admissible in court, since they would not be part of the entire contract. However, the Conditional Receipt is **not** part of a life insurance policy. It is part of the application and is completed and given to the applicant when he/she pays the initial premium at the time of application.

20. **B**   As owner of the policy, this "third party" has the right to control the policy, including the beneficiary designation, taking a loan or even surrendering the policy for cash. However, under the Doctrine of Insurable Interest, the policyholder would need the written consent of the insured to increase the policy limits. ***Remember:*** *Life insurance policy limits may not usually be increased once the policy is in force unless the policy contains the Guaranteed Insurability rider.*

21. **A**  Once the insured's policy lapses the insurer has to offer the insured the choice of what they want to do with their cash value. The three non-forfeiture options are: Cash Surrender, Extended Term and Reduced Paid-up. If the insured wants permanent life insurance they would select the Reduced Paid-up non-forfeiture option. If selected, the insurer uses the insured's cash value to purchase the insured a single premium whole life policy, with a reduced face amount. Since the insured will never pay another premium, the face amount will be reduced from that of the original policy.

22. **D**  This is an example of third party ownership. Remember, the owner and the insured are not always the same person. In this example the parent is the policy owner and the child is the insured. The policy owner retains all the rights of ownership, such as paying the premium, designating the beneficiary, and taking loans. In this situation if the parent died, the policy would NOT pay a death benefit, since the parent is not the insured, the child is.

Once the child reaches a certain age the parent could execute an absolute assignment and assign ownership of the policy to the child. If done, the child would now be the owner/insured and would be responsible for paying the premium, could change the beneficiary, or even take cash surrender.

23. **B**  Typically, the insured or policyholder may change the beneficiary designation at any time. This is called a Revocable Beneficiary designation. However, if the insured or policyholder elects to appoint an Irrevocable Beneficiary, the designation may not be changed without the consent of the irrevocable beneficiary nor may a policy loan be taken. Some 99% of all beneficiary designations are revocable. Irrevocable designations are usually made only in rare situations, such as when the policy's cash value becomes part of a divorce settlement.

24. **B**  Automatic Premium Loan (APL) is a rider attached to Whole Life or Endowment policies, never Term. It must be elected by the policyholder, even though it is usually free. The purpose of the rider is to keep the policy in force if the insured forgets to pay the premium. The policy, with this rider attached, would automatically borrow from itself to pay the overdue premium, therefore avoiding lapse. Of course, the policy would have to have a cash value before such a "loan" could be taken. Also, all loans must be subtracted from policy proceeds (plus interest on the loan) in the event of the insured's death, so benefits will be reduced. Whole Life and Endowment policies are required to have a cash value no later than the end of the third full year.

25. **C**  Often the insured will name a Contingent Beneficiary to receive policy proceeds if the Primary Beneficiary has predeceased the insured. If no Contingent Beneficiary had been named in this instance, the policy proceeds would go to the estate of the insured to be distributed under the terms of the insured's Last Will and Testament. There are no such things as Alternate and Collateral Beneficiaries!

26. **D**  Under the Misstatement of Age clause, the insurance company is protected against clients who state they are younger than they really are in order to obtain a lower rate. Although lying about your age will not void the policy, the company will adjust your Death benefit to the amount that the correct premium would have purchased had you told the truth.

27. **B**  Grace Periods are: 30 days on Whole Life, Term, and Endowment; 28 days on Industrial Life, and 31 days on Group Life. If the insured dies within the grace period, the overdue premium is subtracted from policy proceeds and the beneficiary receives the remainder.

28. **A**  The owner of the policy can designate the beneficiary anyway they choose. The designation described in the question is a class designation such as "all my children."

29. **C**   The waiver of premium rider can be added to any policy and will waive the insured's premium after a six month waiting period if the insured becomes totally disabled. During the six month period the insured is responsible for paying their premium. If, after the six months, they are still totally disabled, the rider goes into effect and will pay the insured back the premium they paid during the six months and waive the ongoing premium as long as they are disabled. Waiver of premium is a rider NOT a non-forfeiture option.

30. **B**   The re-entry option is a common feature on many term policies that gives the insured the opportunity to pass a physical exam at the end of the term in order to qualify to renew the policy at a lower premium rate than the guaranteed rate available. Of course, if the insured fails the physical, he/she can always renew at the rate guaranteed in the policy.

31. **A**   The insured/owner of the policy has the right to pre-designate how they would like the beneficiary to receive the face amount of the policy upon their death. However, if the insured does not, the beneficiary has the right to select from the settlement options offered by the insurer. It is the beneficiary's choice, not the insurers. If no option is selected, the automatic settlement option is cash.

32. **D**   In order to discourage a possible "run on the bank," so to speak, life-insurance companies do have six months to defer the granting of a policy loan or a cash surrender. However, most insurance companies will grant a loan or a cash surrender immediately, in the interest of good public relations.

33. **B**   Collateral Assignments, in which the insured pledges his/her policy to the bank as collateral for a bank loan, are very common. When the loan is paid off, the Collateral Assignment drops off. A Collateral Assignment assures the bank that if the insured dies with the loan outstanding, the bank will be paid.

34. **D**   This is the reverse of the typical situation, in which the insured usually understates their age in order to have a lower premium. If the insured had overstated their age, then of course, they would have been paying a higher premium than they should have. So the formula works in reverse, too: The company would adjust the face amount to be higher, based on the amount the incorrect premium would have bought at the insured's correct age.

35. **A**   When the insured dies, the beneficiary may select any one of five Settlement Options. They are: Cash; Fixed Amount (for example, the beneficiary elects to receive $1,000 a month for as long as the money lasts); Fixed Period (the beneficiary chooses to be paid out over a 20-year period); Interest (the beneficiary leaves all the proceeds with the company to accumulate additional interest), and Life Income (the beneficiary takes the policy proceeds as cash and buys a Straight Life or Pure Life Annuity).

36. **B**   Automatic Premium Loan (APL) is a rider, usually free, that may be attached to any life-insurance policy that has or will have a cash value. It is not a Non-forfeiture option or Dividend option. If the insured fails to make a premium payment when due, the rider will cause the policy to borrow from itself to make the premium payment. Of course, this creates a policy loan, which eventually must be repaid, plus interest, upon the death of the insured. If a policy continues to borrow from itself until there is no cash value left, the policy would eventually lapse.

37. **B**   The Incontestability clause states that the policy is "contestable" for the first two years for material misrepresentation by the insured on the application for insurance. Life-insurance policies do not have a change-of-occupation clause. The Misstatement of Age clause permits the insurance

company to adjust benefits up or down in the event the insured has lied about his/her age at the time of application.

38. **B** Some insurers offer a "Change of Insured" rider, which allows the policy owner to transfer coverage from one key person to another, subject to proof of insurability.

39. **D** Some participating life insurance policies offer a dividend option known as "one year term" insurance. If a policy holder has borrowed against his/her policy, then part of the dividend can be used to buy one year term insurance equal to the face value of the policy. If the insured should die during the one year term before paying back the loan, the beneficiary will still receive the full value of the policy.

40. **B** A person with a terminal illness may elect to sell their policy to a viatical settlement provider in order to obtain money to pay their medical bills. In a viatical settlement agreement, such a person is known as the "viator."

41. **D** A life settlement is a contract between a policy owner and a third party, who agrees to buy the owner's policy for more than its cash value but less than its face amount. The owner then assigns the ownership of the policy to the third party, who names themselves as beneficiary. A life settlement is very similar to a viatical settlement, except on a life settlement, the policy owner does not have a terminal illness.

42. **B** The Accidental Death Benefit (ADB) rider may be added to a life insurance policy at issue for an additional premium. It usually pays double the face amount of the policy if the insured dies within 90 days of an accident, occupational or not. However, the ADB rider usually drops off the policy at a specified age (often 65), so accidents occurring after that age would not be covered, although the policy would still pay single indemnity.

43. **D** The fixed period settlement option specifies that the beneficiary will receive monthly payments from the insurer for a specified period of time, such as 10 years. At the end of that time, all funds will be exhausted and payments will stop. However, since the proceeds will continue to earn interest over this 10 year period, each monthly payment will vary based upon the current account value divided by the total number of monthly payments remaining.

44. **C** On a 10 year fixed period settlement option, $1/10^{th}$ of the policy proceeds will be payable tax free to the beneficiary each year, which in this case would be $10,000. If the annual payout exceeds that amount, the difference must be the interest earned on the unpaid balance, which is taxable as ordinary income.

45. **C** The "spendthrift" clause takes away the rights of the beneficiary to change the time of payments or the amount of installments payable upon the death of the insured. Further, it also prohibits the beneficiary from borrowing against or assigning the unpaid installments, which prevents the beneficiary from making unwise decisions that they may regret later on.

46. **A** Mutual insurers often pay dividends, although they are not guaranteed. If the insurer does pay a dividend, the policy owner may select one of several dividend options. If they select the "paid-up" additions option, each dividend will be used as a single premium to buy a small, additional whole life insurance policy. Since each policy purchased develops its own cash value over a period of time, the policy owner will end with more cash value than that guaranteed by his/her initial policy. Remember, "reduced paid-up" is a non-forfeiture option, not a dividend option.

47. **B** A "war clause" is an exclusion in some life insurance policies that states that there is no coverage if the insured dies as a result of war. However, the premiums paid will be refunded to the beneficiary.

# SECTION 6

# Annuities

## ANNUITY PRINCIPLES AND CONCEPTS

Annuities are the opposite of life insurance. Life insurance creates an estate for your heirs when you die, while annuities are designed to liquidate an estate through a series of systematic, guaranteed (in most cases) payments to the annuitant as long as that person lives. For example, if someone died and left you $100,000 cash, you could buy an annuity that would pay you a predetermined amount of money per month, as long as you lived.

Although annuities are the opposite of life insurance, they are regulated under the insurance laws and a life insurance license is required in order to sell them. They are often called "fixed annuities," in that they guarantee a certain fixed interest rate to you, although they often pay more than the guaranteed rate. Fixed annuities are considered very safe since they are backed by the state Life Insurance Guaranty Fund. If an insurance company that sold an annuity goes broke, the annuitant's funds (invested capital) are protected by law. However, it is against the rules to refer to the Life Insurance Guaranty Fund's safety provision in your sales presentation, unless asked.

So, annuities are unique in that they pay only if you live, not if you die. Of course, you may designate a beneficiary on some annuities to receive your invested capital in case you die, but this is a return of your own money, not a life insurance death benefit. You do not have to be in good health to buy an annuity. The company does not care. In fact, you are betting that you will live, since the company will pay you until you die. The insurance company is betting that you will die and the company can then keep your invested capital. Fixed annuities are not securities, although often sold by stockbrokers who have a life insurance license, as well.

## IMMEDIATE VERSUS DEFERRED ANNUITIES

**Single Premium Annuities:** Purchased with a lump sum by the annuitant. For example, if you came into $100,000 and decided to buy an annuity with it, you could start receiving monthly payments next month. The amount of your payments would be based on your life expectancy, your sex and what type of annuity you purchased. Or, you could buy the annuity with your lump sum, but tell the insurance company to hang on to your money until you reach a certain age, say 65. Of course, the insurance company will pay you, at least, the guaranteed minimum interest rate (or more) during the time they have your money. This type of annuity is called a SPDA (Single Premium Deferred Annuity) and has the benefit of tax-deferred interest accumulation during the Pay-In (accumulation) period. It is up to you when you want to start receiving your funds (plus interest) from the insurance company. *Remember: Most annuities are purchased with after-tax dollars, so when you annuitize, you just have to pay tax on the accumulated interest as you withdraw it.*

Also, it is important to remember that you cannot outlive the income from a Straight or Pure Life Annuity. It will pay you as long as you live, and you can even be paid back more than you invested!

So, a Single Premium Annuity may be purchased to start paying you back right away (<u>Immediate Annuity</u>) or to start paying you back at some time in the future (<u>Deferred Annuity</u>). In either case, remember, it is your money. You are the one who invested the funds. It is similar to stashing your money in the bank, except for the lifetime-pay-out provisions.

**Deferred Annuities:** This type of annuity could be purchased with <u>either a single lump-sum payment</u> or <u>with level premium payments</u> over a period of time. For example, a person, age 30, could buy a Deferred Annuity with a $20,000 premium payment. This premium is <u>not</u> tax-deductible, since you should assume that most annuities are purchased with non-qualified money. However, one of the most important features of a Deferred Annuity is the premium paid ($20,000) will earn interest on a tax-deferred basis during the Accumulation Period. This interest (which could be paid at either a fixed or variable rate) is not taxed to the annuitant until it is withdrawn.

Let's say our client elects to start withdrawing the principal and tax-deferred interest (assume earnings of $80,000 in interest for a total account value of $100,000) at age 60. While the initial $20,000 is not taxable (it was paid with after-tax dollars), the <u>interest is now subject to taxation</u>, so if he/she took the money as a $100,000 lump-sum distribution, $20,000 would be nontaxable and the other $80,000, which is accumulated interest, is taxable in the year withdrawn. However, few annuitants will select lump-sum cash at that point. Instead, most elect to <u>annuitize</u>, which means they will withdraw their money over the <u>remainder of their expected life span</u>, which is, of course, the other main feature of an annuity. <u>All annuity pay-out options are for life</u>!

Of course, if our client did not have $20,000 in after-tax dollars to buy this Deferred Annuity, he/she could have accomplished the same goal by paying <u>monthly installments</u> over the next 30 years into an annuity account. By age 60, he/she would have accumulated a certain amount of money and could elect to stop paying into the annuity and annuitize, which means he/she could take lump-sum cash or select from a number of lifetime annuity options available. Again, upon withdrawal, <u>only the accumulated interest is taxable and all pay-out options are for life</u>.

Remember, although annuities are life insurance products, they contain <u>no</u> life insurance protection. For example, if you paid $1,000 into a Deferred Annuity and died during the accumulation period, your beneficiary would only receive that $1,000 plus any accumulated interest. In other words, the death benefit is limited to the contract's cash value. Also, <u>annuities may be purchased regardless of age or health</u>. You are betting you are going to live a long time and the insurance company is betting you are going to die. Annuities are the <u>opposite</u> of life insurance.

**Flexible Premium Deferred Annuities (FPDAs):** This simply means that the annuitant has purchased a Deferred Annuity and has the option to pay in whatever amount he/she chooses, or nothing at all. The amount you pay for an annuity is called the <u>premium</u>. For example, if someone age 30 were to purchase a $10,000 annuity with cash, would it cost more or less than someone age 60 buying the same annuity? The answer is that they would both cost the same! The premium is $10,000.

## <u>ANNUITY (BENEFIT) PAYMENT OPTIONS</u>

Most annuities are purchased for <u>retirement purposes</u>. Annuities have non-forfeiture options and a 30-day grace period for installment payments that apply during the Pay-In period. Due to the early-withdrawal penalties that most insurance companies build into their contracts and a 10% IRS early-withdrawal penalty that applies to interest withdrawn prior to age 59½ (except for death or disability), annuities should be considered to be long term investments.

Remember our example earlier with the annuitant that had purchased a Deferred Annuity and had $100,000 in the account at age 60? Well, now he/she can elect several annuity options that will pay him/her as long as he/she lives. The insurance company uses an Annuity Table to project what the monthly lifetime payments will be. Factors plugged into this table include:

1. *The expected life span (remember, women live longer than men, so that is a factor)*

2. *The amount of money accumulated*

3. *The type of pay-out option selected (fixed or variable pay-out):* Regardless of the type selected, they all will pay the client as long as he/she lives. However, since some are much riskier than others, the amount of the monthly payment will depend upon the option selected. In all cases, if the annuitant lives longer than the projected life span, he/she will recover more than the value of the account. Once selected, the pay-out option may never be changed.

**Pure (Straight) Life Annuity:** This option pays the annuitant for as long as he/she lives, but payments cease entirely upon death with no refund to survivors. So, if our client died at 65, the insurance company would keep the balance of the account, with no refund (there is no beneficiary on this option). But, if he/she lived long enough, he/she could collect far more than the value of the account. This is the most-risky option.

**Life Income Annuity with Period Certain:** Sometimes called an Annuity Certain or a Period Certain Annuity, this annuity guarantees benefits will be paid for a fixed minimum period of time to be selected by the annuitant when he/she annuitizes, say 10 years. If the annuitant were to die during the period certain, the beneficiary would receive what the annuitant would have received had he/she lived until the end of the period certain.

For example, if an annuitant were to receive $1,000 a month for a 10-year Period Certain, and died after the fifth year, the beneficiary would receive $1,000 a month for the next five years. However, if the annuitant lived longer than the Period Certain and then died, nothing would be paid to the beneficiary. Death must occur during the Period Certain. If the annuitant lives, he/she is still paid for as long as he/she lives and could collect more than the value of the account if he/she lived long enough. The Period Certain feature of this annuity makes it less risky than the Life Income Annuity, but the annuitant's monthly payments would be lower. ***Remember the concept of risk and reward:*** *The higher the risk, the higher the potential reward.*

**Refund Life Annuities (Cash or Installments):** This option has very little risk since the insurance company promises to make a refund of the balance of your account if you die before you collect it all. For example, if you had a $100,000 account balance and died after collecting only $50,000, your beneficiary or estate would collect the balance. It could be paid either in cash (lump sum) or in installments over a period of time. However, if the annuitant lived long enough, he/she could still collect more than the value of the account. **Remember**: *Most annuity options are for the life of the annuitant.*

**Single Life vs. Multiple Life:**

1. *Joint and Survivor Annuity:* Payments on this type of annuity are paid for the lifetime of two or more annuitants, usually husband and wife. If the husband dies first, payments will continue for the wife until her death, or vice versa. Often, the amount paid to the survivor is reduced upon death of the first party.

2. *Joint Life Annuity*: Joint Life Annuities are very similar to Joint and Survivor Annuities, except payments stop entirely when the first party dies. So, if husband and wife choose this option and the husband died, there would be no further payments to the wife. Of course, while both where alive, the amount of the monthly payment would be higher than they would have received under a Joint and Survivor option, since there is obviously more risk involved.

**Fixed Period and Fixed Amount Payment Options:** These annuity payout options may be selected by those who prefer not to have their monthly benefits based upon their life expectancy. Assuming it is a fixed annuity, the fixed period payout will provide fixed monthly payments for a fixed period of time, such as 10, 15 or 20 years. A fixed amount payout will provide the same amount of money each month, until the account is exhausted. Monthly payments would be higher than those payable under the fixed period option.

## ANNUITY PRODUCTS

**Fixed Annuities:** This type of annuity has a fixed rate of return, usually a minimum of around 4%. However, insurance companies will often pay a higher "current rate" of interest, which is guaranteed for one year only and is subject to change (up or down) annually, but never below the minimum. With this product, the annuitant is assured of level monthly payments for life during the annuity period. The insurance company bears the investment risk. Fixed annuities are not considered to be securities products, and all you need to sell them is a life-insurance license. They are backed by the Guaranty Fund, since funds are invested in the insurer's general account.

**Variable Annuities:** With this type of Annuity, the annuitant's monthly payments will vary during the Annuity (Pay-Out) period, since no rate of return is guaranteed. The client's funds are invested into the stock market directly and the insurance company maintains a separate investment account (similar to a mutual fund) for that purpose. Funds are invested more aggressively by the insurance company, since it knows that the client is looking for a better rate of return. The annuitant bears all the investment risk in this type of product. Since Variable Annuities are considered to be securities products and are not backed by the Guaranty Fund, producers selling this product must also have a securities license, FINRA Series 6 or 7. Variable annuities are purchased to hedge against inflation.

**Market Value Adjusted Annuities:** A type of variable annuity where a policy owner commits a sum of money for a certain period of time, usually one year, two years or three years. The longer the commitment, the higher the interest rate. The value at the end of the term is guaranteed, but may be adjusted if surrendered early. At the end of the term, the policy owner may either withdraw the entire sum plus all the interest earned or he/she can reinvest the money for another time period at the rates currently offered by the company.

If, however, funds are withdrawn prior to the end of the term, a "market value adjustment" is made to the value of the account, which requires the client to bear some of the risk. This adjustment is either positive or negative. If interest rates rise, for example, the value of the adjustment would be negative. On the other hand, if interest rates fall, the adjustment would be positive.

**Equity Indexed Annuity:** An EIA is a fixed annuity where both the principal and the interest are guaranteed. However, excess interest earnings above the guaranteed rate may accrue since performance is calculated using an indexing method that is usually linked to the Standard and Poor's 500 index. EIAs are not classified as securities and a FINRA license is not required.

## USES OF ANNUITIES

Most <u>Deferred annuities</u> are purchased for <u>retirement planning</u> or a child's future <u>educational expenses</u>. Immediate annuities are usually purchased to <u>supplement the annuitant's pension or Social Security</u>. Remember, <u>Fixed annuities</u> have a guaranteed rate of return, and the <u>insurance company bears the investment risk</u>. <u>Variable annuities</u> have <u>no guaranteed</u> rate of return, so the <u>annuitant bears</u> the <u>investment risk</u>. Variable annuities are usually purchased by those seeking to <u>hedge against inflation</u> by investing their Annuity funds into the stock market, which historically, has out paced the rate of inflation. Annuities are also used in "structured settlements" and in business to fund such things are guaranteed sports contracts, real estate contracts, and even the lottery! Also, remember, annuity values are measured in "<u>units</u>," which are similar to shares in a mutual fund. During the pay-in period, annuity values are measured in "<u>accumulation units</u>." During the pay-out period, annuity values are measured in "<u>annuity units</u>."

**Lump-sum Settlements:** Annuities are often used in structured settlements. For example, if you won an injury lawsuit for $1,000,000, the defendant's insurance company will most likely ask you to accept an annuity instead of cash. Of course, this will save the insurance company money but it also allows you to structure the award in a manner best suited to your financial situation. Lottery pay-outs, professional sports contracts and some real estate transactions also utilize annuities paid out over a period of time, such as 10 or 20 years instead of life, rather than lump sum payments for tax reasons.

**Tax Sheltered Annuities (TSAs):** Under Internal Revenue Code Section 403(b), employees of public educational institutions (such as public schools and universities), tax exempt non-profit organizations and church organizations may exclude from their gross income, within limits, premiums paid on a contract that will provide for an annuity upon retirement. Employees of for-profit private schools are not eligible, nor are students.

Generally, TSAs are considered to be tax "qualified" plans in that contributions are excluded from the participant's income and earnings accumulate on a tax-deferred basis until distribution. Since neither the contributions nor the earnings have ever been taxed, all distributions from TSAs are taxable as ordinary income and 10% IRS early withdrawal penalties may apply if a participant is under age 59 ½.

# Annuities

# KEY FACTS

- <u>Endowments</u> provide life insurance protection. <u>Annuities</u> do not.

- You cannot outlive the income from a life annuity.

- Annuities are the opposite of Life insurance. Life insurance creates an estate. <u>Annuities</u> systematically liquidate your estate over a period of time.

- <u>Fixed Annuities</u> guarantee a fixed rate of return and are backed by the State Guaranty Fund.

- If you die during the <u>Accumulation Period</u> of an Annuity, the account value will be paid to your beneficiary, who is responsible for taxes on interest earned.

- A <u>Life Income Annuity</u> (Straight or Pure Life Annuity) has no beneficiary, and is the most risky.

- A <u>Refund Annuity</u> has the least amount of risk.

- The premium for a $100,000 <u>Immediate Annuity</u> is $100,000, regardless of the client's age, health or gender. It is the <u>Pay-Out</u> that depends on these factors.

- <u>All annuities are insurance products, although often sold by bankers with Life insurance licenses.</u>

- Most annuities are used for <u>retirement purposes</u> and are considered to be long-term investments.

- Annuity tables are different than mortality tables since there is no <u>insurance protection</u>.

- Annuities are often used as life insurance <u>settlement options</u>.

- The death benefit on an annuity during the accumulation period is equal to its cash value.

- Deferred annuities are usually purchased to generate income for retirement.

- Lottery payouts and structured settlements are often funded by annuities.

- The proceeds of an annuity are payable to the policy owner, who is not necessarily the annuitant. The annuitant is the party whose life the benefits are based upon.

- Although annuity benefits paid to a beneficiary are usually taxable upon the death of an owner/annuitant, beneficiaries who are spouses may continue the contract on a tax deferred basis as the "contingent" owner.

- Single premium immediate annuities (SPIAs) are often purchased with a lump sum upon retirement.

- Deferred annuities are purchased by making periodic payments over a period of time.

- Life insurers often levy a "surrender charge" for taking cash surrender of an annuity during the early years of the contract.

- A "tax sheltered" (403b) annuity (TSA) is funded by making voluntary before-tax contributions.

- A "life annuity" does not start making payments at death. Payments stop at death.

- Fixed annuities are backed by the insurer's "general" account.

- When a policy owner surrenders an annuity for cash, they have exercised a "non-forfeiture" option.

- Fixed annuities usually pay an interest rate that is similar to other types of conservative investments.

- Single Premium Immediate Annuities start making payments to the contract owner right away.

- Annuities waive surrender charges for death or disability.

- Producers selling annuities must have reasonable grounds for believing that the transaction is "suitable" based upon a customer's financial status, tax status and investment objectives.

- Fixed annuities pay a "current interest rate" the first year, which could decline to the minimum guaranteed rate in subsequent years.

- On a "joint life annuity," payments stop when the first annuitant dies.

- Insurers take the money from annuitants who die too soon and pay it to those who live too long.

- One purpose of an annuity is to keep customers from outliving their savings.

- 403b TSAs are owned by the employee, not the employer.

- The owner of an annuity is responsible for paying the premium.

- Equity Indexed Annuities (EIAs) have little purchasing power (or inflation) risk since their rate of return is based in part on an equity (stock) index, such as the S&P 500.

- A corporation cannot use an annuity to build tax deferred growth on corporate assets. Only individuals are entitled to tax deferred annuity earnings.

- An annuitant would select the "period certain" annuity pay-out option if they want payments to continue to a beneficiary after their death.

- If an annuitant selects a pay-out option that will pay them $500 a month for an unspecified period of time, they have selected the "fixed-amount" option.

- If an annuitant selects a pay-out option that will pay them for a specified period of time, they have selected the "fixed-period" option.

- An annuity with no accumulation period that is used to annuitize a lump sum right away is known as an "immediate" annuity.

- Upon annuitization, a life annuity will pay the annuitant a monthly income for life.

- A deferred annuity can only be surrendered for cash during its accumulation (pay-in) period.

- Employers may use annuities to fund deferred compensation plans, but not corporate pension plans.

# Annuities

# PRACTICE EXAM

1. Which contract requires a series of benefit payments to be made at specified intervals:

   A. Endowment
   B. Annuity
   C. 20-Pay Life
   D. Modified Whole Life

2. A husband and wife are co-annuitants and decide to select the joint life payout option upon annuitization. They will receive monthly annuity payments from the insurer until:

   A. Either the husband or wife dies
   B. Both the husband and wife have died
   C. The oldest spouse reaches age 59 ½
   D. The youngest spouse reaches age 59 ½

3. Cash Surrender is available on an annuity in which of the following situations:

   A. During the accumulation period
   B. Once the annuitant has selected the Pure Life payout option
   C. Once the annuitant has selected the Life Income with Period Certain payout option
   D. Once the annuitant has selected the Refund Life payout option

4. A woman has inherited a sum of money. She is age 60 and desires to purchase an annuity that will appreciate with market and economic conditions. What type of annuity should she consider?

   A. Fixed
   B. Deferred
   C. Variable
   D. Refund

5. The Joint and Survivor Life Annuity contract calls for the surviving annuitant to receive a:

   A. Lump sum benefit on the death of the annuitant
   B. Payment each month for 10 years
   C. Predetermined income for life
   D. Deferred income to be paid when the age of 65 is reached

6.  Which of the following Annuities will start paying the annuitant a monthly payment right away for the rest of their life:

    A.  Deferred Annuity
    B.  Flexible premium
    C.  Immediate
    D.  Fixed premium

7.  Which of the following is a characteristic of an annuity:

    A.  Their main function is the creation of an estate upon death
    B.  They provide protection for a retired individual from outliving their savings
    C.  They provide tax free death benefits
    D.  Cash surrenders can be taken at any age without 10% penalty

8.  The principal use of a Life Annuity is to:

    A.  Create capital for the annuitant's heirs
    B.  Provide for the liquidation of debts at retirement
    C.  Provide for the beneficiary's lifetime income
    D.  Arrange an income for old age

9.  On a fixed annuity, the interest rate that is paid the first year, which could decline thereafter is known as the:

    A.  Guaranteed minimum interest rate
    B.  Current interest rate
    C.  Variable interest rate
    D.  Flexible interest rate

10. Upon death, annuity proceeds payable to a beneficiary are generally taxable. However, if the beneficiary is the spouse of the deceased annuity owner/annuitant, they may continue the contract on a tax deferred basis as the _____ owner:

    A.  Contingent
    B.  Substitute
    C.  Primary
    D.  Surviving

11. All of the following are true regarding annuities EXCEPT:

    A.  On a life annuity, payments begin upon the death of the annuitant
    B.  Cash surrender of an annuity in the early years may result in a surrender charge
    C.  A deferred annuity is purchased with periodic payments over a period of time
    D.  A single premium immediate annuity is often purchased with a lump sum at retirement

12. An annuity where both the principal and the interest are guaranteed, but excess interest may accrue since performance is calculated using an indexing method that is usually linked to the S&P 500 is known as a:

    A.    Variable annuity
    B.    Market value adjusted annuity
    C.    Equity indexed annuity
    D.    Performance enhanced annuity

13. All of the following are true regarding an IRC Section 403(b) Tax Sheltered Annuity EXCEPT:

    A.    They are similar to IRC 401(k) plans
    B.    They are funded with voluntary before-tax contributions
    C.    They are available to anyone with earned income
    D.    All distributions are taxable as ordinary income

14. Annuity payments will cease upon the death of an annuitant who has selected which of the following annuity pay-out options:

    A.    Life income
    B.    Life income with period certain
    C.    Life income with refund
    D.    Joint and survivor

15. When recommending the purchase or exchange of an annuity, a producer shall have reasonable grounds for believing that the transaction is _____ based upon the customer's financial status, tax status and investment objectives:

    A.    Compatible
    B.    Suitable
    C.    Appropriate
    D.    Reasonable

16. The individual whose life an annuity is based upon is known as the:

    A.    Beneficiary
    B.    Owner
    C.    Insured
    D.    Annuitant

17. All of the following are true regarding deferred annuities EXCEPT:

    A.    They may be used to fund an IRA
    B.    They provide a source of retirement income
    C.    They provide tax-deferred growth
    D.    They provide an immediate source of education funds

18.  All of the following are true regarding Single Premium Immediate Life Income annuities EXCEPT:

    A.    Payments begin upon the death of the annuitant
    B.    There is no beneficiary
    C.    They may not be surrendered for cash
    D.    They have no accumulation period

19.  Which of the following is NOT true regarding deferred annuities:

    A.    They have a beneficiary during the accumulation period
    B.    They are purchased with periodic payments over a period of time
    C.    Cash surrender in the early years will result in a surrender charge
    D.    They are often used to fund lottery pay-outs or structured settlements

20.  Mr. Jones has contributed a total of $30,000 into a tax-deferred annuity over a period of time, which has now grown to $50,000 due to tax-deferred interest. If he dies now at age 50 prior to annuitizing the contract, what is the tax implication:

    A.    No taxes are due since annuities are life insurance products
    B.    $20,000 is taxable to the beneficiary as ordinary income
    C.    $30,000 is taxable to the beneficiary as ordinary income, plus a 10% penalty
    D.    $50,000 is taxable to the beneficiary as capital gain

21.  A client purchased a single premium deferred annuity in 2001 for $13,000. Ten years later, after his/her account has grown to $24,000, he/she withdraws $15,000. How much is taxable:

    A.    $ 2,000
    B.    $11,000
    C.    $13,000
    D.    $24,000

22.  A client might purchase an immediate annuity for all of the following reasons EXCEPT:

    A.    To save money for a child's future college expenses
    B.    To supplement social security retirement benefits
    C.    To annuitize the proceeds of a life insurance policy
    D.    To annuitize the proceeds of a property/casualty insurance claim settlement

23.  If a client annuitizes an annuity to pay him/her $250 a month for life or for 15 years, whichever is longer, he/she has chosen which annuity pay-out option:

    A.    Life income
    B.    Period certain
    C.    Refund
    D.    Fixed amount

24. During the accumulation period, the earnings in a non-qualified deferred annuity purchased by an individual are:

    A.  Taxed as ordinary income
    B.  Tax free
    C.  Tax deferred
    D.  Taxed as capital gain

25. An annuity that will make monthly payments to the owner/annuitant while living, but has no value at his/her death is known as:

    A.  Refund
    B.  Life income
    C.  Period certain
    D.  Fixed period

26. When an owner/annuitant with a life income annuity dies before receiving the value of their account, the remaining funds will be:

    A.  Distributed according to the terms of the annuitant's will
    B.  Paid to the designated beneficiary
    C.  Retained by the insurer
    D.  Paid to the annuitant's estate

27. What type of annuity will make a cash payment to the beneficiary when the owner/annuitant dies during the annuity period:

    A.  Period certain
    B.  Refund
    C.  Fixed amount
    D.  Life income

28. All of the following are true regarding Market Value Adjusted annuities EXCEPT:

    A.  They are considered to be a type of variable annuity
    B.  The customer is required to bear some of the investment risk
    C.  They are also known as Equity Indexed annuities
    D.  Producers are required to have a FINRA securities license to sell them

29. A penalty that some insurers levy when an annuitant makes a withdrawal in the early years of the contract is known as a:

    A.  Premature distribution penalty
    B.  Distribution fee
    C.  Surrender charge
    D.  Withdrawal fee

30. A customer paid $15,000 in premiums into his/her non-qualified deferred annuity over a period of time. If his/her account balance is now $26,000 and he/she withdraws $17,000, how much is taxable:

    A.    $11,000
    B.    $15,000
    C.    $17,000
    D.    $26,000

31. Fixed annuities are backed by:

    A.    The Federal Deposit Insurance Corporation (FDIC)
    B.    The insurer's general account assets
    C.    The Securities Investment Protection Corporation (SIPC)
    D.    The insurer's separate account assets

32. Which type of annuity requires that the customer bear part of the risk:

    A.    A fixed deferred annuity
    B.    An Equity Indexed annuity
    C.    An immediate fixed annuity
    D.    A Market Value Adjusted annuity

33. On which type of annuity must a producer disclose that excess earnings above the guaranteed rate may vary:

    A.    A fixed deferred annuity
    B.    An Equity Indexed annuity
    C.    An immediate fixed annuity
    D.    A Market Value Adjusted annuity

34. All of the following are true regarding fixed annuities EXCEPT:

    A.    They do worse when the cost of living is going up
    B.    They can be sold by any licensed Life insurance producer
    C.    They do better when the cost of living is going down
    D.    They have no guaranteed rate of return

35. Annuities must be written by which of the following:

    A.    Banks
    B.    Life insurance companies
    C.    Stock brokerages
    D.    Mutual funds

# Annuities

# PRACTICE EXAM ANSWERS AND RATIONALES

1. **B** When an annuity policy is in the pay-out period, it will pay the annuitant back all the money the annuitant paid in, plus interest, over his/her lifetime. The principal amount is guaranteed and will be paid out as long as the annuitant lives. The amount paid is based upon the annuitant's expected life span, sex, and the annuity pay-out option selected. Annuity benefit payments to the annuitant are usually paid out monthly. Insurance companies offer annuities to the beneficiaries of insureds who have died, enabling these beneficiaries to reinvest the policy proceeds with a high degree of safety and the guarantee of lifetime income.

2. **A** When the Joint Life Annuity payout option is selected the insurer will send a check to the husband and wife once a month until the first person dies. Regardless of who dies first (the husband or wife), monthly payments will be discontinued at that point.

   If they had selected the Joint and Survivor payout option the insurer would send them monthly payments until the last surviving spouse died. Since the Joint Life payout option will pay only until the first person dies, they would receive a higher monthly payment than if they selected the Joint and Survivor payout option, since the insurer will be paying the money out over a shorter period of time. Age 59 ½ has no relevance to Annuity payout options.

3. **A** Cash surrender is only available on an Annuity during the accumulation or pay-in period. Once the annuitant annuitizes and selects a payout option they can no longer take cash surrender. An annuitant can annuitize the contract at any age without a 10% penalty (even under 59 ½). However, if the annuitant instead of annuitizing, decides to take cash surrender under 59 ½ they will have to pay a 10% IRS early withdrawal penalty on any interest they withdraw. The 10% penalty DOES NOT apply to the annuitant's cost basis, only to interest withdrawn prior to age 59 ½. Partial surrenders of annuities are taxed as withdrawal of interest first and return of cost basis second (LIFO), similar to Modified Endowment Contracts (MECs).

4. **C** A Variable Annuity is the most risky type of annuity. The insurance company invests the annuitant's funds in a "separate account" that is usually invested in equities (stocks). This type of annuity MAY appreciate with market and economic conditions and it MAY NOT. This type of annuity is not backed by the State Guaranty Fund and it is considered very risky, meaning the client could lose their invested capital due to poor performance of the stock market. Salespersons selling Variable Annuities need to have a life insurance license plus a Financial Industry Regulatory Authority (FINRA) license. In addition, the State Department of Insurance requires a Variable Annuities endorsement on your life insurance license.

   Fixed Annuities are much safer, since the insurance company invests the funds of the annuitant in its "general account" in much the same way it invests its other funds. A Fixed Annuity has a guaranteed, fixed minimum rate of return, guaranteed by the insurance company and backed by the State Insurance Guaranty Fund, so the annuitant cannot lose his/her invested capital. The fixed minimum rate of return may be quite low, such as 4%, but companies often pay more than the minimum. A life insurance license is all that is needed to sell Fixed Annuities.

A Deferred Annuity may be either Variable or Fixed. It is simply an Annuity that is bought over a period of time, say by investing $100 a month from age 35 to age 65. This is called the Accumulation period, or Pay-In period. If the annuitant should die during the Pay-In period, all invested capital up to that point, plus interest, would go directly to his/her beneficiary or estate. Remember, this is not a life insurance Death benefit, it is a return of the annuitant's invested funds. The interest earned during the Pay-In period accumulates on a tax-deferred basis; the annuitant is not taxed on his/her earnings until he/she starts the Pay-Out (Annuity) period, and then only on the interest earned, since the initial contributions were made with after-tax dollars.

An Immediate Annuity means that the annuitant purchases either a Fixed or Variable Annuity with a lump-sum amount, say $100,000. This would be considered the "premium" paid for the annuity. The annuitant wants the insurance company to start paying him/her back immediately, starting with monthly payments based on his/her expected life span, sex, and annuity option selected. Remember, most annuity pay-out options pay the annuitant for life. You cannot outlive the income from a life annuity. As you can see, insurance companies began to offer annuities as a way to keep the money when a life insurance client died. By offering the surviving beneficiary the option to purchase an annuity with a lifetime income, the company was in a position to reinvest the policy proceeds they would have otherwise had to pay out as a lump-sum cash Death benefit.

When the annuitant starts the pay-out period or annuity period, he/she must select an annuity pay-out option. Of course, he/she could always select lump sum cash at that point and pay tax on all interest earned up to that point. Annuity "settlement" options include:

> Straight Life or Pure Life Annuity: The most risky option, it also has the highest pay-out. Based on your expected life span and sex, the insurance company will pay you an amount monthly that would "annuitize" your invested capital over a period of time. If you die, payments stop immediately and the insurance company keeps what is left of your funds. If you live, the insurance company will continue to pay you until you die, even if you collect more then you invested.

> Period Certain Annuity: With this option, either you or your designated beneficiary or estate is guaranteed to receive funds from the insurance company for a period of time designated by the annuitant, say 10 years. If you die after five years, the payments for the remaining five years go to your beneficiary or estate, so there is less risk, although the amount paid monthly is less. If you die in the eleventh year, the insurance company keeps your remaining funds. However, if you live to be 105, they will continue to pay you. The Period Certain can be 5, 10, 15, or 20 years.

> Refund Annuity: The Annuity settlement option with the least risk. If you die before receiving back everything you invested, your designated beneficiary or estate will continue to be paid by the insurance company, either on an installment basis or on a lump-sum cash basis until it has paid out everything you paid in. This is less risky, but the pay-out is lower.

> Joint and Survivor Annuity: This option has two or more annuitants, and benefits are payable as long as the last survivor lives. Usually selected by husband and wife, the benefits are reduced if the husband dies, but the wife continues to be paid until she dies (or vice versa).

5. **C**   Joint and Survivor Annuity option pays benefits, although reduced, to the death of the last survivor.

6. **C**   Annuities can be paid for in a number of ways, which are very similar to life insurance. The annuitant could purchase an annuity with a flexible, fixed or single premium. The only annuity that would begin payments to the annuitant right away would be a single premium immediate annuity. A deferred annuity is any annuity where the annuitant does not enter the pay out period (annuitize) right away.

7. **B**   If a retired person has $200,000 in savings and they start withdrawing $60,000 a year to live on, they could potentially run out of money, depending on the return on their investment and length of their lifespan. A life annuitant can never outlive payments from an annuity. They will be paid as long as they live. Life insurance creates an immediate estate upon death of the insured. The main function of an annuity it to liquidate an estate over an individual's lifespan. Annuity death benefits are not tax free. The beneficiary would have to pay ordinary income tax on any interest they receive. Cash surrenders taken from an annuity prior to age 59 ½ have a 10% IRS early withdrawal penalty that applies to the interest only. Life insurance cash surrenders can be taken at any age without penalty, but tax is still due on any amounts received in excess of premiums paid.

8. **D**   A Life Annuity will pay the annuitant as long as he/she lives. The funds are paid out to the living policyholder, not the beneficiary. Life income annuities do not have a beneficiary, except during the Pay-In period. Remember, during the Pay-Out period of a Life income annuity, the company pays you as long as you live, but if you die, the company keeps the money.

9. **B**   Fixed annuities guarantee not only the amount of payments but also the interest rate paid on the invested capital. Each fixed annuity contract specifies an interest rate, for example 5%. If the portfolio earns only 4%, the company is still obligated to pay the 5% rate.

   To minimize risk, an insurance company uses its general account to fund fixed annuity contracts. The portfolio of the general account is invested in medium term fixed income producing debt securities such as bonds and real estate mortgages. The insurer may also guarantee a higher earnings rate, which may vary from year to year (the current rate).

   For example, the interest rate stated in the contact, say 5%, is the guaranteed base rate. The account will never earn less than 5% for the life of the contract. However, a current interest rate, such as 7½%, may be guaranteed for one year. The account is credited for interest at 7 ½% for the one year period; thereafter, a new rate may be effective, but will never be less than the guaranteed 5%.

10. **A**   If the designated beneficiary on an annuity is the surviving spouse of the owner, then the distribution requirements are applied by treating the spouse as the contingent owner of the annuity contract, which means that they can treat the contract as their own and defer taxes until they elect to annuitize.

11. **A**   On a life annuity, payments stop upon the death of the annuitant.

12. **C**   An EIA is a fixed annuity where both the principal and the interest are guaranteed. However, excess interest earnings above the guaranteed rate may accrue since performance is calculated using an indexing method that is usually linked to the Standard & Poor's 500 index.

13. **C**  TSAs are generally available only to employees of public educational institutions, tax exempt non-profits and church organizations. TSAs are funded with voluntary before-tax contributions, usually on a payroll deduction basis.

14. **A**  A Life income annuity has no beneficiary, so payments will cease upon the death of the annuitant.

15. **B**  Annuity recommendations must be "suitable," based upon a customer's financial status, tax status and investment objectives.

16. **D**  The person whose life an annuity contract is based upon is known as the "annuitant." Although the contract owner is often also the annuitant, that is not always the case.

17. **D**  It is "immediate" annuities that provide an immediate source of education funds.

18. **A**  On immediate annuities, payments will begin to the annuitant immediately upon purchase, but payments will stop upon their death. Remember, Life Income annuities have no beneficiary. An immediate annuity is annuitized right away, so it has no accumulation period. Once an annuity has been annuitized, it can no longer be surrendered for cash.

19. **D**  It is immediate annuities that are used to fund lottery pay-outs and structured settlements.

20. **B**  Although proceeds payable from a Life insurance policy are tax free, that portion of an annuity death benefit that consists of the earnings will be taxable to the beneficiary as ordinary income.

21. **B**  Partial withdrawals from a deferred annuity during the accumulation period are considered to be interest first and a return of principal second. To find the interest portion of the $15,000 withdrawal, subtract the client's cost basis of $13,000 from his/her $24,000 account balance. This $11,000 is taxable as ordinary income. The remainder of the $15,000 withdrawal is a tax free return of principal.

22. **A**  An immediate annuity is purchased with a lump sum and is annuitized right away, meaning that the client will start to receive monthly payments immediately. Remember, an immediate annuity has no accumulation or pay-in period. It is a deferred annuity that would be used to save money for a child's college expenses.

23. **B**  A period certain annuity guarantees that payments will be made to the annuitant for a specified period of time, 15 years in this case. For example, if the annuitant died after 10 years, the beneficiary would receive payments for five years. However, although the beneficiary disappears when the period certain ends, if the annuitant continues to live, payments would continue on until their death.

24. **C**  The earnings during the accumulation period of a deferred annuity purchased by an individual are tax deferred until the contract is surrendered for cash or annuitized, at which time the earnings above the annuitant's cost basis are taxable as ordinary income. However, the earnings during the accumulation period of a deferred annuity owned by a corporation are taxable to the corporation as they accrue.

25. **B**  Life income annuities have no beneficiary, so they only make payments to the annuitant until they die. Since they are the most risky, they offer higher monthly payments than some of the other annuity pay-out options, such as period certain or refund.

26. **C**   Remember, annuities are the opposite of life insurance. When an annuitant buys a life annuity, they are betting that they will outlive the insurer's annuity tables and the insurer is betting that they won't. Based upon the law of large numbers, the insurer will take the money of their life annuitants who die too soon and pay it to those who live too long.

27. **B**   Refund annuities have very little risk, since if the annuitant dies before they receive the value of their account back, the beneficiary will receive the balance, either in cash or in installments. However, if the annuitant continues to live, monthly payments will be made until their death.

28. **C**   Market Value Adjusted annuities are a type of variable annuity, so a life insurance producer must also have a FINRA securities license in order to sell them. Clients who purchase Market Value Adjusted annuities bear some of the risk in that if they withdraw their invested funds early, their account is subject to a market value adjustment, which could result in negative performance. Equity Indexed annuities are not considered to be securities, since both the principal and the rate of return are guaranteed in the contract.

29. **C**   Most annuities are subject to surrender charges, which are levied by the insurer during the early years of the contract, as well as premature distribution penalties, which are levied by the IRS upon cash surrender prior to age 59 ½. Surrender charges usually apply on a declining basis and will gradually disappear over a period of time. Their purpose is to discourage customers from investing in annuities on a short-term basis.

30. **A**   Partial surrenders on annuities are treated as interest first and a return of principal last. In this case, the customer has earned $11,000 in interest, which means of the $17,000 withdrawn, $11,000 will be taxable as ordinary income and $6,000 will be treated as a tax free return of principal. There could also be a 10% IRS penalty on the interest portion of the withdrawal if the customer was under age 59 ½.

31. **B**   FDIC covers bank deposits. SIPC covers securities brokerage firm insolvency. Although fixed annuities are not backed by either, they are backed by the insurer's general account assets. However, variable annuities offer no such backing, since they are invested in the insurer's separate account, which is very similar to a mutual fund.

32. **D**   Market Value Adjusted annuities are considered to be a type of variable annuity, so the customer must bear part of the investment risk.

33. **B**   Although Equity Indexed annuities are considered to be a type of fixed annuity with a guaranteed minimum rate of return, excess earnings above the minimum may or may not accrue, since performance is calculated using an indexing method that is usually linked to the S&P 500 index.

34. **D**   Since fixed annuities have a guaranteed rate of return, they do better when the cost of living is going down and worse when the cost of living is going up. In other words, fixed annuities have purchasing power risk and will suffer in an inflationary economy. Customers often buy variable annuities to hedge against inflation.

35. **B**   All annuities are life insurance products and must be written by life insurance companies. Although many bankers and stock brokers sell annuities, they do so through a life insurance company, who pays them a commission for selling their products.

# SECTION 7

# Federal Tax Considerations

## TAXATION OF PERSONAL LIFE INSURANCE

Life insurance has been granted favorable tax treatment by the Internal Revenue Service. Death benefits are usually excluded from a beneficiary's gross income.

Premiums paid on an individual plan of life insurance are viewed as a "personal" expense and are not deductible. Those paid on Group Life plans are deductible by the employer if a noncontributory type plan is involved. These premiums are viewed as a business expense. If the group plan is contributory, premiums paid by the employee are usually not deductible.

Policy proceeds are generally exempt from income taxation, even though they may exceed the cost of the insurance (the premiums paid). Any payment made to a beneficiary out of policy proceeds is not taxable. However, if no beneficiary was named, the proceeds paid out to the estate will be included when valuing the estate and may be subject to estate taxes.

Policy loans are not considered income and are not taxable. Any interest accrued and paid is taxable. For example, if the proceeds are left with the insurer under the "interest only" settlement option, the interest payments would be taxable. Dividends received on a participating policy are not taxable since they are considered a return of "overpaid premiums."

Cash Surrenders, however, may generate taxable income if the amount withdrawn exceeds the total amount of the premiums paid in. For example, you bought a Whole Life policy with a face amount of $100,000 at age 30 with an annual premium of $1,000. At age 65, your cash value will be approximately $40,000, which is $5,000 more than the total premiums you paid in. The difference, of course, is the tax-deferred interest that your cash value has earned over the years. If you take cash surrender of the entire $40,000 at age 65, you will have to pay ordinary income taxes on the $5,000 of interest. The $35,000 is not taxed, since it is a return of the money you paid in over the years which, of course, was already taxed since you paid your premiums in after tax dollars.

## MODIFIED ENDOWMENT CONTRACTS (MECS)

The Technical and Miscellaneous Revenue Act (TAMRA) established special rules for life insurance contracts, including endowments, which fail to meet the "seven-pay" test. An insurance contract will fail to meet the seven-pay test if the amount paid in premiums during the first seven contract years exceeds the sum of the seven level annual premiums required to pay up the policy.

As a result, any endowment contract that fails this seven-pay test is defined as a Modified Endowment Contract (MEC) and distributions from Modified Endowments are subject to taxation rules that differ from the rules governing the taxation of endowments and life insurance policies that do not fail the seven-pay test.

Distributions, including loans, from a modified endowment are taxable as income at the time received to the extent that the cash value exceeds the premiums paid. This means that distributions from MECs are taxed as income first and recovery of cost basis (premium paid in) second. In addition, a 10% penalty tax is imposed on distributions received under a MEC unless the taxpayer is disabled or past age 59½.

The seven-pay test is administered when the contract is first issued and once classified as a "Modified Endowment Contract," the MEC is subject to these special tax rules for the life of the contract. Further, persons considering making a "material change" to their life insurance policy may also find themselves subject to the rules concerning Modified Endowments (MECs). A "material change" is defined as any increase in the death benefit under the contract and will cause the seven-pay test to apply again.

All MECs issued by the same insurer to the same policyholder within any calendar year are treated as one MEC.

## TAXATION OF NON-QUALIFIED ANNUITIES (EXCLUSION RATIO)

Since most annuities are non-qualified (purchased with after-tax dollars), the amount of money you put in (your tax "basis") will someday be returned to you tax-free, since you have already paid taxes on that amount before you put it in. However, since the earnings in your annuity account are tax-deferred, this portion will be taxed when you take the money out. For example, at age 30 you purchased a Single Premium Deferred Annuity (SPDA) with a lump sum of $20,000. You had already paid tax on this money. During the accumulation stage of your annuity, this money will earn interest, which is not taxed (tax-deferred) until you take the money out. At age 60, you take Cash Surrender and retire. Your account balance has grown to $100,000. Of this distribution, $80,000 would be taxable to you in the year you took it out at ordinary income-tax rates. You never incur capital gains on an annuity. If you were in a 28% tax bracket, this distribution would cost you $22,400 in taxes.

However, you could spread your tax bill over your lifetime by annuitizing instead of taking cash surrender. In this case, the insurance company would pay you monthly for as long as you live. Your tax liability would look like this: At age 60, you might be expected to live another 20 years, so the insurance company will return your $20,000 basis to you tax-free over this 20-year period. So, the first $1,000 you receive each year is a tax-free return of capital. Any amount you receive above that each year would be taxed as ordinary income. If you lived longer than 20 years, all your payments would be 100% taxable, since you would have already recovered your cost basis. This calculation is known as the exclusion ratio.

The IRS also levies early-withdrawal penalties against annuitants who take cash surrender prior to age 59½, unless they have died or become disabled. These are the same penalties that exist for early withdrawal of an IRA or KEOGH plan. In the above example, had you taken cash surrender of $100,000 at age 59 instead of age 60, the IRS would have levied a 10% early-withdrawal penalty on the interest portion of your account. Since the interest portion was $80,000, your penalty would have been $8,000, in addition to your income taxes. Please note that the penalty is a bottom line penalty, and is added to your tax due. Also note, that this penalty only applies to cash surrenders prior to age 59½. You can annuitize at any age without penalty, but of course, you would have to pay tax on the interest portion of your distributions in the year received.

However, if the annuitant took a partial withdrawal or loan instead of full cash surrender, these amounts are treated as distributions of interest first and only second as recovery of cost. In addition, taxable amounts may also be subject to the IRA 10% penalty tax.

If an annuitant dies during the accumulation (pay-in) period, the beneficiary will be paid as a death benefit the amount of premiums paid or the accumulated value of the contract, whichever is more. The gain, if any, is taxable as ordinary income to the beneficiary. Beneficiaries may choose a lump sum cash settlement or elect to receive monthly payments based upon their life expectancy. However, payment of the death benefit at the death of the owner during the accumulation period may be deferred when there is a surviving spouse that has been named beneficiary. The Internal Revenue Code allows a surviving spouse to "step into the shoes" of the deceased contract owner and continue the accumulation period without change as the new owner of the contract.

If it is a corporation who owns the deferred annuity, the contract will not be treated for tax purposes like an annuity. Instead, income on the contract is treated as ordinary income received by the corporation during the taxable year.

## TAXATION OF INDIVIDUAL RETIREMENT ANNUITIES (IRAs)

**Traditional IRAs:** Almost anyone with earned income who is under the age of 70 ½ is eligible to open an IRA. IRAs help individuals to save money for their retirement by allowing them to deduct contributions to these accounts from their pre-tax dollars for income tax purposes. These deductible contributions are a form of deferred compensation and will only be taxed when the individual withdraws them from the account at retirement (usually a time when the individual is in a lower tax bracket).

Any individual who earns wages may participate in an IRA. A qualified person may contribute 100% of annual earned income, subject to specified maximum limits. A person may deduct the maximum contribution if:

1. He/she is a wage earner and does not actively participate in an employer maintained retirement plan *or*

2. He/she is a wage earner who actively participates in an employer-maintained retirement plan, but has an adjusted gross income less than a certain amount.

An individual who is eligible to begin an IRA may also create a Spousal IRA with a non-wage-earning spouse. Two separate IRA accounts must be established.

The owner of an IRA must begin to receive payments from his/her account by the time he/she reaches age 70½. Any benefits withdrawn from an IRA prior to age 59½ will be assessed a 10% penalty. In addition, amounts withdrawn must also be added to the owner's taxable income for the year in which it was received. However, individuals may roll over IRA funds into another IRA without tax liability if the proceeds are reinvested in the new IRA within 60 days following receipt of the distribution. Otherwise, the distributions will be taxable in the year received. Any amount may be rolled over, but rollovers are allowed only once a year. Rollovers may be subject to withholding tax, unless it is a trustee-to-trustee direct rollover.

Further, Traditional IRAs are subject to Required Minimum Distribution (RMD) rules, which state that if the participant does not begin withdrawals by age 70 ½, a 50% penalty will be levied by the IRS upon the amount that should have been withdrawn, but wasn't.

However, the minimum distribution requirements that apply after the death of an IRA owner depend on whether he/she died before or after his/her required beginning date. If an IRA owner dies before his/her required beginning date, distributions must be made under either the life expectancy method **or** the five year rule.

Under the life expectancy rule, if any portion of the interest is payable to a designated beneficiary, that portion must be distributed over the life expectancy of the beneficiary, beginning within one year of the owner's death. Under the <u>five year rule</u>, the entire interest must be distributed within five years after the death of the IRA owner, regardless of who receives the distribution.

However, <u>if a surviving spouse is the sole designated beneficiary</u>, they may elect to treat the IRA as their own. The result of a surviving spouse making the election to treat an IRA as their own is that the surviving spouse will then be considered to be the IRA owner for all other income tax purposes, meaning they may continue the IRA as their own or roll it over to a new one. In either case, the surviving spouse would have to begin taking required minimum distributions no later than April 1st of the year following the year they turn age 70 ½.

If an IRA owner dies after distributions have begun, but before his/her entire interest has been distributed, the entire remaining balance must be distributed at least as rapidly as under the method of distribution in effect as of the owner's death.

**Roth IRAs:** Contributions to a Roth IRA are not tax deductible. Interest earned and distributions made are tax free if the Roth IRA is maintained for at least five years and the distributions are used to buy a first home, for qualified higher education expenses or the recipient has attained age 59½, died or has become disabled. Funds may be rolled over from a regular IRA to a Roth IRA without incurring the 10% IRS early withdrawal penalty, but the rolled over funds are taxable and must be reported as ordinary income.

Although Roth IRA owners do not have to begin taking distributions at age 70 ½, the Required Minimum Distribution Rules do apply once the IRA owner dies. Generally, these rules require that the designated beneficiary withdraw the entire IRA balance over their lifetime. However, if the spouse is the beneficiary, they can elect to be treated as the IRA owner, and distributions would not have to begin until they die.

## <u>WAIVER OF IRA PREMATURE DISTRIBUTION PENALTIES</u>

In general, distributions from an IRA prior to age 59 ½ are subject to a 10% premature distribution penalty tax to the extent that the distribution is taxable. However, the premature distribution penalty does not apply to distributions:

1. Made to a beneficiary or to the owner's estate, made after death of the owner
2. Attributable to the owner's disability
3. Which are part of a series of substantially equal periodic payments
4. Made for medical care, to the extent that the payment exceeds 7.5% of adjusted gross income
5. Made to an unemployed owner for payment of health insurance premiums
6. Made to pay qualified higher education expenses, and
7. Made to first-time homebuyers ($10,000 lifetime limit), who is someone who has not owned a house for at least two years

It is important to note that although the 10% premature distribution penalties may be waived, premature distributions <u>may still be taxable</u>.

Further, since Roth IRAs are purchased with after-tax dollars, owners may always withdraw their contributions without tax or penalty. Remember, penalties only apply to that portion of a premature distribution that is taxable, which on a Roth, would be the account earnings. However, if a Traditional IRA was purchased with before-tax dollars, the entire amount of a premature distribution would be subject to income tax and penalties, since none of the money has ever been taxed.

## SECTION 1035 EXCHANGES

If you take cash surrender but you use the money to purchase a new policy, you may be able to <u>defer paying tax</u> on the accumulated interest by following the special rules on "Life Insurance Policy Exchanges" as spelled out under the <u>Internal Revenue Code Section 1035</u>.

Under Section 1035, the IRS has ruled that the following exchanges are <u>tax-deferred:</u>

1. The exchange of a life policy for another life policy or for an endowment or annuity contract
2. The exchange of an endowment for an annuity contract
3. The exchange of an annuity contract for another annuity contract
4. The exchange of a life policy, endowment or fixed annuity for a variable annuity contract

Although the exchange may be made with the <u>same insurance company or a different company,</u> if the exchange involves life insurance policies, <u>the policies must be on the life of the same insured</u>.  If the exchange involves an annuity, the contracts must be <u>payable to the same person</u>.

# Federal Tax Considerations

# KEY FACTS

- Premiums paid for <u>Individual</u> Life insurance are NOT tax-deductible, nor are benefits taxed. This is true of <u>Key Person</u> Life insurance as well.

- The owners of a <u>Mutual</u> insurance company are the <u>policyholders</u>. <u>Dividends</u> received by the owner of a Mutual policy are NOT taxable.

- Dividends received by the owner of stock in a <u>Stock</u> company are taxable as ordinary income; Dividends are NEVER taxed as capital gains.

- <u>Qualified plans</u> have early-withdrawal penalties. The IRS levies a 10% penalty for <u>cash surrenders</u> on Annuities, IRAs, TSAs, and Keogh Plans prior to age 59½ <u>unless</u> the client has died or become disabled. This penalty is in addition to income taxes due.

- <u>Traditional IRA contributions</u> may be tax-deductible even though the client is an <u>active participant</u> in another qualified plan, if income is below a certain level.

- Contributions to a ROTH IRA are not tax deductible.

- Distributions from a ROTH IRA are not taxable as long as the participant is at least age 59 ½ and has had the ROTH for at least five years.

- <u>Modified Endowment Contracts</u> are classified that way for the life of the contract.

- Modified Endowment Contracts have a <u>10% IRS penalty</u> for premature distributions.

- On cash surrender of a life insurance policy, amounts received in excess of premiums paid in are <u>taxable</u>.

- Upon death, Life insurance proceeds paid to beneficiaries are <u>tax-free</u>.

- All or part of a distribution from a qualified plan may be <u>rolled over</u> into an IRA without tax.

- A "trustee to trustee" roll over <u>eliminates</u> the withholding tax requirement.

- Under Section 1035 of the Internal Revenue Code, an annuity may be exchanged for another annuity, but not for life insurance.

- Making a "material change" to a cash value life insurance policy may cause the "seven-pay test" to be applied again and could cause the policy to be classified as a "modified endowment contract," or MEC.

- If a policy owner has paid premiums into a "whole life" policy in the amount of $10,000 and surrenders the policy for its cash value of $12,000, $2,000 would be taxable.

- Listing a beneficiary on a life insurance policy will avoid "probate."

- Taxes may be deferred when exchanging one life insurance contract for another under Section 1035 of the Internal Revenue Code.

- Deferred interest earned on an annuity is taxable when withdrawals begin.

- Use the "exclusion ratio" to determine how much of an annuity payment is taxable during the annuity (pay-out) period.

- Life insurance policy owners who gift their policy to a charity are entitled to a tax deduction in the year of the gift.

- When surrendering a 403b TSA for cash under age 59 ½, all the proceeds are taxable as ordinary income plus the proceeds are subject to an IRS 10% premature distribution penalty.

- Although IRC Section 1035 exchanges "defer" taxes, they do not avoid them.

- In regard to Modified Endowment Contracts (MECs), a "material" change is defined as any increase in the death benefit. A material change could cause the seven-pay test to be applied again.

- If a surviving spouse is the beneficiary of an IRA owner who died before distributions begin, they may elect to treat the IRA as their own, by continuing it or rolling it over to a new one.

# Federal Tax Considerations

# PRACTICE EXAM

1. A client pays $4,000 in premiums on his/her $50,000 Whole Life policy that has a cash value of $5,000. If he/she takes cash surrender, his/her tax implication will be:

   A. $5,000 capital gains
   B. $5,000 ordinary income
   C. $1,000 capital gains
   D. $1,000 ordinary income

2. A 54 year old client surrenders his/her 403B TSA for cash. His/her tax implication will be:

   A. Only the growth in the account is taxed as ordinary income
   B. Only the growth in the account is taxed as capital gains
   C. The full amount is taxed as ordinary income plus a 10% penalty on the growth in the account
   D. The full amount is taxed as ordinary income plus a 10% penalty on the full amount distributed

3. A client with a $300,000 Modified Endowment Contract (MEC) paid in $70,000 in premiums. His/her cash value is now $100,000. If he/she takes cash surrender what percentage of the distribution is taxed as ordinary income?

   A. 0%, since MEC distributions are taxed as capital gains
   B. 30%
   C. 70%
   D. 100%

4. When a customer takes cash surrender and then transfers their policy to another insurance company in order to defer tax, it is referred to as a:

   A. Collateral assignment
   B. 1035 exchange
   C. Absolute assignment
   D. Viatical settlement

5.    In order to avoid withholding tax applied to a qualified plan rollover an individual should do which of the following:

    A.    Take a distribution and roll it over within 60 days
    B.    Purchase a whole life policy
    C.    Make a trustee to trustee roll over
    D.    There is no withholding tax applied as long as the distribution is rolled over within 60 days

6.    On IRAs, the 10% early withdraw penalty that applies to distributions taken prior to age 59½ is waived in all of the following situations EXCEPT:

    A.    Disability
    B.    Medical expenses
    C.    Bankruptcy
    D.    First time home buyer expenses

7.    If a distribution is taken from a deductible IRA to pay for qualified higher education expenses, the distribution is:

    A.    Not subject to income taxes
    B.    Subject to a 10% premature distribution penalty, but not income taxes
    C.    Subject to income taxes, but not a 10% premature distribution penalty
    D.    Not subject to penalties or taxes

8.    The gift of a life insurance policy to a charity:

    A.    Does not create any tax deductions
    B.    Creates an income tax deduction at the time of the gift
    C.    May be accomplished by designating the charity as revocable beneficiary
    D.    Creates an income tax deduction at the time of death

9.    If a policy owner who paid $10,000 in premiums into a whole life policy now surrenders the policy for its $12,000 cash value, what are the tax implications:

    A.    None, since life insurance proceeds are not taxable
    B.    $12,000 is taxable as a capital gain
    C.    $10,000 is tax free and $2,000 is taxable as ordinary income
    D.    $12,000 is taxable as ordinary income

10.   The maximum lifetime distribution that can be made from an IRA for qualified first-time home buyer expenses without incurring a 10% premature distribution penalty is:

    A.    $10,000
    B.    $15,000
    C.    $20,000
    D.    $25,000

11. On a cash value life insurance policy, a "material change" could cause the seven-pay test to apply again which could result in the policy being classified as a:

    A. Variable life policy
    B. Universal life policy
    C. Modified premium policy
    D. Modified Endowment Contract

12. A client contributed $20,000 to a non-qualified tax-deferred annuity over a period of time, which has now grown to $30,000 due to interest earnings that were credited to the account. If the client, who is now age 45, wants to take a partial withdrawal of $5,000, what will be his/her tax implication:

    A. None, since he/she is withdrawing less than the amount that he/she has contributed
    B. $5,000 capital gain
    C. $5,000 ordinary income
    D. $5,000 ordinary income, plus a 10% penalty

13. A client contributed $20,000 to a non-qualified tax-deferred annuity over a period of time, which has now grown to $30,000 due to interest earnings that were credited to the account. If the client, who is now age 45, wants to take cash surrender, what will be his/her tax implication:

    A. $10,000 capital gain
    B. $10,000 ordinary income
    C. $10,000 capital gain, $20,000 ordinary income
    D. $10,000 ordinary income, plus a 10% penalty

14. A client contributed $20,000 to a tax-qualified IRC 403 (b) Tax Sheltered Annuity over a period of time, which has now grown to $30,000 due to interest earnings that were credited to the account. If the client, who is now age 45, wants to take cash surrender, what will be his/her tax implication:

    A. $10,000 ordinary income, plus a 10% penalty
    B. $10,000 capital gain
    C. $30,000 ordinary income, plus a 10% penalty
    D. $30,000 capital gain

15. A client contributed $20,000 cash to purchase a non-qualified Single Premium Deferred Annuity years ago, which has now grown to $50,000 due to interest earnings that were credited to the account. If the client is now age 60 and annuitizes over his/her 20 year life span, how much of his/her income from this annuity will be excluded from taxes each year for the next 20 years:

    A. None
    B. $1,000
    C. $1,500
    D. $2,500

16. Regarding the rules applicable to Modified Endowment Contracts (MECs), if a "material change" to an existing whole life insurance policy occurs:

    A. The policy will be considered to be surrendered
    B. The policy will be considered to be a security
    C. The seven-pay test will be applied again
    D. The IRS will consider a 1035 exchange to have occurred

17. If a client makes an IRC Section 1035 exchange, what are the tax implications when the second policy is surrendered for cash:

    A. No taxes are due
    B. Ordinary income
    C. Capital gain
    D. Tax deferral

18. Upon death, all of the following taxes could apply EXCEPT:

    A. Inheritance tax
    B. Income tax
    C. Luxury tax
    D. Estate tax

19. All of the following are true regarding IRC Section 1035 exchanges EXCEPT:

    A. Qualified exchanges will avoid future taxes
    B. Exchanges do not have to be made with the same insurer
    C. A life insurance policy may be exchanged for an annuity
    D. A variable annuity may be exchanged for a fixed annuity

20. Proceeds of a life insurance policy paid to a beneficiary:

    A. Are taxable
    B. Are not included in the insured's estate
    C. Avoid probate
    D. May be assigned prior to receipt

# Federal Tax Considerations

# PRACTICE EXAM ANSWERS AND RATIONALES

1. **D**   When taking cash surrender the insured only has to pay tax on the amount withdrawn that exceeds the amount that they paid in. Since premiums for individual life insurance are paid with after tax money, the premiums paid represent the insured's cost basis. When withdrawn, the cost basis is returned to the insured without tax. When taking cash surrender the IRS treats the distribution as return of cost basis first and interest second (First-In-First-Out or FIFO). Since the insured paid $4,000 in premiums and they are withdrawing $5,000 they would have to pay ordinary income tax on the difference ($5,000-$4,000=$1,000). There are never capital gains tax on life insurance cash surrenders.

2. **D**   Since the individual is under age 59 ½ they will have a 10% IRS early withdrawal penalty on the full amount that is distributed. Knowing this alone would be enough to select the correct answer to this question. Since tax sheltered annuities (TSAs) are funded with pre-tax money, the individual has NO cost basis. When a distribution is taken the full amount will be taxable as ordinary income. The individual can avoid current taxation by rolling over the distribution, if done within 60 days.

3. **B**   MECs have tax implications that differ from other types of life insurance policies. MECs are policies that fail the seven-pay test, which means that the cash value is building too rapidly within the policy. Once a policy is classified as a MEC it will remain a MEC for the life of the contract. In general, when an insured takes cash surrender of a life insurance policy they are only taxed to the extent that the amount they withdraw exceeds the amount they paid in, since life insurance cash surrenders are taxed first-in-first-out (FIFO). However, MEC distributions are taxed as a withdrawal of interest first and return of premium second, or last-in-first-out (LIFO). MECs are also subject to a 10% penalty tax on the interest withdrawn, if taken when the insured is under age 59 ½. Since this question does not mention age, we can assume the insured is older than 59 ½.

   Since the insured is taking a full cash surrender, they would only have to pay ordinary income tax on the interest they are withdrawing ($30,000), which equals 30% of the total amount withdrawn ($100,000). However, using the same numbers in this question, if the insured instead took a partial withdrawal of $30,000 from the MEC, 100% of the distribution ($30,000) would be taxable.

4. **B**   A 1035 exchange is very similar to a rollover of a qualified plan. If an insured takes cash surrender of their life insurance policy or annuity they must pay ordinary income tax on any interest they received. The IRS will allow the insured/annuitant to defer paying this tax if they execute a 1035 exchange. The 1035 exchange guidelines state that the new life insurance policy must be written on the life of the same person and the new annuity benefits must be payable to the same person. The exchange does not have to be done with the same insurance company, and there is no limit on the amount that can be exchanged. Certain exchanges are not allowed, such as an exchange of an annuity for a life insurance policy. This is not an allowable 1035 exchange since it will put the individual in a better tax position (annuity death benefits are taxable and life insurance death benefits are not). 1035 exchanges are usually utilized to obtain a policy with a higher rate of return.

A viatical settlement is utilized when a terminally ill insured sells their life insurance policy to an investor for cash.

5. **C** Mandatory income tax withholding of 20% applies to most taxable distributions paid directly to you in a lump sum from employer retirement plans regardless of whether you plan to roll over the taxable amount within 60 days. The only way this 20% withholding can be avoided is by executing a trustee-to-trustee direct rollover.

6. **C** The IRS levies a 10% IRS early withdrawal penalty on distributions taken from IRAs by an individual under age 59½. However, this penalty is waived under certain circumstances, such as distributions due to: death of the IRA owner, disability of the IRA owner, medical expenses that exceed 7.5% of the individual's adjusted gross income, made to an IRA owner who is unemployed for payment of health insurance premiums, made for qualified higher education expenses for the IRA owner, the IRA owner's spouse, or children or grandchildren of either, made for first time home buyer expense ($10,000 lifetime limit), but NOT for bankruptcy.

7. **C** Distributions made from a tax deductible IRA to pay for qualified higher education expenses are taxable, but the 10% premature distribution penalty is waived.

8. **B** When a policy owner gifts their life insurance to a charity, they are entitled to a current income tax charitable deduction. The deduction is limited to the policy owner's cost basis in the policy, which is generally the amount of premiums they have paid in to date.

9. **C** Cash surrenders of life insurance policies will generate taxable income to the policy owner only to the extent that the cash surrender value exceeds the amount of premiums paid in. In this case, the $2,000 excess would be taxable as ordinary income.

10. **A** The maximum lifetime distribution that can be made from an IRA for qualified first-time home buyer expenses is $10,000. Although such distributions are taxable, the 10% premature distribution penalty is waived.

11. **D** Cash value life insurance policies that fail the seven-pay test, which is administered when the policy is first issued, are considered to be Modified Endowment Contracts (MECs) and as such lose some of their favorable tax treatment. Although a policy may initially pass the seven-pay test, making a "material change" to the policy later on could cause the seven-pay test to be administered again, thereby causing the policy to be considered a MEC from that point on. A "material change" is defined as any increase in the death benefit under the contract.

12. **D** On partial withdrawals from annuities, the first money out is considered to be the interest earnings, so in this case, the entire $5,000 would be taxable as ordinary income. In addition, since the client is under age 59 ½, a 10% premature distribution penalty would also be levied by the IRS.

13. **D** On the cash surrender of an annuity, that portion that is withdrawn that is above the client's cost basis is taxable as ordinary income, so in this case the client would have to pay ordinary income taxes on the $10,000 in interest earnings, plus a 10% penalty since he/she is only age 45. Cost basis is defined as the amount of money invested that the client has already paid tax on.

14. **C** A TSA is a tax-qualified annuity, meaning that they are purchased with before-tax dollars. Since none of the money in the account has ever been taxed, the client would have to pay ordinary income taxes on the entire balance of the account, plus a 10% penalty due to his/her age.

15. **B** This is an example of how the annuity "exclusion ratio" works. Since this annuity was purchased with after-tax dollars, the client's "cost basis" consists of the entire amount invested, which in this case was $20,000. When he/she annuitizes the contract, his/her cost basis will be returned to him/her as a tax-free return of principal over his/her life span. Since he/she has a 20 year life span, he/she will receive $1,000 a year tax-free. Anything he/she receives over that amount will be considered to be interest earnings and will be taxable as ordinary income.

16. **C** To determine whether or not a policy is a Modified Endowment Contract (MEC), the seven-pay test is administered when the policy is first issued. However, even though the policy was not initially determined to be an MEC, the seven-pay test will be administered again whenever a "material" change, such as a substantial increase in the cash value, takes place. Remember, a whole life policy could lose its favorable tax treatment as life insurance if its "risk corridor" (the difference between the policy limit and the cash value) does not satisfy IRS rules.

17. **B** An Internal Revenue Code Section 1035 exchange does not avoid taxes, it just defers them until the second policy is surrendered. When the second policy is surrendered for more than the client's original cost basis, any gain is taxable as ordinary income. Life insurance products and retirement plans are not eligible for capital gain tax treatment.

18. **C** Luxury taxes are not levied upon death, although all of the other taxes listed may apply.

19. **A** On an IRC Section 1035 exchange, taxes are deferred until the second policy is surrendered, but they are not avoided. The rules state that an exchange may be made with the same insurance company or a different company, but if the exchange involves life insurance, both policies must be on the life of the same person. Life insurance may be exchanged for life insurance or annuities, and annuities may be exchanged for other annuities, but annuities may not be exchanged for life insurance.

20. **C** Although the amount of life insurance that a customer has is included in the value of their estate upon death, the proceeds payable to a designated beneficiary are paid free of taxes and probate. If there is no designated beneficiary, the proceeds will be payable to the insured's estate, which is subject to probate, and his/her assets will be distributed according to the terms of his/her will, if any.

# SECTION 8

# Qualified Plans

## GENERAL REQUIREMENTS

**Qualified Plan:** A retirement plan that meets the criteria of the Employees Retirement Income Security Act (ERISA) of 1974. This Federal law requires compliance with the following three areas in order to form a plan to be considered a "Qualified Plan" by the IRS:

1. *Vesting:* Vesting means ownership. All Qualified Plans must establish a vesting schedule where all employer contributions to the plan will belong to the employee no later than the end of the sixth year (three years for some plans). Once vested, even if the employee quits or is terminated, those amounts contributed by the employer to the plan belong to the employee and may remain in the plan for withdrawal at retirement or be rolled over to another qualified plan or an IRA without tax implication. Some plans vest a certain percentage each year while others vest 100% at the end of the third year. Any employee contributions are vested immediately.

   **Remember:** *Those contributions were placed into the plan on a pre-tax basis by the employer and earn interest on a tax-deferred basis over the years.* So, upon withdrawal, they will be fully taxable as ordinary income in the year withdrawn. If withdrawn prematurely (prior to age 59½), they are subject to early withdrawal penalties (10%).

2. *Eligibility:* ERISA prescribes that all full time employees (those working 1,000 hours a year or more) who have worked for at least one year, and are age 21 or more, must be covered in a Qualified Plan, if offered.

3. *Non-Discrimination:* ERISA specifies that all workers must be treated alike, that is, the employer must contribute the same percentage for lower paid workers that is contributed for higher paid workers, such as managers.

So, generally speaking, when using the word "qualified" in connection with any type of retirement plan, we are speaking of a plan that follows ERISA and the money contributed is paid in pre-tax (before tax) dollars. In other words, it is money that has not yet been taxed, so when you take it out, all of it will be taxable!!

Most qualified plans are "defined contribution," meaning that the employer contributes the same fixed percent of each eligible employee's salary to the plan. Future benefits are based upon plan performance and length of service. Smaller employers with older employees often establish "defined benefit" plans, where the employee determines what they will need at retirement and the employer funds it accordingly.

**Non-qualified Plans:** Retirement plans that do not meet the requirements of ERISA are known as non-qualified plans. Since these plans often discriminate in favor of the highly paid employees and often have no vesting prior to retirement age, the contributions paid in by employers are not tax deductible until the employee actually receives the funds.

Non-qualified plans are not filed for IRS approval, but usually will be in the form of a written agreement between the employer and employee.

The most common of these is a Deferred Compensation plan, where the employee agrees to defer receipt of current earnings until retirement. This type of plan may be funded or unfunded. If funded, the employer might utilize an annuity as the funding device. If unfunded, the plan amounts to an unsecured promise by the employer to provide the compensation in the future, which could be risky for the employee if the employer goes broke.

Even if funded, the employer receives no current tax deductions but the employee is not currently taxed. Upon receipt of the deferred amount at retirement, the employee will be taxed on the amount received and the employer will be allowed to deduct the amount paid into the plan.

## FEDERAL TAX CONSIDERATIONS

So, as you can see, qualified plans have advantages to both the employer and the employee. For the employer, the money contributed is tax deductible as a business expense in the year paid in. For the employee, the money paid in by the employer earns interest on a tax-deferred basis and neither the contribution nor the interest is taxable to the employee until withdrawn.

However, taxes may be deferred further if the withdrawal is "rolled over" into another qualified plan, such as an IRA. Rollovers to IRAs are permitted once each year, but are subject to a withholding tax, unless the rollover goes directly from one trustee to another. There is no limit to the amount that can be rolled over into an IRA.

## PLAN TYPES, CHARACTERISTICS AND PURCHASERS

**Simplified Employee Pensions (SEPs):** Employer-sponsored IRAs. This type of plan offers corporations the opportunity to establish an employer-funded pension plan for eligible employees. With the exception of annuities, IRAs may not be funded by life insurance products.

Under a SEP, an employer contributes specific amounts directly into IRA accounts of eligible employees. Since an IRA is already a qualified plan, the employer does not have to bother with setting up a pension plan, which is very expensive to administer.

Contributions to the plan are not included in the employee's taxable income for the year, to the extent that the contribution does not exceed the maximums allowed. Distributions from the SEP will be taxable as ordinary income when received at retirement. SEPs are qualified plans and must follow ERISA.

**Self-employed Plans (HR-10 or Keogh Plans):** This type of retirement plan is also known as an HR-10 plan. This vehicle is provided for self-employed individuals or partners, and their employees, who wish to establish a retirement plan that will provide tax deferral and a reduced tax liability. Corporate officers, shareholders/employees and limited partners are not eligible.

Like a Traditional IRA, annual contributions to a Keogh plan are tax-deductible. Keogh plans may be funded by Life Insurance. They have the same early withdrawal penalties as IRAs.

**Profit Sharing and (401(k) Plans):** Under a 401(k) plan, an employee may elect to <u>reduce his/her current income</u> by deferring amounts into a qualified retirement plan. These plans are voluntary, and if an employee elects to participate, amounts deferred are not included in taxable gross income and earnings credited to the account will grow tax-free until distributed. Many employers will match the employee's contribution. Maximum contributions are <u>indexed for inflation</u>. Distributions are treated similarly to IRA and KEOGH plans, including a <u>10% penalty for early withdrawal prior to age 59½</u>, which is typical of all qualified plans.

Remember, contributions to qualified plans are generally made in "before-tax" dollars, since this money has never been taxed, 100% is taxable as <u>ordinary income</u> upon distribution.

An employer may elect to establish a qualified profit sharing plan, under which contributions to the plan are made only if profits are made. Usually, the amount of the contribution will be a specified share of company profits (such as 20%) up to a maximum percentage of an employee's salary (such as 5%). If there is no profit in a given year, there would be no contribution made.

When the payment of profit sharing proceeds is deferred, life insurance products are often used to accumulate funds and make disbursements. Many employers also allow their employees to participate in group annuities.

**SIMPLE (Savings Incentive Match Plan for Employees) Plans:** A simplified retirement plan for small employers (less than 100 employees) who do not have another type of retirement plan to offer their employees. This plan may be structured as an IRA or a 401(k) and allows for elective contributions by employers. Plans must meet vesting and participation requirements, but are generally not subject to the nondiscrimination rules applicable to other qualified plans.

Employee contributions to a SIMPLE IRA may only be made through a qualified salary deduction plan, according to a set percentage of compensation. Employer contributions may be made either as dollar-for-dollar matching contributions or a non-elective contribution for each eligible employee. All contributions must be non-forfeitable and are vested immediately.

In general, distributions from a SIMPLE IRA received before age 59 ½ are subject to a 10% penalty tax on premature distributions. However, any amount received by an employee participant from a SIMPLE IRA within the first two years is subject to a premature distribution penalty of 25%.

**403 (b) Tax Sheltered Annuities (TSAs):** Employees of qualified (tax-exempt) organizations are permitted, under the Internal Revenue Code (Section 403B), to contribute funds to annuities with "tax-free" dollars. Those eligible for TSAs include public-school teachers, school superintendents, college professors, and employees of religious-affiliated hospitals and charities. Early withdrawal penalties also apply. <u>Voluntary before-tax dollars are subtracted from the individual's gross income</u> by way of a <u>salary reduction</u>. This amount must be placed in the tax-sheltered Annuity and accumulates on a tax-deferred basis. Amounts to be contributed are determined in accordance with an <u>exclusion-allowance formula</u>, subject to certain maximum limits.

# Qualified Plans

# KEY FACTS

- Although Keogh plans are available to self-employed sole proprietors, partners, and their employees, they are NOT available to corporate officers.

- IRAs may be funded with Annuities, but NOT with Whole Life policies.

- Amounts contributed to qualified plans are limited by the IRS.

- Children cannot buy an IRA unless they have earned income.

- IRS rules determine the maximum contributions that may be made to "qualified" plans.

- Trustees must manage qualified plan assets exclusively for the benefit of the participants.

- Contributions made to SIMPLE IRA Plans are "vested" immediately.

- Premature distributions may be made to a first-time homebuyer from an IRA without incurring a 10% penalty, subject to a life-time limit of $10,000.

- Premature distributions made from a deductible IRA for qualified educational expenses are exempt from the 10% penalty, but they are not exempt from income tax.

- If an IRA participant dies before distributions begin, his/her surviving spouse may roll the account over to their own IRA.

- Deferred annuities may be used to fund an IRA.

- Contributions made to qualified plans are generally made before taxes, which benefits employees.

- When a trustee of a qualified plan splits the funds with a participant's separated spouse against the participant's wishes, it is a violation of ERISA known as "alienation."

- Qualified retirement plans offer special tax advantages to both employers and employees, in that employers can tax deduct contributions although they are not taxable to employees until distributed.

- The Employee Retirement Income Security Act (ERISA) is administered and enforced by the Federal Department of Labor.

- Premature distribution penalties are not waived due to bankruptcy.

- When a corporation sets up a qualified retirement plan to contribute a portion of their net income for the benefits of employees, it is known as a "profit sharing" plan.

- There is no maximum dollar limit that applies to roll-overs from one qualified plan to another.

# Qualified Plans

# PRACTICE EXAM

1. Which of the following organizations is responsible for enforcing the Employees Retirement Income Security Act of 1974 (ERISA) pension plan requirements:

    A.   IRS
    B.   Department of Health
    C.   Pension Benefit Guaranty Corporation
    D.   Department of Labor

2. A corporation may set up a qualified plan to contribute a percentage of their net earned income. This is known as a:

    A.   SEP IRA
    B.   Keogh plan
    C.   TSA 403B
    D.   Profit sharing plan

3. If the trustee of a qualified plan splits a participant's funds with his/her separated spouse against his/her wishes, the trustee has committed a violation of ERISA known as:

    A.   Alternation
    B.   Accumulation
    C.   Alienation
    D.   Attribution

4. The maximum contribution limits for qualified plans are governed by:

    A.   State law
    B.   ERISA
    C.   IRS rules
    D.   The Department of Labor

5. An employee's contributions to a SIMPLE IRA vest:

    A.   Immediately
    B.   After two years
    C.   After five years
    D.   At age 59 ½

6. A 403(b) Tax Sheltered Annuity (TSA) is purchased with:

    A. Involuntary after-tax contributions
    B. Voluntary before-tax contributions
    C. Involuntary before-tax contributions
    D. Voluntary after-tax contributions

7. If an IRA participant dies before distributions begin, his/her surviving spouse as beneficiary:

    A. May roll the account over to another IRA
    B. Must take the funds out over his/her expected life span
    C. Must take the funds out within five years of the death of the owner
    D. Must take the funds out over the owner's expected life span

8. All of the following are eligible for Keogh plans EXCEPT:

    A. Partners
    B. Sole proprietors
    C. Self employed
    D. Corporate officers

9. A ROTH IRA is purchased with:

    A. Involuntary after-tax contributions
    B. Voluntary before-tax contributions
    C. Involuntary before-tax contributions
    D. Voluntary after-tax contributions

10. All of the following are true regarding SEP IRAs EXCEPT:

    A. They are employer sponsored
    B. They are owned by the employee
    C. They have higher contribution limits than traditional IRAs
    D. Employer contributions may be discriminatory

11. Which of the following is true when a person with an IRA dies and their surviving spouse is the beneficiary:

    A. The spouse is entitled to the marital deduction
    B. The distribution is tax free
    C. Capital gains taxes are due on the amount of the distribution
    D. 100% of the distribution is taxable to the beneficiary in the year the owner died

12. Which of the following could occur if the owner of a corporation takes out of series of interest free loans from his/her company's qualified retirement plan:

    A. The IRS could disqualify the plan under the Top Heavy rules
    B. This violates the provisions of the Pension Benefit Guaranty Corporation
    C. The IRS could disqualify the plan under the Exclusive Benefit rules
    D. This is permissible since the owner of the company is in control of the plan

13.     If four business partners start a new business and establish a Keogh plan, which of the following would not be eligible to participate:

      A.     An employee who works 10 months a year
      B.     A partner who is also an employee
      C.     A limited partner who is not active in the business
      D.     A full-time employee who started work before the plan was established

14.     A client who has contributed $20,000 to his/her Traditional IRA over a period of time now has an account balance of $30,000. How much of his/her account balance may he/she elect to roll over to another IRA:

      A.     The account earnings only
      B.     The contribution limit that applies in the year of the roll-over
      C.     The contributions only
      D.     The entire amount in the account

15.     A 35 year old client who has contributed $20,000 to his/her ROTH IRA over a period of time now has an account balance of $30,000. How much can he/she withdraw without tax or penalty:

      A.     None
      B.     $10,000
      C.     $20,000
      D.     $30,000

# Qualified Plans

# PRACTICE EXAM ANSWERS AND RATIONALES

1. **D**   The Employee Retirement Income Security Act of 1974 (ERISA) is a Federal law that sets minimum standards for pension plans in private industry. ERISA does not require any employer to establish a pension plan. It only requires that those who establish plans must meet certain minimum standards. The law generally does not specify how much money a participant must be paid as a benefit. ERISA requires plans to regularly provide participants with information about the plan including information about plan features and funding; sets minimum standards for participation, vesting, benefit accrual and funding; requires accountability of plan fiduciaries; and gives participants the right to sue for benefits and breaches of fiduciary duty.

   ERISA also guarantees payment of certain benefits through the Pension Benefit Guaranty Corporation, a Federally chartered corporation, if a defined benefit plan is terminated.

   The Department of Labor's (DOL) Employee Benefits Security Administration (EBSA) enforces ERISA.

2. **D**   A profit sharing plan is an arrangement by an employer in which employees share in profits of the business. To be a qualified plan, a predetermined formula must be used to determine contributions to the plan and benefits to be distributed once a participant attains a specified age, becomes ill or disabled, severs employment, retires, or dies. An advantage to an employer is that in low or no profit years, the business does not have to contribute to the plan, since contributions are voluntary.

   SEP IRAs are employer sponsored IRAs, Keogh plans are for self-employed individuals or partners, and 403B tax sheltered annuities (TSAs) are for public-school teachers, school superintendents, college professors, and employees of religious-affiliated hospitals and charities.

3. **C**   Under a Federal law known as ERISA, trustees of qualified plans may not allocate funds to anyone other than the participant without their consent. To do so is a violation of ERISA known as "alienation."

4. **C**   It is the Internal Revenue Service (IRS) that establishes the maximum contribution limits on qualified plans.

5. **A**   All contributions to a SIMPLE IRA account must be fully vested immediately. However, the premature distribution penalty for withdrawals is increased to 25% during the first two years of participation.

6. **B**   TSAs are generally sold only to employees of public educational institutions, non-profits and charitable organizations. Eligible employees make voluntary, before-tax contributions on a payroll deduction basis, up to specified limits. 403(b) plans are very similar to 401(k) plans.

7. **A**    Generally, when an IRA owner dies before distributions begin, distributions must be made under either the life expectancy method or the five year rule. However, when a surviving spouse is the sole designated beneficiary of the IRA, they may elect to treat the IRA as their own and may either continue the account as owner or roll it over to their own IRA account.

8. **D**    Corporate officers are not eligible for Keogh plans unless they have separate self-employment income.

9. **D**    Individual contributions to a ROTH IRA are voluntary and are not tax-deductible.

10. **D**    SEP IRAs are employer sponsored IRAs that are owned by the employees. Although contributions may not be made on a discriminatory basis, contribution limits are much higher than permitted on Traditional IRAs.

11. **A**    When an IRA participant dies before required minimum distributions start and their surviving spouse is listed as beneficiary, the spouse may take the entire distribution within five years of the account owner's death or treat the IRA as their own and delay distributions until they reach age 70 ½. In either event, ordinary income taxes will eventually apply.

        However, although the value of the IRA is included in the value of the account owner's estate at death, under the estate tax "marital deduction," the entire estate will pass to the surviving spouse with no estate taxes due until the surviving spouse eventually dies.

12. **C**    Qualified corporate pension plans are regulated by the Employee Retirement Income Security Act of 1974 (ERISA) which states that such plans must be set up for the "exclusive benefit" of the employees. Violation of ERISA rules may result in plan disqualification and reclassification as a non-qualified plan.

13. **C**    Limited partners in a partnership would not be eligible to participate in a Keogh plan, since they are not actively involved in the partnership.

14. **D**    There are no limits governing the amount that may be rolled over. In other words, a participant may roll over all or part of their IRA to another IRA. If the roll-over is done trustee-to-trustee direct, then no taxes will be withheld.

15. **C**    Since contributions to a ROTH IRA are never tax deductible, the client's cost basis consists of the amount of after-tax dollars he/she contributed, which in this case was $20,000. IRS rules state that on a ROTH, a client may withdraw the amount of after-tax dollars he/she invested at any time, without tax or penalty.

# Life Insurance

# FINAL EXAM A

1. A life insurance customer misstates his/her age as being five years less than it really is. The rate he/she pays is $13 per $1,000 of coverage, but the correct rate is $15 per $1,000. If he/she dies, how much will the insurer pay:

   A. None, since the policy is voided if the client dies within the first two years
   B. All, since misstatement of age is not a material misrepresentation
   C. 13/15s of the face amount purchased
   D. All, but the overdue premium is subtracted from the face amount at death

2. Most group life insurance is what type of coverage:

   A. Level Term
   B. Whole Life
   C. Decreasing Term
   D. Interest Sensitive Whole Life

3. A 30-year mortgage obligation is best protected by what type of insurance:

   A. Decreasing Term
   B. Annual Renewable Term
   C. Credit Life
   D. Level Term

4. An insurable interest exists in all of the following situations, EXCEPT:

   A. A son-in-law on the life of his father-in-law
   B. A business partner
   C. A key person
   D. A creditor upon the life of a debtor

5. If the initial premium is not received along with the application, the agent upon delivery of the policy must obtain it as well as:

   A. Results of a new physical exam
   B. A statement that the applicant's health has not changed since initial application
   C. A certified statement from the applicant's regular physician
   D. Nothing additional is required

6. All are true about a preferred risk for life insurance, EXCEPT:

   A. The premium will be discounted from the standard rates
   B. The applicant has a longer than average life expectancy
   C. The rates and benefits of the policy are based on the Standard Mortality Table
   D. The premiums will be lower than for an applicant who smokes

7. All are true about the agent's duties, EXCEPT:

   A. Applicants must approve all changes in the application in writing
   B. The agent must explain all policy ratings at the time of policy delivery
   C. The agent must cash the applicant's check prior to delivering the policy
   D. If the policy is issued with an exclusion, the agent must explain to the applicant that they can either accept it or refuse it and receive a full premium refund

8. Which of the following avocations is not important when underwriting an individual policy:

   A. Fire fighting
   B. Hang gliding
   C. Scuba diving
   D. Sky diving

9. All of the following are true when a life insurance premium is overdue, EXCEPT:

   A. The policy will lapse at the end of the grace period
   B. Non-forfeiture provisions apply to lapsed whole life policies
   C. A policy may be reinstated if certain conditions are satisfied
   D. A policy will be reinstated without a physical exam if overdue premiums are paid

10. A life insurance policy sold to each spouse, rather than a joint life insurance policy sold to cover both spouses, would have all, EXCEPT:

    A. Two separate premiums
    B. A combined higher premium
    C. Coverage only for whichever spouse dies first
    D. Coverage for both spouses whenever either dies

11. All of the following are true about annuities, EXCEPT:

    A. They are used to create an estate for the insured's family
    B. They are tax deferred during the pay-in period
    C. Deferred interest is taxable as ordinary income upon receipt
    D. The annuitant cannot outlive the income from a life annuity

12. To calculate a net single premium, a life insurance company would subtract which of the following from the cost of mortality:

    A. Interest
    B. Commissions
    C. Expenses
    D. Loading for contingencies

13. When an insured sells or assigns their life insurance policy to another party in order to get money to pay for terminal expenses, it is known as a(an):

    A. Absolute assignment
    B. Collateral assignment
    C. Accelerated benefit
    D. Viatical settlement

14. All of the following are true regarding accelerated benefits, EXCEPT:

    A. They are treated as a policy loan
    B. They reduce the amount payable to the beneficiary at death of the insured
    C. They are added as a rider to some policies but built into others as a provision
    D. They pay a portion of the death benefit prior to death of the insured

15. All of the following should be considered when determining the amount of life insurance a client needs, EXCEPT:

    A. Mortgage pay-off
    B. Child's education
    C. Final expenses
    D. Self-maintenance costs

16. Universal life policies have all of the following, EXCEPT:

    A. A choice of a fixed or level premium
    B. Flexibility in premium payments
    C. The cash value invested in a separate account
    D. A minimum guaranteed interest rate on the cash value

17. Taxes on the accumulated interest in the cash value account of a whole life policy are due:

    A. Never
    B. Upon cash surrender
    C. At death
    D. When taking a loan

18. Which type of life insurance offers only pure protection:

    A. Universal Life
    B. Variable/Universal Life
    C. Variable Life
    D. Term

19. All of the following are dividend options on a life insurance policy issued by a mutual insurer, EXCEPT:

    A. Extended term option
    B. Cash
    C. Apply to premium when due
    D. Paid-up additions

20. The interest adjusted cost comparison index includes all of the following factors, EXCEPT:

    A. The time value of money
    B. The interest rate to be earned on the cash value
    C. The amount of the premium paid
    D. The earnings in the separate account

21. Which of the following riders is added to a policy written on the life of a child to make sure the premium is paid if the policyholder dies or becomes disabled:

    A. Automatic premium loan
    B. Extended term option
    C. Payor benefit rider
    D. Accelerated benefits rider

22. Ryder buys an annuity naming Gerry and Cheryl as co-annuitants. The amount of the monthly payments during the annuity period will be based upon:

    A. Ryder's life span
    B. Gerry's life span
    C. Cheryl's life span
    D. The joint life span of both Gerry and Cheryl

23. Mr. Jones bought an annual renewable term policy with a face amount of $200,000 on April 1, 2010 for an annual premium of $400. If he died on May 15th, 2011 without paying his renewal premium when due, his insurer would pay:

    A. $199,600
    B. $200,000
    C. $200,000 less any outstanding loans
    D. Nothing

24. The Spendthrift Clause on a life insurance policy keeps the beneficiary from doing any of the following, EXCEPT:

    A. Commuting the proceeds
    B. Spending the proceeds
    C. Assigning the proceeds
    D. Transferring the proceeds

25. When a creditor has a temporary interest in a life insurance policy, it is known as a:

    A. Lien
    B. Absolute assignment
    C. Ownership provision
    D. Collateral assignment

26. Upon your death, if your beneficiary chooses the interest only settlement option, the:

    A. Proceeds are taxable
    B. Interest is taxable
    C. Principal reverts to the insurer
    D. Both the proceeds and the interest are taxable

27. All are true about a Limited Pay Whole Life policy, EXCEPT:

    A. The cash value will be paid to the policy owner upon cash surrender
    B. The face amount of the policy will be paid to the policy owner at policy maturity
    C. The policy will cover the insured until death or age 100, whichever occurs first
    D. The policy will reach maturity at the end of the premium paying period

28. All are true about the rider called Accidental Death Benefit, EXCEPT:

    A. It has a lower cost per $1,000 than does life insurance
    B. It pays double when the insured dies as a result of sickness
    C. It requires death to occur within a certain period of time
    D. It drops off the policy automatically at a certain age, causing the overall premium to decrease

29. A rider added to a life policy to create coverage for your entire family is the:

    A. Family Income Rider
    B. Family Rider
    C. Family Maintenance Rider
    D. Other Insured Rider

30. The amount of annuity benefits included in the value of the estate of a deceased life income annuitant is:

    A. The amount of premium paid
    B. The interest earned in the annuity account
    C. The amount of future benefits to be paid
    D. Zero

31. All are true about immediate annuities, EXCEPT:

    A. There is no cost basis for the annuitant
    B. They are used in structured settlements
    C. There is no accumulation period
    D. They may provide a lifetime pay-out

32. All of the following are true about annuities, EXCEPT:

    A.    TSA (403b) annuities are sold to employees of public educational institutions and non-profit entities
    B.    Interest earned during the accumulation period is tax deferred
    C.    Insureds invest annuity premiums into their general account
    D.    Annuities create an estate and are therefore subject to underwriting

33. When selling a market value adjusted annuity, you must state all, EXCEPT:

    A.    The market value may be adjusted up or down in the future
    B.    Future income generated will be based upon future market value
    C.    Upon annuitization, the annuitant may receive an income for life
    D.    Future payments will be based upon past investment experience

34. Once classified as a Modified Endowment Contract (MEC), the contract will remain that way:

    A.    Until the proper adjustments are made
    B.    Forever
    C.    Until age 59½
    D.    For seven years

35. A valid 1035 Exchange of a life insurance contract must be:

    A.    On the life of the same person
    B.    With the same person designated as owner of the policy
    C.    With the same insurer who issued the initial policy
    D.    To the same type of policy

36. What are the tax implications when an annuitant elects to take a cash surrender of a deferred annuity during the accumulation period at age 56:

    A.    All the funds distributed are taxable as ordinary income
    B.    Only the interest is taxable as ordinary income, but a 10% penalty applies to the entire distribution
    C.    All of the funds distributed are taxable as a capital gain
    D.    Only the interest is taxable as ordinary income, but the interest is also subject to an IRS 10% early withdrawal penalty

37. All of the following are true regarding qualified plans, EXCEPT:

    A.    Trustee-to-trustee rollovers are permitted without actual distribution of funds
    B.    Qualified plans have special tax advantages under ERISA
    C.    Rollovers are subject to tax unless reinvested within 30 days
    D.    TSA (403b) Plans are salary reduction plans with contributions in before-tax dollars

38.     All of the following are true about orders from the Commissioner or Director, EXCEPT:

      A.     They have the validity of law
      B.     They are issued only after holding a hearing
      C.     They are final
      D.     They are designed to protect the insurance-buying public

39.     All are true regarding replacement of life insurance, EXCEPT:

      A.     Producers must review the existing policy prior to replacing to see if it contains any limitations that may not be covered by the new policy
      B.     Replacement is unlawful
      C.     Special forms must be given to clients electing to replace coverage
      D.     Making misrepresentations in order to induce replacement is known as "twisting"

40.     Under the Fair Credit Reporting Act, if a customer is rejected due to adverse information contained in a consumer report, all of the following are true EXCEPT:

      A.     The insurer must send the client a list of all parties who have requested a report during the last six months
      B.     The client must get a court order to be able to access such reported information
      C.     The insurer must inform the client of where they can obtain a copy of the report
      D.     Inaccurate information must be corrected by the consumer reporting agency

41.     A client can make the "Presumption of Agency" if agent Smith does any of the following, EXCEPT:

      A.     Gives out business cards with the name of XYZ Insurance Company
      B.     Uses XYZ Company applications and forms
      C.     Uses the XYZ Company rate manual
      D.     Represents the client in finding the best coverage and premium available

42.     Reinsurance is used for all of the following purposes, EXCEPT:

      A.     To increase unearned premium reserves
      B.     For maintaining stability of rates
      C.     To cover catastrophic claim situations
      D.     To increase capacity to write more business

43.     An insurer selling life and health insurance to their own members only is a:

      A.     Reciprocal company
      B.     Mutual company
      C.     Fraternal company
      D.     Stock company

44. Insurance companies doing business in this State may be _____ corporations:

    A.    Foreign
    B.    Domestic
    C.    Alien
    D.    Any of the above

45. An insurance company that is domiciled in another country, but authorized to do business in this state is considered to be:

    A.    Foreign
    B.    Domestic
    C.    Alien
    D.    Surplus Lines

46. Generally, all of the following are true EXCEPT:

    A.    Mutual life insurers cannot guarantee their future dividend scale
    B.    Misrepresentation on an application can void coverage, if material
    C.    Agents act in a fiduciary capacity when handling premiums
    D.    Producers may project future dividends on a non-participating policy

47. All are true about life insurance, EXCEPT:

    A.    An Automatic Premium Loan rider will keep a Whole Life policy from lapsing
    B.    A policy that was surrendered for cash may not be reinstated
    C.    The cash value of a Whole Life policy may be used to supplement retirement
    D.    The 1035 Exchange must always be with the same company that issued the first policy

48. In which of the following areas could the actions of an insurance agent cause a company to be liable:

    A.    Implied agency
    B.    Waiver
    C.    Estoppel
    D.    Errors and omissions

49. Which one of the following provides the clearest source of authority that can be exercised by an agent:

    A.    The Code of Ethics published by the National Association of Life Underwriters
    B.    The agent's contract with the insurance company
    C.    Model legislation from the National Association of Insurance Commissioners
    D.    The insured's outline of coverage

50.     If a life insurance policy is purchased and fails to meet the seven-pay test, it is considered by the IRS to be a:

        A.      Modified Endowment Contract (MEC)
        B.      Annuity
        C.      Whole Life policy
        D.      Modified Whole Life policy

51.     All of the following are true regarding credit life insurance EXCEPT:

        A.      If the policy is cancelled, the unearned premium must be returned
        B.      If the borrower dies, the proceeds are paid to the lender
        C.      It is usually written as level term coverage
        D.      The policy limit may not exceed the amount of the loan

52.     Which type of life insurance allows a policy owner to take a partial surrender:

        A.      Traditional whole life
        B.      Universal life
        C.      Endowment
        D       Limited-pay whole life

53.     All of the following are typical exclusions in a life insurance policy EXCEPT:

        A.      Auto
        B.      War
        C.      Aviation
        D       Suicide

54.     All of the following are true regarding a mutual insurer EXCEPT:

        A.      The governing body is elected by the policy holders
        B.      They have no capital stock
        C.      They guarantee the payment of future dividends
        D.      They issue participating policies

55.     All of the following are considered to be misrepresentation EXCEPT;

        A.      Making comparisons between policies
        B.      Twisting
        C.      Misstating dividends
        D.      Misstating financial condition

56.     Which of the following life insurance beneficiaries is not exempt from the claims of creditors:

        A.      Estate
        B.      Spouse
        C.      Children
        D.      Business partner

57. Which type of life insurance pays a guaranteed minimum rate of return, but could pay more:

    A. Variable life
    B. Whole life
    C. Universal life
    D. Endowment

58. An adjustable whole life policy allows for the adjustment of all of the following EXCEPT:

    A. Premium paying period
    B. Face amount
    C. Expense loading
    D. Premium

59. Grandma has $250,000 to invest. Although she needs income, she also wants to leave money to her five grandchildren when she dies. What should she buy:

    A. Life income annuity
    B. Deferred annuity
    C. Immediate annuity with refund option
    D. Period certain annuity

60. Most life insurers will permit the owner of a lapsed policy to apply for reinstatement for up to _____ years:

    A. 2
    B. 3
    C. 5
    D. 7

61. Which life insurance non-forfeiture option will result in a face amount that is lower than that of the original policy:

    A. Reduced paid-up
    B. Automatic premium loan
    C. Reduced term
    D. Extended term

62. If, after discussing the customer's investment objectives and needs, the customer and the producer agree upon an annuity, the purchase would be considered to be:

    A. Appropriate
    B. Suitable
    C. Approved
    D. Accredited

63.    All of the following are true regarding the rules regarding the replacement of life insurance EXCEPT:

      A.    Producers must list all policies that are being replaced
      B.    They require direct response insurers to ask the question regarding replacement
      C.    They reduce the opportunity for misrepresentation and incomplete comparisons
      D.    They apply when replacing all types of life insurance

64.    All of the following are true regarding life insurance loans EXCEPT:

      A.    The cash value in the policy is the collateral for the loan
      B.    Loans are not taxable
      C.    Policy owners may borrow up to the face amount of their policy
      D.    Insurers charge annual interest on policy loans

65.    The rules regarding replacement always apply when replacing which of the following types of life insurance:

      A.    Credit life
      B.    Whole life
      C.    Group life
      D.    Term life

66.    All of the following are true regarding the advertising of life insurance EXCEPT:

      A.    Advertising is prohibited
      B.    The name of the insurer must be disclosed in all advertisements
      C.    A Life Insurance Buyer's Guide is not considered to be advertising
      D.    Advertisements are the responsibility of the insurer whose products are advertised

67.    Which of the following is considered to be irrevocable:

      A.    Settlement options
      B.    Beneficiary designations
      C.    Absolute assignments
      D.    Dividend options

68.    A joint life insurance policy will pay:

      A.    On a second-to-die basis
      B.    Only when both insureds die in a common disaster
      C.    On a first-to-die basis
      D.    50% of the proceeds upon the death of the first to die and 50% upon the death of the second to die

69.    All of the following are true regarding immediate annuities EXCEPT:

      A.    They have no accumulation period
      B.    They do not provide life insurance protection
      C.    They may not have a beneficiary
      D.    They may pay for the life time of the annuitant

70. All of the following are true regarding employee Group Life insurance EXCEPT:

    A. Insurers are responsible for claims that occur during the grace period
    B. Employees receive Certificates of Insurance summarizing their coverage
    C. Upon conversion, the premium is based upon the employee's age at enrollment
    D. The rules regarding replacement do not apply when replacing group life

71. The mode of premium provision addresses:

    A. The method of payment
    B. The frequency of payment
    C. The amount of payment
    D. The premium due date

72. All are part of the "entire contract" EXCEPT:

    A. The policy
    B. The application
    C. Riders, if any
    D. Changes made by the agent

73. When the living beneficiaries on a life insurance policy share the proceeds equally, it is known as a _____ beneficiary designation:

    A. Per capita
    B. Class
    C. Per stirpes
    D. Individual

74. A customer buys a whole life policy and pays $700 a year for the first five years. After that, the premium increases to $1,100 a year and stays level at that amount thereafter. What type of life insurance did he/she buy:

    A. Graded premium
    B. Adjustable premium
    C. Modified premium
    D. Flexible premium

75. An IRA purchased by an employer to cover employees is known as a:

    A. 401k plan
    B. Defined contribution plan
    C. 403b plan
    D. Simplified Employee Pension plan

76.　A business has an insurable interest in all of the following EXCEPT:

　　A.　Key persons
　　B.　Customers
　　C.　Corporate officers
　　D.　Partners

77.　Which of the following transactions is not an eligible for an IRC 1035 Exchange:

　　A.　Annuity to whole life
　　B.　Variable life to universal life
　　C.　Whole life to annuity
　　D.　Variable annuity to fixed annuity

78.　A 30 year old client buys a 30 year level term life insurance policy with a face amount of $200,000. If he/she dies at age 45, the insurer will pay his/her beneficiary:

　　A.　Zero
　　B.　$100,000
　　C.　$150,000
　　D.　$200,000

79.　A client has a whole life policy with a stated cash value of $1,500 and a loan outstanding in the amount of $500. What is his/her cash surrender value:

　　A.　$1,500
　　B.　$1,000
　　C.　$ 500
　　D.　Zero

80.　All of the following are true about Group life insurance EXCEPT:

　　A.　The employees receive Certificates of Insurance
　　B.　Groups cannot be formed just to buy insurance
　　C.　They provide a source of income for the employer
　　D.　The employer is the master policy holder

81.　All of the following are true regarding Key Person life insurance EXCEPT:

　　A.　Employers may deduct the premiums paid as a business expense
　　B.　The employer is the beneficiary
　　C.　It is written on employees who make significant contributions to the business
　　D.　Proceeds payable upon death are tax free

82.　On adjustable whole life, the policy owner may do all of the following EXCEPT:

　　A.　Adjust the premiums
　　B.　Adjust the face amount
　　C.　Extend the period of protection
　　D.　Use non-forfeiture provisions to buy additional insurance

83. If an insured covered by a $100,000 life insurance policy dies and the beneficiary elects to take the proceeds and interest at $5,000 a month, they have selected which of the following settlement options:

    A.      Fixed period
    B.      Cash
    C.      Fixed amount
    D.      Interest

84. On an annuity, which of the following can surrender the contract for cash during the accumulation (pay-in) period:

    A.      The annuitant
    B.      The beneficiary
    C.      The policy owner
    D.      The insured

85. Which type of annuity will make payments only until the death of the annuitant:

    A.      Life income
    B.      Person certain
    C.      Refund
    D.      Joint and survivor

86. All of the following are true about annuities EXCEPT:

    A.      The pay-out period is also known as the "annuitization" period
    B.      During the accumulation period, the cash value consists of the premiums paid in plus interest
    C.      An immediate annuity requires the policy owner to make periodic payments into the general or separate account
    D.      An annuity that pays out a level amount every month is a fixed annuity

87. All of the following are true regarding 529 College Savings plans EXCEPT:

    A.      Contributions grow on a tax deferred basis
    B.      A 10% penalty applies to non-qualified distributions
    C.      Contributions are tax deductible
    D.      Qualified distributions are tax free

88. Which of the following is true about life insurance policy dividends:

    A.      They are guaranteed
    B.      They may be used to reduce premiums, when due
    C.      They are taxable
    D.      They are a feature of all life insurance policies

89.　A life insurance policy may include provisions that do all of the following EXCEPT:

A.　Restrict coverage if death is caused by suicide
B.　Require evidence of insurability to reinstate coverage
C.　Extend the contestable period beyond two years
D.　Adjust proceeds if the insured's age is misstated on the application

90.　Term life is usually sold to clients who:

A.　Need permanent protection
B.　Want rapid cash value accumulation
C.　Need a lot of coverage but cannot afford permanent insurance
D.　Want coverage until they die

91.　The "cost of insurance" rider is attached to which type of life insurance policy:

A.　Universal life
B.　Term life
C.　Endowment
D.　Traditional whole life

92.　All of the following are true regarding variable life insurance EXCEPT:

A.　Producers need a state life insurance license and a FINRA securities license
B.　Premiums are invested in the insurers "separate" account
C.　The minimum rate of return is guaranteed by the insurer
D.　The minimum death benefit is guaranteed by the insurer

93.　Regarding life settlements, the difference between the face amount and the cash value is known as the:

A.　Gross value
B.　Surrender value
C.　Net value
D.　Adjusted value

94.　Who does a life settlement broker represent:

A.　Insurer
B.　Settlement provider
C.　Beneficiary
D.　Policy owner

95.　The authority that an agent has, but is not expressed in their contract is known as _____ authority:

A.　Written
B.　Implied
C.　Conditional
D.　Apparent

96. Which clause in a life insurance policy states "This policy is issued in consideration of the premium paid and the statements made on the application":

    A.    Conditions
    B.    Insuring agreement
    C.    Consideration
    D.    Mode of payment

97. All of the following are true about life insurance policies EXCEPT:

    A.    They are unilateral since only the insurer makes an enforceable promise
    B.    If the policy language is ambiguous, claims may be paid based upon reasonable expectations
    C.    The policy may be rescinded if the client made a material misrepresentation
    D.    A policy holder may revoke an absolute assignment

98. To determine a life insurance applicant's human life value, a producer must consider:

    A.    The amount of their mortgage
    B.    Their lifetime earnings potential
    C.    Their children's future educational expenses
    D.    The cost of their funeral

99. If the initial life insurance premium is not pre-paid, coverage will be effective:

    A.    Upon passing a physical examination
    B.    When both the agent and the applicant sign the application
    C.    When the underwriter approves the application
    D.    When the policy is delivered and the first premium is paid

100. The premium on annual renewable term life insurance:

    A.    Will remain level for at least five years
    B.    Will increase every year
    C.    Will remain level until the insured reaches age 65
    D.    Will never change

# Life Insurance

# FINAL EXAM A ANSWERS AND RATIONALES

1. **C** It is too late to adjust the premium, so the insurer will adjust the face amount instead. The adjustment is based on what the premium that the client paid would have purchased if he/she would have disclosed his/her true age. He/she did pay $13 per $1,000 but he/she should have paid $15 per $1,000, so the insurer will only pay 13/15ths of the face amount.

2. **A** Most group policies are purchased by employers who want to pay as little as possible, so most group policies are annual renewable level term contracts. Premiums are based on the average age of the group and often consider past claims experience of the group.

3. **A** Credit life is generally written to cover relatively short-term consumer loans. However, decreasing term policies may be written for any length of time, often up to 30 years or longer.

4. **A** Insurable interest must exist at the time of application. If you would benefit if a person continues to live, then you have an insurable interest in that person. Insurable interest is based on economics or immediate family relationships.

5. **B** There is never any coverage unless the premium has been paid. On a submittal application, the agent "submits" the application to the underwriter to see if the client is acceptable. If he/she is, the underwriter will issue the policy, but there is no coverage since the premium has not yet been paid.

   When delivering the policy, the agent must have the client sign a statement that his/her health has not changed since the date of the original application and pay the premium. If the client's health has changed, the agent should not deliver the policy.

6. **C** The Commissioner's Standard Mortality Table is used to calculate the rates and benefits for the "standard" or average person. The rates for a "preferred" risk are discounted from the standard.

7. **C** The client's premium check is usually submitted to the insurer along with the application.

8. **A** A lot of questions deal with definitions. An "avocation" is a hobby. A "vocation" is your job. Fire fighting is a vocation, not an avocation.

9. **D** Although the right to apply for reinstatement is a mandatory provision in a life policy, the insurer will usually require that the insured pass a physical exam as well as pay the overdue premiums prior to reinstatement.

10. **C** A joint life policy is usually written to cover only the first party to die. A survivorship life policy only covers the last party to die and is usually used to pay estate taxes. If both spouses want coverage to apply when either dies, they need separate policies.

11. **A**   Life insurance is used to create an estate. Annuities are the opposite, and are used to liquidate an estate by paying the beneficiary monthly payments over a period of time, usually for life.

12. **A**   Commissions, company expenses and loading for contingencies are added to the cost of mortality, but since the insurer invests the advance premiums paid, any interest earned by the insurer is subtracted out prior to establishing the net premium.

13. **D**   If you get a terminal illness, you may need money to pay for the cost of care prior to your death. You can sell your policy to an investor at a discount by assigning your rights of ownership to the investor, who now names himself as beneficiary. When you die, they get the policy proceeds, which is more than they paid you. This is known as a viatical settlement.

Some insurers now include a provision or rider in their policies called "accelerated" or "living" benefits. This allows an insured to receive funds from their own policy in advance of death and eliminates the need to make a viatical settlement.

14. **A**   Accelerated or living benefits are not treated as a loan and no interest will accrue, although any amounts paid will reduce the amount payable at death.

15. **D**   There are two ways to determine the amount of life insurance to be sold to a client. The "needs" approach is often used for older clients to determine the amount necessary to take care of their final expenses, children's education and mortgage.

The "human life value" approach is used for younger people to measure the amount of future income their family will lose if they die. Neither method includes funds for self-maintenance.

16. **C**   Variable life utilizes a separate account that is similar to a mutual fund, which is why an agent also needs a FINRA license. Universal life does offer a "current" interest rate, but funds are invested in the insurers "general account" which does have a minimum guaranteed rate of return.

17. **B**   If you surrender your whole life policy for cash and the amount of cash you receive exceeds the total amount of the premiums you have paid over a period of time, the difference must be interest and is taxable as ordinary income. Loans are not taxable, however.

18. **D**   In this context "pure" protection means coverage for mortality only. Term insurance has no cash value and therefore offers the most pure protection for the lowest cost.

19. **A**   Be sure to know the difference between the "non-forfeiture" options and the "dividend" options. All policies with a cash value must have non-forfeiture options but only policies issued by mutual insurers have dividend options. The three non-forfeiture options are cash surrender, reduced paid up and extended term. You should understand them fully.

20. **D**   Only variable contracts use separate accounts and since there are no guarantees in separate accounts, they are not a component of the interest adjusted cost comparison index which uses a fixed interest rate to measure the future value of premiums paid.

21. **C**   The payor benefit rider is like waiver of premium, except it is added to a policy written on the life of a child.

22. **D**   This is an annuity option known as "joint and survivor" which pays until the last party dies, so the joint life span of both annuitants is considered.

23. **D**   This policy lapsed at the end of its grace period, so the insurer would pay nothing.

24. **B**   The spend thrift clause prevents the beneficiary from changing the way you specified you want the proceeds to be paid when you die. For example, you specified that the proceeds be paid to your beneficiary over a 20-year period in the event of your death.

   However, when you die your beneficiary would rather have the cash up front. The spend thrift clause prevents the beneficiary from commuting, assigning or transferring the proceeds to other parties in lieu of a lump sum cash payment. The proceeds must be paid out over the 20-year period as you specified.

25. **D**   There are two types of assignments, absolute and collateral. An absolute assignment would occur when you sign over your ownership of a life policy you bought on your child to the child when they attain age 21. You are giving up all rights of ownership irrevocably.

   A collateral assignment is temporary. For example, you take out a loan from the bank who asks you to provide life insurance to pay off the loan if you should die. Since you already have life insurance, you direct your insurer to pay off the loan out of the proceeds of your life policy. Neither type of assignment is valid unless the insurer is notified in writing.

26. **B**   Proceeds of a life policy are never taxable. However, if the beneficiary selects the interest option, which means that the insurer will save the proceeds for the beneficiary and pay them interest in the meantime, the interest is taxable as ordinary income in the year paid.

27. **D**   Although limited pay policies are a type of whole life insurance, the premium is paid during a limited period of time, such as 20 years. However, the policy does not reach maturity until age 100. Limited pay policies are very expensive, but build cash values very rapidly.

28. **B**   ADB or accidental death benefit rider is a type of health insurance that can be added to a life policy by means of a rider. The rider costs about $1.00 per $1,000 of coverage, but drops off the policy at older ages since the chance of accidental death increases. It does not cover sickness.

29. **B**   A Family Rider allows the breadwinner to add level, convertible term insurance as a rider to his/her whole life policy to cover their spouse and all their children. The term insurance on the spouse is often written for 10, 15 or 20 years. The children's coverage expires when they turn 18. Both the spouse and children can convert to whole life without a physical exam at expiration of their term. This is the cheapest way to provide a lot of coverage for your entire family.

30. **D**   Remember, on the life income option, all payments cease when the annuitant dies and there is no beneficiary. The insurance company keeps any monies remaining in the account when the annuitant dies. Obviously, this is a risky option.

31. **A**   Be sure to know the difference between an immediate annuity and a deferred annuity. On an immediate annuity, you give the insurer the money and they start paying you back with monthly payments right away. Your cost basis is the amount of money you gave them, which was money you already paid taxes on (after-tax dollars).

32. **D**  Life insurance creates an estate and is subject to underwriting. Annuities are the opposite. The insurer does not care about your health at all, since on some options, they get to keep the money if you die.

33. **D**  It is illegal to base future performance on past investment experience.

34. **B**  An MEC is a life insurance policy where the cash value builds too fast. If the cash value will exceed the total amount of premiums paid over the first seven years of the contract, the IRS will classify the policy as an MEC and it will lose its favorable tax treatment. This determination is made when the policy is first issued, and once so classified, it will stay that way forever.

35. **A**  A 1035 exchange allows a person to switch from one life policy to another without incurring any present tax liability. However, both policies must be on the life of the same person.

36. **D**  Most annuities are non-qualified plans, so upon surrender, taxes are only due on the amount above the annuitant's cost basis. However, since this client is under age 59½, there is also an IRS 10% penalty on the interest portion of the proceeds.

37. **C**  Tax-free rollovers may be made on qualified plans up to 60 days after a distribution.

38. **C**  The Commissioner or Director of Insurance has rule making powers, but all rules are subject to appeal in a court of law.

39. **B**  Replacement of insurance is not unlawful, unless detrimental to your client. However, special rules must be followed. Misstating the facts regarding replacement is called "twisting."

40. **B**  The Federal Fair Credit Reporting Act requires that rejected applicants may obtain copies of a consumer report from the investigating agency upon their written request. No court order is required.

41. **D**  An agent represents the insurer under the doctrine of agency law. The agent does not represent the insured. Brokers represent the insured.

42. **A**  Although insurers do purchase reinsurance for various reasons, it does not increase their unearned premium reserves.

43. **C**  Fraternal insurers are non-profit with a lodge system and ritualistic form of government. They sell life and health only to their members. A reciprocal is a P&C insurer operated by an "attorney in fact" who arranges the inter-exchange of agreements of indemnity among insureds.

44. **D**  Many insurers operating in this state are foreign with their home office in some other state. However, some are domestic with their home office here and some are alien with their home office in another country.

45. **C**  Although all insurers selling in this state need to have a Certificate of Authority, they may be domestic, foreign or alien.

46. **D**  Only "participating" policies issued by mutual insurers might pay dividends to policyholders. Non-participating policies are issued by stock insurers and may pay dividends only to shareholders. In either case, it is illegal to guarantee future dividends.

47. **D**  IRC Section 1035 allows the same person to defer taxes when switching from one life insurance policy to another as long as all the conditions are met. However, policies do not have to be with the same insurer.

48. **A**  An insurer is liable for the acts of its agents. If an insurer gives you business cards, for example, that would imply to a customer that you represent that company.

49. **B**  The agent represents the insurance company. The agent's authority is expressed in writing in a contract between the agent and the insurer.

50. **A**  Once the IRS classifies a life policy as an MEC, it will lose its favorable tax treatment.

51. **C**  Credit life is usually written as decreasing term life insurance.

52. **B**  It is Universal Life that allows policy holders to make partial surrenders.

53. **A**  There is no exclusion in a life insurance policy relating to death caused by an auto accident.

54. **C**  Although a mutual insurer is a corporation, they do not issue stock. Mutual insurers are owned by their policy holders, who have the right to vote to elect the Board of Directors. Although policy holders might receive dividends, they are not guaranteed.

55. **A**  It is not considered to be misrepresentation to make fair comparisons of policies.

56. **A**  Life insurance proceeds payable to a designated beneficiary are generally exempt from the claims of creditors. However, if there is no beneficiary designated, the proceeds are payable to the insured's estate, who is responsible for paying creditor claims.

57. **C**  Universal life is also known as "interest sensitive" whole life, since it pays a guaranteed minimum rate of return on the accumulated cash value, plus a current interest rate, which may exceed the minimum guaranteed rate.

58. **C**  Adjustable whole life insurance is sold to clients who have fluctuating incomes, who may make adjustments in the premium paying period, the face amount and/or the amount of the premium. However, no adjustments may be made in the amount of the expenses the insurer has "loaded" into the policy.

59. **C**  Grandma should buy an immediate annuity with a refund provision. Since this type of annuity will start making monthly payments to her right away, there is no accumulation period like there is on a deferred annuity. However, since she selected a refund option, in the event of her death before she recovers all of her invested capital, a refund of the remaining balance will be made to her five grandchildren as beneficiaries.

60. **C**  Most insurers will allow a policy owner whose policy has lapsed to apply for reinstatement for up to five years, although some limit it to 3 years. However, reinstatement is subject to proof of insurability (physical exam) and the repayment of all overdue premiums, plus interest.

61. **A**  The three non-forfeiture options are 1) cash surrender; 2) reduced paid-up; and 3) extended term. Automatic premium loan is a rider, not a non-forfeiture provision. If the owner of a cash value life insurance policy selects the reduced-paid up option, the insurer will issue him/her a new

whole life policy, without a physical exam, that is paid up until age 100, but with a reduced face amount.

62. **B**   Producers must make sure that annuity sales are "suitable" based upon the customer's investment objectives and needs.

63. **D**   The rules regarding replacement do not apply when replacing credit life, group life and some types of term life.

64. **C**   Although policy owners may often borrow as much as 90% of their cash value as a policy loan, they cannot borrow the face amount of their policy. Insurers will charge an annual rate of interest on policy loans as stated in the policy and if the interest is not paid, it will be added to the amount of the loan. Loans are not taxable.

65. **B**   The rules regarding replacement always apply when replacing cash value insurance products, such as whole life, universal life, endowments and even annuities.

66. **A**   Advertising is not prohibited, as long as the rules are followed.

67. **C**   An "absolute assignment" is an irrevocable change in the ownership of the policy, and is required whenever the policy owner makes either a viatical settlement or a life settlement. Although there is such a thing as an "irrevocable" beneficiary designation, most beneficiary designations are "revocable," meaning they can be changed.

68. **C**   Although a "joint life" policy covers two insureds, it only pays when the first party dies. However, there is such a thing as a "survivorship" life policy, which also covers two insureds, but only pays upon the death of the second party. Survivorship life policies are often used to pay estate taxes, which are due when the surviving spouse dies.

69. **C**   Immediate annuities are purchased with a single lump-sum and are annuitized "immediately," meaning that monthly payments begin right away. The annuity owner may elect to annuitize with a life income annuity, which has no beneficiary, or with a period certain or refund annuity, both of which have beneficiaries.

70. **C**   When converting group life coverage, the premium for the new individual policy is based upon the employee's current age at the time of conversion.

71. **B**   The various modes of paying life insurance premiums address the frequency of premium payments. Modes of payment include annual, semi-annual, quarterly and monthly. Since insurers usually levy a service fee on each payment other than annual, the more frequent the mode, the higher the cost. The least expensive mode of payment would be annual, and the mode with the highest cost would be monthly.

72. **D**   Since the agent is not a party to the contract, changes they make are not included in the "entire contract" provision. However, an agent is a party to the application, and they may make changes to it as long as such changes are initialed or signed by the applicant.

73. **A**   Under a "per capita" beneficiary designation, if you name two people as beneficiaries, they will share in the proceeds equally. But, if one of those people dies before the insured dies, then all the proceeds will go to the beneficiary who is still living. However, under a "per stirpes"

designation, if two people are named as beneficiary and one of those people dies before the insured dies, then their heir will move up to take their place as beneficiary.

74. **C** This is known as a "modified" premium policy. On a "graded" premium policy, the premium goes up gradually over a period of time.

75. **D** A Simplified Employee Pension (SEP) is an employer sponsored IRA. Contributions to the plan are not included in the employee's taxable income for the year, to the extent that they do not exceed the maximums allowed. Distributions from a SEP are taxable as ordinary income when received at retirement.

76. **B** Insurable interest must exist at the time of application, and must be based either on family relationships or economics. A business has an economic insurable interest in their key employees, corporate officers and partners, but not in their customers.

77. **A** Section 1035 of the Internal Revenue Code permits life insurance and annuity contract holders to exchange one insurance product for another while deferring taxes. However, exchanges may not be made unless they leave the contract holder either in the same overall tax position or worse. Since annuity benefits payable to beneficiaries are taxable and life insurance proceeds are not, annuities cannot be exchanged for life insurance.

78. **D** Since the face amount of a level term policy never changes, this policy would pay $200,000 to the insured's beneficiary no matter when he/she dies, as long as he/she dies within the term of coverage.

79. **B** Since loans have to be subtracted from the policy owner's stated cash value, his/her cash surrender value would only be $1,000.

80. **C** Group life must be written to benefit employees and their beneficiaries, so the policy proceeds payable from a group life policy would not be a source of income to the employer.

81. **A** Since group life coverage is written to benefit employees, premiums paid by employers are tax deductible as a business expense. However, since key person is written to benefit the employer if the key person dies, premiums are not tax deductible, but policy proceeds payable to the employer would not be taxable.

82. **D** Although adjustable whole life insurance does have non-forfeiture benefits, they cannot be used to buy additional life insurance. Remember, non-forfeiture benefits are designed to protect the policy owner's cash value, and there are three of them: cash surrender, reduced paid-up and extended term.

83. **C** When a beneficiary elects to take the same amount every month as a settlement option, they have chosen the "fixed amount" option. This same amount will be paid out every month until all the proceeds plus interest have been distributed.

84. **C** Remember, the annuitant and the policy owner of an annuity are not necessarily the same person. Only the contract owner can take cash surrender.

85. **A** A "life income" annuity will make payments only until the annuitant dies. This pay-out option is seldom selected since it has no beneficiary.

86. **C** An "immediate annuity" is purchased with a single lump sum, and is annuitized right away. In other words, an immediate annuity does not have any accumulation (pay-in) period.

87. **C** 529 plans allow individuals to contribute to an account to pay a beneficiary's qualified higher education expenses. Contributions are made with after-tax dollars, but earnings accumulate on a tax-deferred basis. Although qualified distributions are free from income tax, non-qualified distributions are subject to income tax and a 10% penalty.

88. **B** Only mutual insurers pay dividends, and it is not guaranteed that they will. If paid, policy owners have several dividend options to choose from, including applying the dividend to their next premium, when due.

89. **C** By state law, life insurance policies are "contestable" for a maximum of two years, and are "incontestable" thereafter.

90. **C** Term life insurance is considered to be "temporary" coverage, since it only provides coverage for a specific period of time. Since term has no cash value, it is cheaper than buying permanent life insurance. However, most people who buy term life insurance are not covered when they die, since the "term" has expired.

91. **A** The "cost of insurance" rider provides for a waiver of the premium required to pay for the guaranteed death benefit that is provided by life insurance policies that have variable death benefits, such as universal and variable life, when the insured becomes totally disabled during the term of the policy.

92. **C** Although variable life insurance is considered to be a security, it does have a minimum guaranteed death benefit. If the cash value in the separate account increases beyond what is needed to fund the contract, excess cash value is created which causes the death benefit to increase beyond the minimum amount guaranteed in the contract. However, future fluctuations in the cash value can cause the death benefit to decline, but never below the minimum.

93. **C** A life settlement involves selling a life insurance policy for more than its cash value, but for less than its face amount. The amount the policy owner would receive for selling his/her policy, less expenses, is known as the policy's net value.

94. **D** Life settlement brokers earn a fee for putting a policy owner in touch with a life settlement provider. However, life settlement brokers represent the policy owner, not the provider.

95. **B** An agent's "express" authority is that which is written in their contract with the insurer they represent. However, agents have "implied" authority as well, which although it is not written down, is necessary for the agent to conduct their business.

96. **C** "Consideration" is defined as the exchange of value, which need not be equal. An applicant's consideration for a life insurance policy is the premium they pay plus the statements they make on their application, as stated in the consideration clause. Remember, consideration is a pre-requisite to a valid contract.

97. **D** An "absolute assignment" is executed as part of a life settlement contract. The seller of the policy assigns his/her ownership in the contract to the buyer of the policy, who then lists themselves as beneficiary. Once an absolute assignment is made, it cannot be revoked.

98. **B** There are two ways to determine how much life insurance an applicant needs: 1) the "needs" approach, which takes into consideration how much money will be needed to pay the insured's final expenses; or 2) the "human life value" approach, which takes into account the insured's lifetime earnings potential.

99. **D** Coverage is never effective until the premium is paid.

100. **B** On annual renewable term life insurance, the face amount remains level, but the premium increases every year since the insured is now another year older.

# Life Insurance

# FINAL EXAM B

1. On a Modified Endowment Contract (MEC), the IRS considers which of the following to be a "material change":

   A. Absolute assignment of ownership
   B. Decrease in the amount of dividends paid
   C. An increase in benefits
   D. A change in the beneficiary designation

2. Why would an annuitant consider making a 1035 exchange to another contract issued by the same insurer:

   A. The new contract has a higher interest rate
   B. The new contract has life insurance protection
   C. The old contract has higher interest rates
   D. The new contract will put him/her in an overall better tax position

3. A Survivorship Life insurance policy will pay benefits when the:

   A. First party dies
   B. Beneficiary of the first party dies
   C. The last party dies
   D. The beneficiary of the last party dies

4. Upon death of an annuitant during the accumulation period of a deferred annuity, the proceeds:

   A. Are taxable to the beneficiary above the annuitant's cost basis
   B. Are not taxable
   C. Are not included in the annuitant's estate
   D. Revert to the insurance company

5. All are characteristics of an immediate annuity, EXCEPT:

   A. There is no pay-in or accumulation period
   B. It systematically liquidates your principal and interest over time
   C. They are often used to fund structured settlements or lottery pay-outs
   D. They are purchased with installment payments

6.      The life span of the beneficiary of a life insurance policy is needed to:

   A.   Determine the total amount payable under the policy
   B.   Determine the amount of monthly payments that will be taxable if the life income option is selected
   C.   Determine the amount of taxes due if cash is selected as a settlement option
   D.   Determine the amount of capital gain due

7.      A pure life annuity is also known as a:

   A.   Refund annuity
   B.   Joint and survivor annuity
   C.   Life income annuity
   D.   Period certain annuity

8.      Life insurance sold to fund a small partnership buy/sell agreement is also called:

   A.   Key person
   B.   Cross purchase plan
   C.   Disability buy out
   D.   Split dollar plan

9.      All of the following are true about equity indexed annuities, EXCEPT:

   A.   They keep pace with inflation over a period of time
   B.   Their return is based on the S&P 500
   C.   They have purchasing power risk
   D.   They have little inflation risk

10.     A life insurance rider added to cover a child is usually what type of insurance:

   A.   Whole life
   B.   Level term
   C.   Decreasing term
   D.   Increasing term

11.     Life insurance policy dividends are considered to be:

   A.   A sharing of company profits with the stockholders
   B.   A return of a premium overcharge
   C.   A sharing of company profits with the policyholders
   D.   A guaranteed amount paid to reduce the cost of insurance

12.     Which type of life insurance does not permit changes in death benefits:

   A.   Adjustable whole life
   B.   Universal life
   C.   Modified whole life
   D.   Variable/Universal whole life

13.     Which is not a reason to buy life insurance on the life of a child:

    A.    To provide the child with benefits in the event that a parent dies
    B.    To provide cash value for college
    C.    To provide coverage in the event the child dies
    D.    To provide for the child's retirement

14.     Parents of children ages six and eight are considering IRAs for them.  What would you advise them:

    A.    To go ahead, since there is no minimum age limit to establish an IRA
    B.    To consider alternative investments, since IRAs are only for those with earnings and their spouses
    C.    To go ahead, since IRAs earn tax deferred income which would supplement the children's eventual retirement
    D.    To go ahead, since the children could withdraw all the earnings without income tax for college tuition later on

15.     A Keogh Plan is a qualified plan for:

    A.    Anyone with earned income
    B.    The self-employed
    C.    Corporate officers
    D.    Employees of public schools and universities

16.     Which of the following would have the lowest mortality rate:

    A.    50 year old female
    B.    50 year old male
    C.    60 year old female
    D.    60 year old male

17.     To take cash surrender on an annuity, the insurer needs the permission of the:

    A.    Annuitant
    B.    Insured
    C.    Owner
    D.    Beneficiary

18.     A client who contributes to a 403b TSA on a payroll deduction basis may:

    A.    Also make non-deductible contributions to a ROTH IRA up to specified limits
    B.    Also make deductible contributions to a ROTH IRA up to specified limits
    C.    Not also contribute to a ROTH IRA
    D.    Also make deductible contributions to a ROTH IRA without limit

19.     A life insurance benefit payable while the insured is still living is:

    A.    Double indemnity
    B.    Accelerated benefits
    C.    Fixed amount settlement option
    D.    Accidental death benefit

20. A producer uses the "needs" approach when selling life insurance to determine:

   A. What the premium needs to be
   B. What the commission needs to be
   C. How much coverage is necessary to cover final expenses
   D. The client's human life value

21. A stock insurer who issues non-participating life insurance policies:

   A. Might pay taxable dividends to shareholders
   B. Might distribute taxable dividends to policyholders
   C. Treats dividends as a return of an overpayment of premium
   D. Guarantees dividends to policyholders

22. All of the following are false about single premium whole life insurance, EXCEPT:

   A. They are always participating policies
   B. They have an immediate cash value
   C. The insurer may ask for more premium later if expenses go up
   D. Loans are taxable

23. A preferred risk has a(an):

   A. Longer than average life expectancy
   B. Average life expectancy
   C. Shorter than average life expectancy
   D. Higher than average premium

24. A 10-year level renewable term insurance policy:

   A. May not be renewed
   B. May be renewed without a physical exam
   C. Must be renewed at the same rates
   D. May be renewed with a new contestability period

25. Which whole life non-forfeiture option provides lifetime coverage:

   A. Extended term
   B. Reduced Paid up
   C. Paid up additions
   D. Life income

26. If the beneficiary of a life policy wants the proceeds to be paid out in equal monthly payments, they should select which settlement option:

   A. Period certain
   B. Fixed period
   C. Fixed amount
   D. Interest

27.     A 30-year-old client invests $20,000 in a deferred annuity, which grows to $50,000 in 20 years. At age 50, the annuitant takes a partial withdrawal in the amount of $10,000. How is this taxed:

    A.      100% capital gain
    B.      100% ordinary income
    C.      100% ordinary income plus 10% penalty
    D.      No tax is due since it is less than his/her cost basis

28.     If the interest on a policy loan is not repaid:

    A.      It will be added to the premiums due
    B.      It will be added to the amount of the loan outstanding
    C.      It will have no effect on the policy benefits
    D.      It will be turned over to a collection agency

29.     A revocable beneficiary:

    A.      Must give their consent before a loan may be taken
    B.      Must give their consent before cash surrender may be taken
    C.      Has no vested interest in the policy
    D.      May never be changed

30.     Distributions taken from a tax-sheltered annuity (TSA) are:

    A.      Not taxable
    B.      Taxable as capital gains in the year of the distribution
    C.      Taxable as ordinary income in the year of the distribution
    D.      Never subject to IRS 10% early withdrawal penalties

31.     On her 401k, Dana (age 60) takes a distribution and rolls it over to an IRA within 60 days. Which of the following is true:

    A.      There is a 10% IRS early withdrawal penalty
    B.      The amount distributed is subject to ordinary income tax
    C.      The amount of the distribution is reduced by the amount of a 20% withholding tax
    D.      No taxes are due since she is over age 59 ½

32.     On a refund annuity, who is entitled to the refund:

    A.      The owner
    B.      The annuitant
    C.      The insurer
    D.      The beneficiary

33.     Upon death of an annuitant, proceeds payable to a beneficiary are:

    A.      Tax free
    B.      Taxed as ordinary income above the annuitant's invested capital
    C.      Taxed as capital gains above the annuitant's invested capital
    D.      100% taxable

34. Universal life insurance offers all of the following, EXCEPT:

    A. Tax deferred earnings on the cash value account
    B. Guaranteed minimum rate of return
    C. Flexibility of premium payments
    D. Level costs of insurance throughout the insured's lifespan

35. All of the following are false about insurable interest on life insurance, EXCEPT:

    A. It must be based upon economics
    B. A son-in-law has an insurable interest in his father-in-law
    C. It may be based upon friendship
    D. It must exist at the time of the application

36. On a tax deferred annuity, distributions must begin by age:

    A. 59 1/2
    B. 70 1/2
    C. 75
    D. No age limit applies

37. All are true about Joint Life policies, EXCEPT:

    A. The premium would be lower than it would be for two individual policies
    B. They pay when the last party dies
    C. They are usually whole life insurance
    D. They pay when the first party dies

38. The face amount of a Credit Life policy is limited by:

    A. The age of the insured
    B. The amount of the loan
    C. Federal law
    D. There are no limits

39. Insurable interest does not exist on a:

    A. Sibling
    B. Life long friend
    C. Child
    D. Spouse

40. If an insurer waives a legal right under the policy, they can no longer assert that right. This is known as:

    A. Estoppel
    B. Rescission
    C. Waiver
    D. Assignment

41.  What insurance product has a flexible premium, fixed rate of return, tax deferred growth and a death benefit equal to the cash value:

    A.  Whole life
    B.  Immediate annuity
    C.  Endowment
    D.  Flexible premium deferred annuity

42.  All are true about a fixed annuity, EXCEPT:

    A.  The annuitant bears the investment risk
    B.  The purchasing power goes up in times of deflation
    C.  The purchasing power goes down in times of inflation
    D.  Monthly payments to the annuitant are made in a constant amount

43.  Which of the following beneficiary designations on a life insurance policy is "by class":

    A.  To both my children, Suzy and Scott equally
    B.  To my estate
    C.  To all my children
    D.  To my family trust

44.  The cash value of a life insurance policy may be used for all, EXCEPT:

    A.  To supplement retirement
    B.  To generate funds that will be available 15 years from now
    C.  To serve as collateral for a policy loan
    D.  To meet the expenses of college tuition one year after purchase

45.  Key Person life insurance:

    A.  Helps pay for the cost of training a new employee
    B.  Has tax deductible premiums
    C.  Has taxable benefits
    D.  Pays benefits to the spouse of a key person

46.  On most qualified retirement plans, such as traditional IRAs, distributions must begin no later than age 70 ½. If they don't, an excise tax of _____ applies:

    A.  10%
    B.  20%
    C.  50%
    D.  100%

47.  Death of an annuity owner may create a tax burden for the beneficiary. How can the spouse of an annuity owner, as beneficiary, avoid this burden:

    A.  There is no way to avoid it
    B.  They may continue the contract and defer taxes
    C.  They may receive a non-taxable death benefit
    D.  They may take a lump sum and defer taxes

48.   Tom and Joe are 21 year old identical twins in good health.  Both have $500 a year to spend on Life Insurance.  Tom buys five year renewable term and Joe buys Whole Life.  All are true EXCEPT:

A.   Joe's policy will provide more coverage in the early years
B.   Tom has temporary protection
C.   Joe has permanent protection
D.   Tom's policy will provide more coverage in the early years

49.   A producer's responsibility to the insurer they represent is known as the:

A.   Aleatory nature of contracts
B.   Principal of Indemnity
C.   Doctrine of Agency
D.   Doctrine of Utmost Good Faith

50.   Failure of an insurer to enforce a provision in their policy is known as:

A.   Estoppel
B.   Rescission
C.   Waiver
D.   Breach of warranty

51.   Under Privacy Protection laws, regarding an insurer's release of an insured's non-public information to an unaffiliated third party, all of the following are true EXCEPT:

A.   The insured must agree to the release of such information
B.   The insurer or producer must notify, explain and allow the insured to "opt out"
C.   The producer's obligation to notify and explain the insured's rights may be satisfied by joint notification with the insurer
D.   The phrase "opt out" means that the insured may refuse to allow such information to be released

52.   For tax purposes, all Modified Endowment Contracts (MEC) issued to an insured will be considered to be one Modified Endowment Contract if issued:

A.   On the same day
B.   Within 90 days
C.   Within 12 months
D.   Within 24 months

53.   Which financial services product creates an immediate estate:

A.   Immediate annuity
B.   Deferred annuity
C.   Life insurance
D.   Period certain annuity

54. A product with a flexible premium, guaranteed minimum rate of return, tax deferred earnings and a tax free death benefit is:

    A. Variable life
    B. Flexible premium deferred annuity
    C. Endowment
    D. Universal life

55. In the absence of a monetary interest, insurable interest may be based upon:

    A. Friendship
    B. Distant family relationships
    C. Close kinship
    D. Admiration

56. All of the following are true about the payout period on a Joint and Survivor annuity EXCEPT:

    A. It pays monthly until the last annuitant dies
    B. It has no beneficiary
    C. Monthly payments are reduced when the first annuitant dies
    D. Monthly payments are higher than they would be on Joint Life annuity

57. All of the following are true about Joint Life insurance policies EXCEPT:

    A. They only pay when the first party dies
    B. They are often written to pay estate taxes
    C. Proceeds are tax free
    D. They cover two insureds

58. The Human Life Value approach to Life insurance mainly considers the insured's:

    A. Funeral expenses
    B. Future earnings
    C. Mortgage obligation
    D. Children's college education expenses

59. When an insured with a terminal illness sells their Life insurance policy to an investor, it is known as:

    A. A collateral assignment
    B. Accelerated benefits
    C. Cash surrender
    D. A viatical settlement

60. Producers should be very concerned about possible Errors and Omissions when:

    A. Processing a change of beneficiary designation
    B. Issuing Conditional Receipts
    C. Replacing Life insurance
    D. Accepting premiums

61. Industrial Life insurance is typically sold by:

    A.  Debit agents
    B.  Independent agents
    C.  Captive agents
    D.  Exclusive agents

62. Mr. Smith bought a Life insurance policy on his six year old son, Jimmy, naming himself as beneficiary. Now that Jim is 18 years old, Mr. Smith may transfer all rights of ownership in the policy to him by executing a(n):

    A.  Viatical settlement
    B.  Absolute assignment
    C.  Acceleration of benefits
    D.  Change of beneficiary

63. Which of the following is true when Life insurance is used by an employer as an Executive Bonus plan:

    A.  The employer pays the premium
    B.  The employer is the beneficiary
    C.  The employer owns the policy
    D.  It is a type of group Life insurance

64. When an employer and an employee share the cost of the employee's Life insurance, it is known as:

    A.  Non-contributory group Life
    B.  A split dollar plan
    C.  Key Person Life
    D.  Partnership insurance

65. All are true about Group Life insurance EXCEPT:

    A.  It is convertible to Whole Life for 31 days after termination of employment
    B.  The employer is the master policyholder
    C.  The employer may tax deduct the premiums paid
    D.  Proceeds paid to the beneficiary are taxable

66. All of the following are guaranteed on a Participating Whole Life insurance policy EXCEPT:

    A.  The dividend scale
    B.  The cash value
    C.  The rate of return
    D.  The face amount

67.     All of the following are true about Adjustable Life insurance EXCEPT:

    A.    It is a type of Whole Life insurance
    B.    A physical exam is always required when premiums are adjusted
    C.    The face amount, premium or length of protection may be adjusted
    D.    Adjustments may cause a change in the coverage plan initially selected

68.     All of the following are true about the cash value in Life insurance policies EXCEPT:

    A.    Term insurance has no cash value
    B.    The cash value in a Whole Life policy is based upon the level premium concept
    C.    On limited pay Whole Life, the cash value will equal the face amount at the end of the premium paying period
    D.    Single premium Whole Life policies have an immediate cash value

69.     Investment income earned by Life insurance companies:

    A.    Is added to the cost of insurance
    B.    Helps offset the premiums that insurance companies charge
    C.    Is added to the cost of mortality when calculating premiums
    D.    Is guaranteed to exceed the rate of inflation

70.     All of the following are true about an agent or producer EXCEPT:

    A.    Insurers are responsible for all acts of their agents
    B.    Notice of Claim to an agent is the same as notice to the insurer
    C.    Agents may not change policy provisions
    D.    Agents act as fiduciaries when handling premiums

71.     Annuity contracts are based upon the life of which of the following:

    A.    The beneficiary
    B.    The contract owner
    C.    The annuitant
    D.    The insured

72.     When the initial premium is paid along with the application for Life insurance, the agent or producer should give the applicant a:

    A.    Binder
    B.    Binding receipt
    C.    Conditional receipt
    D.    Certificate of Insurance

73.     All of the following are true about the Fair Credit Reporting Act EXCEPT:

    A.    It regulates Consumer Reporting Agencies
    B.    It requires applicants to be pre-notified that a report may be ordered
    C.    It requires post-notification in the event of an adverse underwriting decision
    D.    It requires applicants to sue in order to get inaccurate data corrected

74. The average person is known as a:

    A.  Standard risk
    B.  Preferred risk
    C.  Non-standard risk
    D.  Sub-standard risk

75. A person who is in good health and does not drink or smoke is known as a:

    A.  Standard risk
    B.  Preferred risk
    C.  Non-standard risk
    D.  Sub-standard risk

76. What changes on a Term Life insurance policy when an insured exercises the re-entry option:

    A.  Face amount
    B.  Premium
    C.  Cash value
    D.  Beneficiary

77. A 60 year old client buys a $100,000 Immediate Annuity.  Which pay out option will pay him/her the highest monthly payment for life:

    A.  Life income
    B.  Refund
    C.  Joint and Survivor
    D.  Period certain

78. Most people buy deferred annuities to:

    A.  Earn tax deferred income to supplement retirement
    B.  Avoid income taxes
    C.  Provide a tax free death benefit to a beneficiary
    D.  Provide funds for a child's education

79. The insuring agreement or clause in a Life insurance policy contains all of the following EXCEPT:

    A.  The name of the insurer
    B.  The name of the insured
    C.  The coverages
    D.  How to change the beneficiary

80. A collateral assignment on a Life insurance policy:

    A.  Is an absolute change of ownership
    B.  Is a partial assignment of some rights to a creditor
    C.  Designates an irrevocable beneficiary
    D.  Allows early payment of proceeds in the event of a terminal illness

81. All of the following are true about the reinstatement of a lapsed Life insurance policy EXCEPT:

    A. Applicants must apply within a certain period of time
    B. Applicants must pay back premiums
    C. Reinstatement is based upon current age
    D. Applicants must pass a physical exam

82. All are false about Automatic Premium Loan on a Life insurance policy EXCEPT:

    A. It is a non-forfeiture provision
    B. It pays premiums due at the end of the grace period
    C. It is a rider requiring the payment of an additional premium
    D. It is attached to all Whole Life and Term Life policies

83. Which Life insurance settlement option takes into account the life span of the beneficiary:

    A. Life income option
    B. Fixed amount option
    C. Fixed period option
    D. Interest option

84. Under Internal Revenue Code Section 1035, an annuity may be exchanged for:

    A. Whole Life insurance
    B. For another annuity written on a different annuitant with the same insurer
    C. Term Life insurance
    D. For another annuity written on the same annuitant with a different insurer

85. An insured on a tight budget who has a Whole Life insurance policy written by a mutual insurer should select which dividend option:

    A. Cash
    B. Reduction of premium
    C. Paid-up additions
    D. Interest option

86. A Life insurance rider that provides Whole Life on the primary insured and Term Life on the insured's spouse and children is the:

    A. Combination rider
    B. Family income rider
    C. Family maintenance rider
    D. Family rider

87. If an insured buys the Return of Premium Rider and dies, the policy will pay the beneficiary:

    A. The face amount only
    B. All premiums paid up until the date of death
    C. The cash value plus the face amount
    D. The face amount plus all premiums paid up until the date of death

88. Which annuity guarantees payments for a specific period of time even if the annuitant dies:

    A.    Refund
    B.    Period certain
    C.    Life Income
    D.    Joint and survivor

89. All of the following are true about annuities EXCEPT:

    A.    The rate of return on an Equity Indexed Annuity is based upon the performance of the Standard and Poor's index
    B.    An immediate annuity is not suitable for a parent planning for a child's college education
    C.    Upon death of an annuitant, proceeds payable to a beneficiary of an annuity are always tax free
    D.    Most annuities are purchased with after-tax dollars

90. The annuitant's cost basis on a non-qualified deferred annuity is:

    A.    Zero
    B.    The amount of the premiums paid in
    C.    The value of the annuity account
    D.    The amount of the interest earned

91. Mary brings in a business partner instead of operating as a sole proprietor. This is a form of risk:

    A.    Retention
    B.    Avoidance
    C.    Sharing
    D.    Transfer

92. On a 403b Tax Sheltered Annuity, all of the following are true EXCEPT:

    A.    Early withdrawals prior to age 59 ½ are subject to a 10% IRS penalty
    B.    The annuitants cost basis is zero
    C.    Distributions are not taxable
    D.    Contributions are made via payroll deduction

93. An employee covered by a Group Life policy elects to cover three dependents as well. How many Certificates of Insurance must the group insurer issue:

    A.    One
    B.    Two
    C.    Three
    D.    Four

94. A producer or agent could go to jail for all of the following EXCEPT:

    A.    Selling insurance in this state with a non-resident insurance license
    B.    Embezzlement
    C.    Writing threatening letters to public officials
    D.    Fraud

95.    Although excluded in the contract, a court may direct the insurer to pay a claim under the Doctrine of:

A.    Utmost Good Faith
B.    Reasonable Expectations
C.    Adhesion
D.    Indemnification

96.    Buying insurance does all of the following EXCEPT:

A.    Help you sleep at night
B.    Eliminates the risk
C.    Helps with the feeling of uncertainty
D.    Transfers the risk

97.    A contract where the outcome depends upon chance and the consideration is not equal is known as:

A.    Unilateral
B.    Aleatory
C.    A contract of Adhesion
D.    A contract of Indemnity

98.    All of the following are true about employer Group Life EXCEPT:

A.    The employer is the master policy holder
B.    The employees receive Certificates of Insurance
C.    It is convertible for 31 days after termination of employment
D.    Conversion is based upon original age

99.    A client bought an annual renewable Term policy with a face amount of $100,000 on June 1, 2010 for an annual premium of $200. If he/she died on June 20$^{th}$, 2011 without paying his/her renewal premium when due, the insurer would pay:

A.    Zero
B.    $99,800
C.    $100,000
D.    $100,000 less any outstanding loans

100.    All of the following are non-forfeiture options on a Whole Life insurance policy EXCEPT:

A.    Cash surrender
B.    Paid-up additions
C.    Extended term
D.    Reduced paid-up

1. **C** Modified Endowment Contracts (MECs) are life insurance policies that build cash value too fast. As a result, under IRS regulations, they lose their preferential tax treatment, meaning that loans are taxable and cash surrenders under age 59 ½ are subject to a 10% penalty.

    Insurers administer the "seven-pay test" at policy inception to determine if the cash value will exceed the amount of the total premiums paid in by the end of the seventh year. If it does, the policy will be classified as an MEC. However, even if a policy is not classified as an MEC, the occurrence of a "material change" (such as the payment of substantial additional premiums to increase the cash value benefits) at any time could cause it to be reclassified as an MEC.

    Single premium Universal Life policies were often considered to be MECs. Remember, UL policies also have flexible premium schedules, which allow policy owners to pay in far more than the minimum premium required. MECs are not illegal, but clients generally don't want them due to the adverse tax consequences.

2. **A** IRC Section 1035 allows a policy owner to exchange a life insurance (or annuity) contract for another as long as the contract holder is still in the same overall tax position (or worse) after the exchange.

    For example, you can exchange traditional whole life insurance for variable whole life insurance, since you would still be in the same overall tax position upon death since life insurance benefits paid to a beneficiary are not taxable. Or, you could exchange a fixed annuity for a variable annuity, since annuity earnings are taxable to your beneficiary upon your death.

    However, you could not exchange an annuity for life insurance, since that exchange would place you in a better overall tax position upon death. But, you could exchange a life insurance policy for an annuity, since you would be worse off tax wise.

    Although a 1035 exchange may be made between different insurers, the contracts must be on the life of the same person. Most exchanges are done to obtain a higher yield (interest rate).

3. **C** There are two types of "joint life" insurance policies. Remember, a joint life policy covers two insureds and would be cheaper than buying separate individual policies on each person. Most joint life policies are set up as "first-to-die," meaning that benefits are paid upon the death of the first insured only, with nothing paid when the second party dies.

    However, a "survivorship" joint life policy pays nothing when the first party dies. It only pays upon the death of the second insured. Historically, survivorship life insurance was sold to provide proceeds to pay estate taxes, which are due when the second spouse dies.

4. **A**  Most annuities are "non-qualified," meaning that the premiums were paid-in with after-tax dollars. Deferred annuities have two distinct stages: 1) the accumulation (or pay-in) period and 2) the annuity (or pay-out) period. Although there is always a beneficiary during the pay-in period, there may or may not be a beneficiary during the pay-out period, depending upon the pay-out option selected.

   If an annuitant dies during pay-in, the value of their account will be paid to their designated beneficiary (or to their estate, if no beneficiary has been listed). However, proceeds paid-out above what the annuitant paid-in will be taxable to the beneficiary as ordinary income. The annuitant's contributions (or cost basis) will be returned tax free, since they have already been taxed.

5. **D**  Although deferred annuities are often purchased with installment payments, immediate annuities must be purchased with a lump sum single premium. For example, Aunt Mary dies and leaves you $100,000. You could use the money to buy an immediate annuity which would start paying you monthly payments right away for life. In other words, an immediate annuity has no pay-in or accumulation period. You buy it for cash and "annuitize" immediately.

6. **B**  Proceeds of a life policy paid-out as cash to a beneficiary are not taxable. However, if the beneficiary selects the life income annuity pay-out option, the insurer would need to know the beneficiary's life span in order to determine how much of the monthly payment would be taxable.

   For example, you died leaving your beneficiary the proceeds of a $100,000 life insurance policy. If the beneficiary elected to take a lump sum settlement in cash, no taxes are due.

   But if your beneficiary elected to instead take monthly payments in the form of a life income annuity of $500 a month (or $6,000 a year) over their 20 year life span, they would receive a total of $120,000. This extra $20,000 represents earnings in the account over the 20 year period and would be taxable as ordinary income to the beneficiary. If the beneficiary continued to live beyond his/her 20 year life span, monthly payments would continue, but would be fully taxable since the tax free proceeds have been recovered.

7. **C**  The "pure" or life income annuity pay-out option is considered to be the most risky since it has no beneficiary. If the annuitant dies during the pay-out period before collecting the value of their account, the insurer keeps whatever is left. However, based upon the concept of "risk and reward," this pay-out option would have the highest monthly payments to the annuitant while they are alive. This option is seldom selected.

8. **B**  Life insurance is often used as a funding vehicle for partnership "buy/sell" agreements. For example, Mr. Q is in an equal partnership with Mr. T. Both partners are married and the business is currently valued at $1 million. The parties hire a lawyer to draft a "buy/sell" agreement which states that if Mr. Q dies, his interest goes to his spouse, but she agrees to sell it to Mr. T for $500,000, who agrees to buy it for that amount and continue the business as a sole proprietorship.

   The agreement also states that if Mr. T dies, his interest will go to his spouse, who agrees to sell it to Mr. Q for $500,000, who agrees to buy it for that amount. However, since neither Mr. Q nor Mr. T have the necessary funds available to make such a purchase, life insurance is often used to "fund" the "cross purchase" agreement.

Mr. T buys a $500,000 life policy on Mr. Q, naming himself as beneficiary. Mr. Q also buys a $500,000 life policy on Mr. T, naming himself as beneficiary. If Mr. Q dies, the tax free policy proceeds are payable to Mr. T, who in turn uses the money to buy out Mrs. Q, and vice versa.

Cross purchase buy/sell agreements are also used in small corporate situations. The corporation buys life insurance on each stockholder, naming themselves as beneficiary. If a stockholder dies, the life proceeds are paid tax free to the corporation that uses the money to buy out the shares now held by the deceased stockholder's spouse. Premiums are not tax deductible.

9. **C** Although an Equity Indexed Annuity (EIA) is not considered to be a security, since performance of an EIA is often linked to the performance of the Standard & Poor's 500 index, EIAs have no purchasing power risk. The S&P 500 index is a broad based index whose performance has outpaced the rate of inflation over a period of time.

   It is fixed annuities that have purchasing power risk, since their fixed rate of return could be less than the rate of inflation. Purchasing power risk is also known as inflation risk.

10. **B** A "rider" is something added to a policy to modify its terms, usually for an additional premium charge. The cheapest way to provide life insurance coverage for your entire family is to add a "family" rider to your whole life insurance policy. This rider provides level, convertible term coverage for your spouse and minor children.

    For example, you have a $100,000 whole life policy on yourself. You could add a family rider to cover your spouse for $50,000 for 10 years and each of your children for $5,000 until they reach the age of majority. "Level" refers to the face amount of the rider, which remains constant until expiration. "Convertible" means that the family members could convert to whole life prior to expiration without a physical exam.

11. **B** Mutual insurers write "participating" policies, which means that their policy owners MAY receive dividends, at the discretion of the Board of Directors. If paid, such dividends are not taxable, since the IRS considers them to be a return of a premium overcharge. Remember, premiums are paid with after-tax dollars. Dividends may never be guaranteed. Stock insurers write "non-participating" policies.

12. **C** Modified whole life modify the premium, not the face amount. For example, an insurer may modify (discount) the premium for the first five years of a new policy in order to attract a client who may be on a limited income because they are in medical school. However, at the end of five years, the premium will increase dramatically.

    Adjustable, universal and variable/universal all permit changes in premiums, which in turn, changes the death benefit (or face amount) of the policy.

13. **A** A policy written on a child will pay benefits if the child dies, not the parent. Parents often purchase life insurance on children, which is a form of third party ownership. The parent is the owner, but the child is the insured. The parent has all the rights of ownership, but could "assign" the policy to the child when they reach the age of majority.

14. **B** IRAs are generally only for those who have earned income and it is unlikely children of these ages would have any. However, married persons with non-working spouses may set up separate "spousal" IRAs on behalf of their spouses who have no earnings.

15. **B** Keogh plans are qualified plans for the self-employed and partners. Corporate officers are not eligible. Employees of public schools are eligible for Internal Revenue Code Section 403b plans, also known as Tax Sheltered Annuities.

16. **A** Life insurance rates and benefits are based upon the Law of Large Numbers, also known as a Mortality Table. This table is developed by actuaries and is used to determine how many people of a certain age will die each year. The table starts at age zero (newborns) and ends at age 100, when everyone is considered to have died.

    Of course, the older you are, the greater the chance of mortality (death). Further, men have shorter life spans than do women. Larger insurers develop their own tables, while smaller insurers tend to use the Commissioners Standard Ordinary (or CSO) table, which is the industry standard. Tables are updated periodically as life spans lengthen.

17. **C** The owner of an annuity and the annuitant are usually the same person, but don't have to be. For example, you (the owner) could buy an annuity on your child (the annuitant). The contract would be based upon the annuitant's life span, but you would retain all the rights of ownership.

18. **A** Anyone with earned income may contribute to an IRA regardless of whether or not they are covered by another qualified plan. However, contributions to a ROTH IRA are NEVER tax deductible. Don't confuse deductibility with eligibility.

19. **B** Accelerated benefits may be paid out to an insured while still living. For example, if an insured has a terminal illness he/she may request that the insurer pay out part of his/her death benefit early. The insured may use the funds for any purpose, but any amount paid out will reduce the amount paid to his/her beneficiary upon his/her eventual death. Accelerated benefits are not considered to be a loan and are not taxable.

20. **C** Agents (or Producers) use one of two methods to determine how much life insurance is appropriate: 1) The "needs" approach calculates how much money the insured's family will need after his/her death to pay for his funeral, mortgage and children's education; 2) The "human life value" approach calculates how much money the insured's family will lose due to his/her premature death. For example, if a 40 year old man making $100,000 a year died, his family will lose $2,500,000 based upon his future earnings over the next 25 years.

21. **A** Stock insurers are owned by their shareholders, who MAY receive taxable dividends, if declared by the company's Board of Directors. However, dividends may never be guaranteed.

22. **B** Although EXCEPT questions are usually looking for the false answer, this one is looking for the response that is true. Although it will usually take three years for a minimum premium whole life policy to develop a cash value, a single premium whole life policy will develop a cash value right away.

    Initially, many Universal Life policies were sold to wealthy persons who could afford to pay up the policy by paying a large single premium. Such policies developed an immediate cash value, which earned high rates of tax deferred interest that resulted in rapid cash value accumulation. Eventually, the IRS recognized that such policies were more like investments than life insurance, and reclassified them as Modified Endowments.

23. **A** Life insurers generally have three categories of risks: 1) Preferred: A client with good health and no dangerous hobbies, occupational hazards or bad habits; 2) Standard: The average person,

upon which the standard mortality table is based; and 3) Non-Standard:  A client who may be expected to have a shorter life span due to bad health, dangerous hobbies, occupational hazards and/or bad habits.  A preferred risk would be expected to live longer and would pay the lowest premium for life insurance coverage.  Non-standard (or sub-standard) would pay the most.

24. **B**   Most term insurance is renewable up to certain ages as stated in the policy.  Remember, the word "term" means time.  A 10 year level term policy has a level premium for 10 years, which is based upon the client's average age.  At the end of 10 years, the client may renew it by simply paying the premium, which will be based upon the client's average age for the next 10 years.  No physical exam is required and neither the suicide clause nor the incontestability clause starts over.

However, some insurers offer a "re-entry option" upon term renewal.  If the insured can pass a physical exam, the insurer will renew the policy at a lower rate than that offered to insureds who either decline to take or fail to pass a physical exam.

25. **B**   All cash value life insurance policies must contain "non-forfeiture" options or provisions, which are also known as "guaranteed" values.  In other words, the cash value in the policy belongs to the policy owner and cannot be forfeited to the insurer if the policy lapses.

There are three non-forfeiture options:  1) Cash surrender; 2) Reduced Paid-Up; and 3) Extended Term.  Upon lapse, the policy owner can simply ask the insurer to send him/her his/her accumulated cash value (cash surrender), which is taxable to the extent that it exceeds the amount of premiums paid in.  Or, the policy owner can ask the insurer to keep his/her cash value and use it as a single premium to buy him/her a new smaller whole life policy that is paid-up for life, or age 100, whichever comes first (reduced paid-up).  Or, the policy owner can ask the insurer to keep his/her cash value and use it as a single premium to buy him/her a new term policy with the same face amount as his/her original policy for as long as the money will last (extended term).

All three of these options (or provisions) are required by state law and the policy owner may choose which one they prefer at any time.  No physical exam is required to exercise any of these options and no agent is involved.  Of course, none of these options apply if the client's original policy was term life, since term has no cash value to forfeit.

26. **C**   There are five life insurance settlement options: 1) cash; 2) fixed period; 3) fixed amount; 4) interest only; and 5) the annuity option.  If the beneficiary selects the fixed amount option, the proceeds will be paid out in equal monthly installments until they are exhausted.

27. **C**   According to IRS rules, partial withdrawals from annuities during the accumulation period are treated as interest earnings first, even if the withdrawal is less than the client's cost basis.  Further, a 10% premature distribution penalty will apply if the client is under age 59 ½.

28. **B**   Interest on life insurance policy loans accrues annually on a pre-paid basis.  Assuming the interest rate on a policy loan is 8% (the maximum allowed in most states), a client borrowing $10,000 from his/her insurer using his/her cash value as collateral would actually owe $10,800 on day one.  Although the client may repay the loan plus interest at any time, there is no requirement that he/she do so.

In other words, the interest on the loan will continue to accrue on an annual basis, which will have the effect of increasing the total amount owed.  Once the amount owed equals the collateral (the cash value in the policy), the policy will lapse unless the client begins repayment.  Of course, if the client dies with a loan outstanding, the amount of the loan plus accrued interest will be subtracted from what the beneficiary will receive.

29. **C**  The owner of a life insurance policy may change (or revoke) the beneficiary at any time, unless he/she initially made an "irrevocable" designation. Irrevocable designations are rare, although they are sometimes required as part of a property settlement in the event of a divorce. Irrevocable beneficiaries have a "vested" interest in the policy, meaning that the owner could not take out a policy loan without their prior permission. Most beneficiary designations are "revocable."

30. **C**  Tax sheltered annuities (or TSAs) are qualified retirement plans that are available to employees of public schools, certain types of hospitals and non-profit charities on a payroll deduction basis. They are also known as IRC 403b plans and are similar to 401k plans. Since contributions to the plan are made with before tax dollars, 100% of amounts distributed (which include tax deferred earnings) are taxable as ordinary income in the year of the distribution.

31. **C**  Distributions from a 401k plans are taxable as ordinary income in the year of the distribution. However, if the distribution is rolled over to a Traditional IRA, taxes are deferred until the required minimum IRA distributions begin (which is generally no later than age 70 ½). However, since this client actually took a distribution (instead of making a trustee-to-trustee roll over), the distribution is subject to 20% withholding tax.

32. **D**  When electing a pay-out option, most annuitants will select the Life Income Annuity option with Refund, which eliminates virtually all the risk. For example, if an annuitant who has $100,000 in his/her account selects this pay-out option, the insurer will guarantee that at least $100,000 will be paid out to someone, either to the annuitant (if he/she lives) or to the beneficiary (if the annuitant dies before recovering his/her $100,000). Although the beneficiary disappears once the $100,000 has been paid out, the annuitant could receive more than $100,000, since payments are guaranteed for as long as he/she lives.

33. **B**  Although life insurance death benefits are tax free, annuity death benefits (which consist of the annuitant's invested capital plus earnings) are taxable as ordinary income to the beneficiary to the extent that they exceed the annuitant's cost basis (or invested capital). Remember, most annuities are purchased with after-tax dollars. Capital gain tax treatment is not available on annuities, retirement plans or life insurance products.

34. **D**  A Universal Life (UL) insurance policy actually has two parts: 1) the protection part, which is actually level term insurance; and 2) the cash value part. Since the protection part is term insurance (which costs more each year as the insured grows older), an increasing portion of the premium paid is allocated to cost of the term coverage each year. In theory, the cost of insurance protection could eventually exceed the minimum premium, which would cause either the premium to go up, or the cash value to start going down.

However, UL does offer policy owners the advantage of flexible premiums, meaning that the owner may pay in more or less than the required minimum. However, if the owner pays in less or skips a premium payment, the insurer will debit (reduce) the insured's cash value account to make up the difference. If the owner pays in more, the additional premium will be credited to the cash value, which could possibly cause the policy to be reclassified as a Modified Endowment Contract (MEC), since the insurer's risk has diminished.

Since UL is not considered to be a security, it does offer a minimum guaranteed rate of return on the cash value. UL is also known as "interest sensitive" whole life, since the current rate of return may vary year to year above the minimum. As with all cash value life insurance, earnings are tax deferred.

35. **D** Insurable interest must exist at the time of application, and is based upon either immediate family relationships or economics. In other words, if you would benefit if another person continues to live, you have an insurable interest in that person. The purpose of insurable interest is to prevent gambling. If insurable interest was not required, you could buy a policy on anyone with a dangerous hobby and name yourself as beneficiary.

    However, insurable interest need not exist at the time of death. For example, you buy a policy on your spouse. You are the owner of the policy and your spouse is the insured. If you should get divorced, the policy is still valid as long as you continue to pay the premiums.

36. **D** Although most qualified retirement plans require minimum distributions to begin no later than April 1st of the year after you turn age 70 ½, no age limit applies to annuities. Remember, most annuities are non-qualified plans, so the annuitant may remain in the accumulation period indefinitely. However, upon death, any amount payable to a beneficiary above the annuitant's cost basis is taxable as ordinary income.

37. **B** Most Joint Life insurance policies are set up as first-to-die. In other words, two people (often husband and wife) are insured on the same policy. The proceeds are payable when the first party dies. Nothing is paid when the second party dies. However, the opposite would be true on a Joint Life Survivorship policy, which are set up as second-to-die.

38. **B** Credit Life insurance is usually a type of decreasing term insurance that is sold by lenders, such as banks and credit unions. The face amount of the policy is limited to the amount of the loan and the policy expiration date must coincide with the maturity date of the loan. Most credit life is sold as Group, with the lender (or creditor) as the Master Policy Holder and the debtor (or borrower) as the insured. The debtor receives a Certificate of Insurance, not a policy. The creditor is the beneficiary and the proceeds are paid directly to them to pay off the loan if the insured dies. Credit Life may not be used as Mortgage Protection Life insurance.

39. **B** On Life insurance, insurable interest must exist at the time of the application, and may be based upon economics or immediate kinship, but not friendship.

40. **A** Waiver and Estoppel are legal terms. A waiver is defined as the voluntary giving up of a legal right. Once given up, that right may no longer be asserted, which is known as "estoppel." Remember, insurance policies are legal contracts and are governed by contract law.

41. **D** Although annuities do not offer insurance protection, they do contain a death benefit which is equal to the contract's cash value at the time of death. Annuities also offer flexible premiums and tax deferred growth at a fixed rate during the accumulation period. Since this is an insurance exam, don't assume they are asking about variable annuities.

42. **A** Fixed annuities offer the annuitant a fixed, guaranteed rate of return, which makes them subject to "purchasing power" or "inflation" risk, which will occur if the rate of inflation exceeds the contract's fixed rate of return. However, since the rate of return is fixed, it is the insurer who bears the investment risk. If the insurer guarantees a 5% rate of return, but only earns 4% in their general account, they must make up the difference.

43. **C**  If you designate "all your children" as primary beneficiaries of your life insurance policy, you have made a "class" designation, rather than an individual designation.  In other words, any person who can prove that they are your child would be entitled to an equal share of the proceeds upon your death.

44. **D**  Although single premium whole life policies will develop a cash value immediately, most life insurance policies take three years to develop a cash value, and even then it will be minimal.  The cash value generally grows very gradually and it will take a long time before the cash value of a policy exceeds the amount of premiums paid.

45. **A**  Don't confuse Key Person Life insurance with Group Life.  If a business owner has a key person, they may purchase a life insurance policy on that person based upon their economic insurable interest.  If the key person dies, the proceeds of the policy are paid to the business owner who uses them to hire and train a new key person.  Premiums are not tax deductible but proceeds are not taxable.  Only Group Life has a tax deductible premium.

46. **C**  On a Traditional IRA, required minimum distributions must begin by April 1st of the year following the year the participant turns age 70 ½.  If they don't, a 50% excise tax is levied on the amount that should have been distributed, but wasn't.

47. **B**  Generally, annuity distributions made to a designated beneficiary when an annuitant dies during the accumulation period are taxable to that beneficiary to the extent that they exceed the annuitant's cost basis.  However, special rules apply if the beneficiary is the annuitant's spouse, which state that the spouse can "step into the shoes" of the deceased annuitant and continue the contract and defer taxes until they elect to annuitize the contract.

48. **A**  Since both Tom and Joe are spending the exact same amount on their life insurance ($500), the brother who purchased term (Tom) will be able to purchase a significantly higher amount of protection (face amount) than the brother who purchases whole life (Joe), since whole life is so expensive.  Term is considered to be temporary protection since it only provides protection for a limited period of time.  Whole life is considered to be permanent insurance since it never has to be renewed and provides protection until the insured dies or reaches age 100, whichever occurs first.

49. **C**  In most states, agents are also known as "producers."  Under the Doctrine of Agency, agents (or producers) represent the insurer as principal, and the insurer is responsible for the acts of their agents as long as they stay within the scope of their agent's authority, which is spelled out in their agent's contract with the insurer.

50. **C**  A "waiver" is defined as voluntarily giving up a legal right.  Once waived, this right may no longer be asserted, which is known as "estoppel".

51. **A**  Under state and Federal Privacy Protection laws, it is assumed that the insured has agreed to the release of their non-public personal information unless the insured specifically "opts out."  However, insurers are obligated to disclose their privacy protection practices to new clients at policy inception and again upon future renewal.

52. **C**  IRS rules state that all cash value life insurance policies issued to the same client within a 12 month period are to be combined for purposes of the seven-pay test, which states that if the total cash value exceeds the amount of the total premiums paid in by the end of the seventh policy year, the contracts are considered to be Modified Endowments (MECs), which would cause them

to lose their favorable tax treatment (loans are taxable and cash surrenders are subject to a 10% penalty).

53. **C**   Upon death, your life insurance policy will create an immediate estate, which your beneficiary may choose to liquidate by using the policy proceeds to purchase an annuity.

54. **D**   All life insurance policies provide the beneficiary with tax free death benefits.   However, Endowments (which are a type of life insurance that reach maturity at a predetermined age prior to age 100) have a fixed, level premium.   Variable life also has a fixed, level premium but does not have a guaranteed minimum rate of return since it is considered to be a securities product. Although annuities do have a death benefit during the accumulation period, it is limited to the account value.   There is no insurance protection feature on an annuity and no underwriting requirements.   However, Universal Life has all these features.

55. **C**   Insurable interest must exist at the time of application, and must either be based upon economics (such as key person life insurance or partnership insurance) or on immediate family relationships (kinship).

56. **D**   A Joint Life annuity is based upon the lives of two annuitants, but upon annuitization, monthly payments stop when the first annuitant dies.   Since a Joint and Survivor annuity will make monthly payments until the last annuitant dies, monthly payments would be lower.

57. **B**   You can assume that a Joint Life policy is written on a first-to-die basis unless the exam question specifically refers to a Joint Life "Survivorship" policy, which is set up to pay only when the second insured dies.   Survivorship Life insurance is often purchased to pay estate taxes, which are due when the second spouse dies.

58. **B**   It is the "Needs" approach to life insurance that considers the insured's immediate financial needs upon death.   The Human Life Value approach considers the future earnings the insured's family will lose in the event of his/her premature death.

59. **D**   One problem with life insurance is that you have to die to collect.   When someone gets a terminal illness, they need money right away for medical expenses, etc., so some policy owners may elect to sell their policy to an investor, which is known as a "viatical settlement."

For example, the insured/owner of a $100,000 policy may elect to sell his/her policy for a discounted price of $85,000 cash and execute an "absolute" assignment, assigning full ownership of the policy to the new owner.   Of course, the new owner will immediately name himself as beneficiary and is responsible for all future premiums.   When the prior owner dies, since he/she is still the person insured on the policy, the new owner will receive the policy proceeds, thereby making a profit of $15,000.

To solve this problem and eliminate the need for an owner/insured to make a viatical settlement, many insurers now include a policy provision entitled "accelerated benefits," which allows a policy owner to receive an advance on the death benefit if they get a terminal illness.   This is not a loan and is not taxable, but will reduce the amount the beneficiary will receive when the insured dies.

60. **C**   Although "replacement" of life insurance is not unlawful, "twisting" the facts in order to replace coverage is.   Replacement is defined as selling a client a new policy to replace one he/she already has.   Twisting is a form of misrepresentation, often related to replacement.

For example, when replacing existing coverage, an agent or producer should explain to their client that the suicide clause and incontestability clause start over on the new policy, even if the new policy is written with the same insurer. Since replacement may be detrimental to the client, it could be grounds for errors and omissions liability. Most states require that producers give clients a Notice Regarding Replacement that explains the possible negative aspects of a replacing transaction.

61. **A**  "Industrial" Life insurance was sold during the great depression of the 1930s by "debit" agents who called on their clients door-to-door to collect a weekly premium. Industrial policies had small face amounts (often $1,000), but did develop cash values. Since the premium was collected weekly, the grace period was 28 days. Most industrial life today is sold via the mail.

62. **B**  The owner of a life insurance policy may absolutely assign (transfer) all their rights of ownership to another party by executing (signing) an "absolute assignment." The new owner would now have all the rights of ownership, including paying the premium, naming the beneficiary, taking a loan or taking cash surrender.

63. **A**  If an employer purchases life insurance on behalf of a business executive, the premium the employer pays would be considered to be compensation to the executive in the form of a bonus. The policy belongs to the executive who may name anyone he/she wants as beneficiary. Executive Bonus plans are not considered to be Key Person life insurance, since the proceeds are not payable to the employer if the executive dies.

64. **B**  Employers sometimes help their employees purchase cash value life insurance in the form of a "split dollar" plan. The employer pays that part of the premium that is allocated to the cash value and the employee pays the difference. The cash value portion of the policy belongs to the employer, so if the employee terminates employment the employer may surrender the policy for cash.

However, if the employee dies during his/her term of employment, the proceeds of the policy are paid to whoever the employee designated as beneficiary. If the employee works until full retirement age, the employer may assign the policy to the employee who may keep it or surrender it for cash to supplement his/her retirement. Split dollar plans are not considered to be Group life or Key Person life insurance.

65. **D**  Group life insurance is considered to be an employee benefit, so the employer may tax deduct the premiums paid. However, the proceeds are payable tax free to the beneficiary selected by the employee. The employer is considered to be the Master Policy Holder, and the insured employee receives a Certificate of Insurance summarizing his/her coverage. Although dependents may be covered, only one Certificate is issued to each covered employee.

Group premiums may be contributory or non-contributory. A group may not be formed just to buy insurance. It must exist for some other reason. By law, Group life coverage is convertible to whole life without a physical exam for 31 days after termination of employment. Conversion is based upon the employee's current age.

66. **A**  Mutual insurers issue "participating" policies, which means that the policy holders may participate in company surplus in the form of dividends, if declared by the company Board of Directors. However, it is unlawful to guarantee future dividends. Dividends paid by mutual

insurers are not taxable since the IRS considers them to be a return of premium, and premiums are paid in after tax dollars.

67. **B**  Adjustable whole life insurance is sold to clients who have fluctuating incomes, such as real estate agents. For example, a 30 year-old realtor buys a $100,000 adjustable whole life policy for an annual premium of $1,000. If his/her income drops, he/she could adjust his/her premium down to $500, which in turn would cause the policy limit to drop to $50,000. If his/her income increases, he/she can adjust his premium up to $750, which in turn will adjust his/her policy limit up to $75,000, without a physical exam. However, he/she cannot adjust his face amount up to more than the $100,000 he/she originally purchased unless he/she can pass a physical exam.

68. **C**  Limited pay Whole Life (such as a 20-pay life or a life paid-up at 65 policy) are variations of traditional Whole Life insurance. All Whole Life insurance is designed to reach maturity at the insured's age 100. So, although a 20 pay-life policy will be paid-up in 20 years from the date it was purchased, it will not reach maturity until age 100. At maturity, the cash value of the policy will equal the face amount of the contract.

69. **B**  To calculate Life insurance premiums, insurers first determine the cost of mortality (death claims). Next, they add in the administrative expenses necessary to operate the company (primarily commissions to agents). Then, they subtract the investment income that they expect to earn from investing the premiums they collect. So, the formula that an insurer would use to calculate Gross Premium would be "Mortality plus Expenses minus Investment Income."

70. **A**  Under the Doctrine of Agency, agents or producers represent the insurer who is responsible for the acts of their agents. However, insurers are responsible only if the agent or producer acts within the scope of their authority, which is spelled out in their contract with the insurer. If an agent acts outside their scope of authority, they may be held to be personally liable, which is why some agents carry Errors and Omissions (E&O) insurance.

Agents may not alter an application without the written consent of the applicant. Further, agents may not modify the terms of a policy once it is issued. However, Notice of Claim to an agent is the same as notice to the company.

71. **C**  The contract owner has all the rights of ownership. Although the contract owner and the annuitant are often the same person, they don't have to be. The annuitant is the person upon whose life the contract is based.

72. **C**  Most Life insurers require their agents to give clients a Conditional Receipt as evidence of the first premium payment. Although this receipt is given, coverage is still conditional upon the applicant's ability to pass a physical exam.

Some Life insurers utilize Binding Receipts instead, which provide a limited amount of coverage between the date of application and the date of the physical exam. Full coverage does not apply until the underwriter approves the results of the physical exam. Binders are used in Property/Casualty insurance, not in Life and Health. Binders are temporary coverage until superseded by the policy, and may be written or oral.

73. **D**  The Fair Credit Reporting Act (FCRA) is a Federal law that regulates investigative consumer reports, such as credit reports. If a report is in error, there are procedures to follow to get it corrected. Filing a lawsuit against the reporting agency is not necessary.

74. **A** The "standard" risk is presented by the average person. Life insurers base their mortality tables on the life expectancies of the standard risk. Mortality tables are used by actuaries to determine life insurance rates and benefits. If a person is a preferred risk, their rate is discounted from the standard. If a person is a non-standard risk, their rate is surcharged above the standard.

75. **B** A "preferred" risk is entitled to a lower rate since they have a very healthy lifestyle and do not have a dangerous occupation or any dangerous hobbies.

76. **B** Most Term insurance is renewable without a physical exam, although the premium goes up as the insured ages. For example, a client buys a five year Level term policy, which has both a level face amount and a level premium for five years. At the end of five years, the policy is renewable, but the renewal premium will be based upon the insured's average age for the next five year period, which will be higher. If the insured is still in good health, they may feel that this increase in premium is unfair, so they may let the policy lapse.

To solve this problem, some term insurers offer the "re-entry option," which states that if the insured can pass a physical exam prior to renewal, the insurer will renew the policy for a premium that is less than that charged those insureds who either refuse to take or fail a physical exam.

77. **A** The riskiest annuity pay-out option will always have the highest rate of return. If the client selects the Life income pay-out option, monthly payments will be made for as long as the annuitant lives. However, this option has no beneficiary, so if the annuitant dies before they receive all their money back, the insurer keeps the balance.

78. **A** Earnings during the accumulation period of a deferred annuity are automatically reinvested without tax. Although banks often sell deferred annuities to older clients who are seeking safety, tax deferral and a competitive rate of return, most annuities are sold to younger clients who are concerned about supplementing their retirement income.

79. **D** The right to designate or change a beneficiary is stated in a section of the contract entitled "owners rights." The insuring agreement states the names of the parties to the contract, the coverage and the consideration for the contract.

80. **B** The owner of a Life policy may pledge the policy as collateral for a loan from a bank, who would then have a temporary lien against the policy. If the insured dies during the term of the loan, the insurer will pay off the bank. Any remaining proceeds are payable to the designated beneficiary.

81. **C** The right to apply for Reinstatement is a mandatory provision in a Life policy. If the policy lapses, the owner has the right to apply, but reinstatement is subject to underwriting and paying all back premiums due, plus interest. If an insurer approves, the original policy is reinstated, which means that future premiums will be based upon the insured's original age. However, a policy that has been surrendered for cash may not be reinstated.

82. **B** Automatic Premium Loan (APL) is a rider that may be added only to a cash value Life insurance policy. Although most riders cost extra, this rider is free, since it is designed to keep the policy from lapsing, which benefits both the insured and the insurer. Although the rider is free, it is not automatically added to a policy unless the owner requests it. It is not a non-forfeiture option and it cannot be added to a term policy.

If this rider is attached and the owner fails to make a premium payment by the end of the grace period, the policy will automatically borrow from itself an amount sufficient to pay the overdue premium, so the policy will not lapse and will not go into non-forfeiture. However, the amount borrowed is a loan and will be subject to interest charges. If the insured dies with a loan outstanding, the amount of the loan, plus interest, will be subtracted from the policy proceeds.

83. **A**   The Life Income settlement option is actually an annuity option. Remember, annuity payouts are based upon the expected life span of the annuitant, who in this case would be the beneficiary of the policy. This settlement option will make monthly payments to the annuitant for as long as they live, which could be longer than their expected life span.

84. **D**   IRC Section 1035 allows for tax deferred exchanges of certain insurance products as long as the exchange does not place the owner in an overall better tax position at death. For example, life insurance may be exchanged for life insurance, since the tax implications are the same. Or, an annuity may be exchanged for another annuity, since the tax implications remain the same.

Further, life insurance may be exchanged for an annuity, since annuity earnings are taxable at death but life insurance proceeds are not. However, an annuity may not be exchanged for life insurance, since that would place the owner in a better tax position.

1035 Exchanges may be made with the same or a different insurer, but on life insurance exchanges, the policies must be on the life of the same insured. Most exchanges involve exchanging contracts to obtain a higher rate of return.

85. **B**   Mutual insurers write "participating" policies, which might pay a dividend to policyholders. If a dividend is declared, the policyholder may choose from five different dividend options: 1) cash; 2) interest; 3) apply to next premium when due; 4) paid-up additions; or 5) one year term insurance.

If a policy owner is on tight budget, he/she will most likely elect to apply a dividend towards his/her next premium, when due. For example, if the annual premium is $1,000 and the dividend is $100, the policy owner will only have to pay $900 out of pocket. A policy owner may change the dividend option at any time, even if the policy has an irrevocable beneficiary.

86. **D**   Adding the Family Rider to your Whole Life policy is the cheapest way to provide coverage for your entire family. For example, you have a $100,000 permanent Whole Life policy on yourself. You add a $50,000 10 year level term rider to cover your spouse and a $5,000 level term rider to cover each of your children until they reach the age of majority. The term coverage on your spouse and children is temporary, but provides coverage for your entire family when you most need it for the lowest possible price.

When the term insurance expires, your total premium will be reduced. Further, the term coverage on your spouse and children is convertible to Whole Life upon expiration, without a physical exam.

87. **D**   The Return of Premium Rider is a type of "increasing" term insurance. If a person wants their beneficiary to have the face amount of their life insurance plus all the premiums they paid-in up to the date of their death, they can add this rider to the policy for an additional premium charge.

A similar rider is known as the Return of Cash Value Rider, which is also "increasing" term insurance. If this rider is added, the beneficiary will receive the face amount of the insured's policy plus all of the cash value in the contract.

88. **B**  There are several annuity pay-out options, which are selected by the annuitant when they annuitize the contract. Once selected, they can never be changed, and some are more risky than others.

The Life income option is the most risky, since it has no beneficiary. However, a client who wants high monthly payments with less risk might choose the Life income with Period Certain option instead. With this option, monthly payments are guaranteed to be paid to the annuitant (or to his/her beneficiary) for a certain period of time, often 10 years. However, if the annuitant lives beyond the period certain, payments will continue until he/she dies.

For example, a 60 year old client annuitizes a $100,000 annuity over his/her 20 year life span with a 10 year period certain. To receive his/her entire $100,000, he/she must live 20 years. However, if he/she lives longer, he/she will continue to receive monthly payments until death.

But if he/she died at age 65, he/she would have only received payments for five years. But since he/she had a 10 year period certain, his/her beneficiary will receive what the annuitant would have received until he/she would have turned age 70. However, if he/she died at age 71, the beneficiary would not receive anything since the 10 year period certain ended at age 70.

So, as you can see in this example, the 10 year period certain eliminated one-half of the risk. The period certain can be 5, 10, 15 or 20 years. The longer it is, the lower the monthly payments to the annuitant will be.

89. **C**  Although Life insurance proceeds are always tax free to a beneficiary, annuity death benefits are taxable as ordinary income to a beneficiary to the extent that they exceed the amount that the owner/annuitant invested in the contract. The death benefit on an annuity consists of the amount invested plus earnings. Since the amount invested consists of after-tax dollars (except on a 403b TSA), only the earnings are taxable to the beneficiary.

90. **B**  Cost basis is defined as the amount of after-tax dollars you invest. Since your cost basis has already been taxed, upon distribution that money will be returned to you (or your beneficiary) tax free as a return of principal. However, certain retirement plans (such as a 403b TSA) are purchased with before-tax dollars, so they have no cost basis. Distributions from such plans are 100% taxable as ordinary income, since neither the amount contributed nor the earnings have ever been taxed.

91. **C**  Risk is defined as the "chance of loss." Once identified, risk may be managed in several different ways. On Health insurance, you could retain some of your risk by increasing the amount of your deductible. In business, you could bring in a business partner to share the risk. Insurance is defined as the "transfer of risk" to the insurer in consideration of a premium.

92. **C**  Internal Revenue Code (IRC) 403b TSAs are qualified retirement plans that are available to employees of public schools, certain hospitals and non-profit charitable organizations on a payroll deduction basis. They are very similar to 401k plans.

Contributions are made in before-tax dollars, so the participants cost basis is zero. As a result, 100% of all distributions are taxable as ordinary income to participants. Further, premature distributions made prior to age 59 ½ are subject to a 10% IRS penalty.

93. **A**   On Group Life, which is usually written as Annual Renewable Term insurance, the employer is considered to be the Master Policyholder. Covered employees only receive one Certificate of Insurance, summarizing their coverage and listing all covered dependents, if any.

94. **A**   A producer or agent must be licensed in every state they sell in. Although you can only have one resident insurance license (in your home state), you could have as many as 49 non-resident licenses in other states. Non-resident licenses are usually issued without exam and are based upon reciprocal agreements between your home state and the non-resident states.

95. **B**   Insurance is based upon the Doctrine of Reasonable Expectations. If you buy life insurance, it would be reasonable for you to expect that coverage would apply if you died, or that your health insurance would cover you if you became sick or injured. Of course, sometimes the question of what is reasonable to expect must be decided in court.

96. **B**   When an individual purchases insurance they are transferring the risk to the insurance company in return for the premium paid. The purchase of insurance does NOT eliminate the risk. Just because you have Life insurance does not mean you are not going to die. The risk is still present!

97. **B**   Insurance contracts have an uncertain outcome, which makes them "aleatory," since the outcome depends upon chance. For example, when you buy Term Life insurance, you may or may not die within the term of coverage. When you buy Health insurance, you may or may not ever become sick or injured. Further, although "consideration" is defined as the exchange of value, this exchange need not be equal. For example, if you bought a $100,000 whole life policy for a premium of $1,000 and died right away, an unequal exchange of consideration would have taken place.

98. **D**   Although Group Life insurance is convertible for 31 days after termination of employment to whole life without a physical exam, the premium for the new Whole Life policy is based upon the insured's current age, not their original age.

99. **B**   "Ordinary" Life insurance, which consists of Whole Life, Term and Endowment, is required by law to have a grace period of at least 30 days. Since this client died within the grace period, the insurer has to pay the face amount, less the overdue premium. If he/she had died after the end of the grace period, there would have been no coverage. The grace period on Industrial Life is 28 days and on Group Life the grace period is 31 days.

100. **B**   There are only three non-forfeiture options: 1) cash surrender; 2) reduced paid-up; and 3) the extended term option. "Paid-up additions" is a dividend option, which is available only on Whole Life policies issued by mutual insurers who issue participating policies.

    For example, an insured owns a Whole Life policy issued by a mutual. He/she would like to buy more life insurance, but can no longer pass a physical exam. However, if his/her insurer declares a policy dividend, he/she could use that dividend as a single premium to buy a small, additional Whole Life policy (without a physical exam) that would be paid-up until his/her death or age 100, whichever comes first. If he/she used his/her dividend in this manner every year, he/her could end up with substantially more insurance coverage.

Don't confuse non-forfeiture options with dividend options. All cash value life insurance policies must contain non-forfeiture options. However, only life insurance policies issued by mutual insurers have dividends options.